"*The Lens of Leadership* is *the* playbook for building any kind of championship team."

– Boomer Esiason, NFL quarterback; Chairman, Boomer Esiason Foundation

"By taking a look at yourself through *The Lens of Leadership*, you'll gain enormous insight into what it takes to become an even better leader and, just as importantly, to develop the untapped leaders around you."

– Michael Zuna, Executive Vice President, Chief Marketing and Sales Officer, Aflac, Inc.

"The Lens of Leadership gets it right: The best leaders know how to share power to get more done."

– Joe Iarocci, CEO of the Robert K. Greenleaf Center for Servant Leadership

"Where in the hell was this book fifteen years ago? *The Lens of Leadership* touches on many of the factors that are the key to successful leadership. It not only motivated me to become a better boss, but I believe it will also inspire everyone to become a better leader. It will definitely put your career in the 'fast lane.'"

– Randy Bernard, CEO, Indy Racing League

"We need government leaders that have great skills *and* strength of character in our capitols and municipalities so they can help build a better future for America. *The Lens of Leadership*'s 'Serve-Build-Inspire' model is just the tool to build those leaders."

– Ed Rendell, former Governor of Pennsylvania and Chairman of the Democratic National Committee

"Cory Bouck's *The Lens of Leadership* is destined to become a seminal piece. The insights will benefit both fledgling and seasoned leaders. Apply its principles to any organization, and you will see serious positive results, both immediate and for the long haul."

– Admiral Joseph W. Prueher, former U.S. Ambassador to the People's Republic of China

"Cory Bouck's *Lens of Leadership* principles are time-tested, and his timing is *perfect*. So much leadership talent is retiring. This book will help build better leaders that are ready to follow, serve, and *lead*."

— **Matt Blunt, former Republican Governor of Missouri; President of The American Automotive Policy Council**

"*The Lens of Leadership* is a very helpful book for individuals who are motivated to become great leaders. Its 'Serve – Build – Inspire' framework is supported by a series of practical examples and exercises to help hone leadership skills. Ultimately, the book contains a strong affirmation of personal accountability coupled with a useful path to achieve leadership impact."

— **Rick Searer, President, Kraft North America (Retired)**

"The leadership exodus has begun: Baby Boomers are retiring in droves and there aren't enough Gen Xers to replace them. The Lens of Leadership is a practical field manual for getting Millennials ready to lead."

— **Haydn Shaw, Practice Leader, Franklin-Covey Co., author of *Sticking Points: How to Get 4 Generations Working Together in the 12 Places They Come Apart***

"This powerful, practical book shows you how to create, lead, manage, and motivate a team of high-performing people—in *any* business."

— **Brian Tracy, Professional Speaker, International Best Selling Author, Entrepreneur, and Success Expert**

"Retiring U.S. workers are taking decades of job skills and leadership experience with them. They are being replaced by a labor force that is ambitious but untested. If America's younger workers can adopt Cory Bouck's 'Serve—Build—Inspire' model, they will strengthen the companies that create great jobs for American families."

— **Dr. Donnie Horner, Education Commissioner, City of Jacksonville, Florida**

"*The Lens of Leadership* uses the best tools from the training world to ensure you convert what you learn from this book into better behaviors that deliver better results."
— Dr. Donald Kirkpatrick, *professor emeritus* of the University of Wisconsin, creator of the four "Kirkpatrick Levels" for evaluating the effectiveness of corporate training programs

"The Lens of Leadership explains how the skills of great followership build better organizations today and better leaders tomorrow."
— Peter Nicholas Lengyel, President & CEO, Safran USA

"No matter who you are, *The Lens of Leadership* will help you achieve your professional goals and leave an enduring and endearing legacy. This book is a blueprint designed to bring leadership and character together."
— Dr. Mark Huberty, DDS, Chairman, American Dental Association's Global Mission of Mercy; Deputy Regent, International College of Dentists

"Emerging markets are growing at an astonishing pace. Businesses attempting to succeed in this arena are in dire need of leaders who can apply Bouck's 'Serve—Build—Inspire' model to unleash the power embedded in the universal human desire to achieve."
— Scott Chandler, Finance Director, Asia, Middle East, & Africa, General Mills, Inc.

"If you are a leader today and you don't understand how to be a follower at the same time, *The Lens of Leadership* should be the next business book you read."
— Chuck Goddard, President & CEO, Marinette Marine Corp.

"Like great actors, great leaders are born *and* made: skilled people still need great coaching. *The Lens of Leadership* brilliantly provides you with your own personal leadership coach. Read it *now*. You simply can't afford to wait until tomorrow."
— Christopher Olsen, Hollywood screenwriter, and producer of the upcoming feature *Lombardi*

"Cory Bouck speaks from and to the heart of leadership. His easy to use tools and practical advice are based on many years of proven experience, and can be readily used by any leader to inspire people working together to achieve exemplary results."
— Dr. Robert O. Brinkerhoff, creator and best-selling author of
***The Success Case Method,* and internationally-recognized**
expert in training effectiveness and measurement

"Looking at your skills through *The Lens of Leadership*, you will see how easy it is to *focus* your development, *magnify* your impact, and set your career *on fire!*"
— Patrick Snow, International Best-Selling Author of *Creating*
Your Own Destiny* and *The Affluent Entrepreneur

"*The Lens of Leadership* clearly defines three imperatives for the next generation of great leaders: Serve, Build and Inspire. I encourage anyone interested in fully developing as a leader to use this book as a practical guide and personal coach."
— Kevin D. Wilde, VP, Organization Effectiveness and
Chief Learning Officer, General Mills; 2007 Chief Learning
Officer Of the Year; author of *Dancing with the Talent Stars:*
25 Moves That Matter Now

"*The Lens of Leadership* provides useful and practical advice for leaders. It's a good resource for first time managers and anyone who wants to expand their knowledge about leadership fundamentals."
— Tamar Elkeles, Ph.D., Chief Learning Officer, Qualcomm,
and the 2010 CLO of the Year

"A company's and country's most cherished asset is its leaders. Weak leadership will guarantee mediocrity and decline. Strong leadership will position the company/institution to be the best. Cory's book is timely in a world where true leadership is in dangerously short supply. *The Lens of Leadership* is a phenomenal book. I wish that I had had Cory's book early in my career. Here comes a much-needed best seller!"
— Neal Whitten, Best-selling author and Project Management
Expert; President, The Neal Whitten Group

THE
LENS OF
LEADERSHIP

BEING THE LEADER OTHERS *WANT* TO FOLLOW

Katy

Good luck leadership

Serve, Build, INSPIRE!!

On your continuing journey.

AVIVA
PUBLISHING
NEW YORK

CORY BOUCK

Please address all inquiries to:

Cory Bouck LLC.

www.TheLensOfLeadership.com

ISBN: 978-1-935586-89-0

Editor: Tyler Tichelaar

Cover and Interior Book Design: Fusion Creative Works, www.fusioncw.com

Impact Map adaptation used with permission of the authors Robert Brinkerhoff & Anne Apking, High Impact Learning, Strategies for Leveraging Performance and Business Results from Training Investments (Basic Books, 2001).

Content found in chapters 15, 18, and 20 is copyright-protected and owned by VitalSmarts and used herein with permission.

"CLOSING TIME"—Words and Music by DAN WILSON
© 1998 WB MUSIC CORP. and SEMIDELICIOUS MUSIC
All Rights Administered by WB MUSIC CORP.

The Lens of Leadership is also available as an e-book.

For additional copies please visit: www.TheLensOfLeadership.com

DEDICATION

To Beth, my one particular harbor.

To my children: You are inheriting a glorious-but-broken world that will require greatness just to solve the simple problems. I know this stuff works, so I wrote it down for you. Use it to become great, along whatever path you choose. Your future – with the families you will Serve, Build, and Inspire one day – is the only legacy that matters.

And to every person around the world who answers the call, and steps up to the challenges of leading: Leadership is Noble.

ACKNOWLEDGMENTS

We often never know the extent to which we impact the lives of others. There are many people—too many to list here—who have no idea that they contributed to this book. In moments big and small, by what was done or left undone, and by their great or not-so-great example: I was changed and inspired by scores of people. I am grateful.

Scotty Chandler, my leadership yardstick. If I could impress you, I knew I was on to something. Thanks for your friendship and help, shipmate.

Tim Ahrens, my right brain and my professional "other half." Thank you for your role in my finding my voice.

Sean Liedman, who taught me how to fight: "Fight to Fly, Fly to Fight, Fight to Win." Bing Lengyel, who taught me how to write. Patrick Snow, whose example inspired me to write a book. And Tyler Tichelaar, who taught me not to split my infinitives.

Ralph, Launa, and Shelly Stayer, Don McAdams, Brian Klepke, Leah Glaub, and 1,400 other Johnsonville members, who have helped build a company where people belong to something very special: a team that builds leaders and helps its members find their voices, so they can achieve their God-given potential.

I am also indebted to my Naval Academy classmates, "Pelican" squadron mates, ProDev "Luce Cannons," and the fine people of General Mills, Newell-Rubbermaid, and my hometowns of Owosso, Michigan and Sheboygan, Wisconsin.

CONTENTS

INTRODUCTION

All glory comes from daring to begin.
— Eugene F. Ware

Leaders don't create followers, they create more leaders.
— Tom Peters

While researching the data that became the book *Good to Great*, Jim Collins cautioned his team against the Siren song of "leadership" being attributed as the "answer to everything." What the team discovered, however, was that great leadership *was* present in all of the "good" companies at the time of their transition to "great," and those strong leadership skills were consistently missing in all of the poorly-performing comparison companies.

- Do you aspire to lead others on a truly high performance team?

- Is your career not progressing as quickly—or in the direction—that you would like?

- Is your paycheck suffering because you are not delivering superior results?

- Are you in over your head as a leader, and you're just waiting to be found out?

If so, this book can help.

During my years as a military leader, all performance—the critical and the mundane—was viewed through what I call "The Lens of Leadership." If a mission failed to achieve its goal or was executed sloppily, it was considered a leadership failure. If the floors were dirty or the brass un-shined in a ship's passageway, that was also a leadership failure. If the meals were bad at the base cafeteria, that was a leadership failure, too. When leaders are held accountable for results, those results almost always improve. Great leadership seeks out accountability.

In my experience outside the military, I have seen business, academic, and community leaders quickly attribute *success* to "leadership," but they often neglect to attribute *failure* to leadership as well. I have seen bosses—and sometimes even the boss' boss—shirk accountability and choose instead to cite a long list of *other* problems, often rationalized as having been beyond someone's control. That's no way to lead an organization to greatness.

My earliest leadership skills were developed in a very intentional and structured way in what I believe is the finest leadership laboratory in the world: the U.S. Naval Academy in Annapolis, Maryland. Students there, called Midshipmen, learn and practice the most powerful principles of leadership using a potent combination of formal learning, social modeling, and experiential immersion. Everything students do there is an opportunity to demonstrate or further develop their leadership skills.

While I learned these principles in the context of a military environment, they are universally-applicable, and have direct relevance to other competitive enterprises like business, entertainment, and not-for-profits. Business titans like Malcolm Forbes, Dave Thomas of Wendy's restaurants, FedEx's Fred Smith, P&G's Bob McDonald and A.G. Lafley, George Steinbrenner of the New York Yankees, Estée Lauder's founder Leonard Lauder, and Sam Walton formed their leadership skills in the military, as did entertainment leaders like Clint Eastwood, Tony Bennett, and Bill Cosby. Great leaders understand the universal, human principles that drive people and teams. This understanding does not have to be developed in the military, but it *does* have to be developed because it does translate into organizational success.

My learning and experience – as a Naval Academy graduate and former leadership instructor, a Naval Flight Officer, a business leader at two Fortune 300 companies and a privately-held firm, and as an elected official – has taught me to see all results through The Lens of Leadership. This book will introduce you to **a new mindset, new skills, and new development tools** for your leadership toolbox.

A NEW MINDSET

The Lens of Leadership is an accountability mindset. All successes and failures have their roots in leadership, and people in positions of leadership bear responsibility for those successes and failures. Great leaders are not afraid to have their results examined through The Lens of Leadership.

This book will introduce you to this uncommon mindset, which is vital to your success as both a follower and as a leader. All intentions, acts, and outcomes should be viewed through The Lens of Leadership to bring focus to the leader's ultimate accountability for results.

NEW SKILLS

In May 2010, *Harvard Business Review* published an article titled, "How to Keep Your Top Talent." In it, researchers from the Corporate Leadership Council revealed that 70 percent of today's high performers—tomorrow's future experts and leaders—lack critical skills essential to their future success.

To bridge that gap, this book offers a powerful set of leadership skills. I have included the highest-leverage tools available for building high performance teams that will consistently deliver winning results. You can apply these skills no matter what your role or level in any kind of organization. These tools are *practical,* not theoretical. You should apply them immediately to earn the recognition you want to earn by improving the results that you and your teammates deliver.

NEW DEVELOPMENT TOOLS

This book also is designed to be a leadership development *handbook.* Each chapter includes a template and resources for you to create your customized personal development plan. This plan should be your commitment—to your organization, to your leader, to your team, and to yourself. If you keep the development commitments you create in this book, your results will improve, your reputation will blossom, and your career will be dramatically enhanced.

This book is a *long-term resource* for you. People can learn to master only one or two new competencies at a time, usually over the course of twelve to eighteen months. This book has plans for an entire career's worth of leadership development. As your skills and responsibilities advance, you can choose the chapters that apply to your current needs and changing situations.

THE LEADERSHIP EXODUS

Across centuries, great leaders have written the history we know today by developing themselves and inspiring others. The great leaders of tomorrow will have to do so as well. But what "leaders" look like in all kinds of organizations is about to undergo a radical transformation driven by a demographic tsunami: The 80 million members of the Baby Boomer generation (born between 1946 and 1964) have begun to retire at a rate that will continue to accelerate over the next ten to fifteen years. Generation X (born between 1965 and 1980) has had a couple of decades to develop its leadership skills and prove itself, but its 50 million members will be insufficient to fill the leadership vacuum created by the retiring Baby Boomers. As a result, some of the younger and less-experienced Gen Xers and a huge number of undeveloped, unprepared Millennials (born between 1981 and 1995, and also called "Generation Y") will soon be sucked up into leadership roles for which their organizations will find them wholly unprepared.

Millennials will make up *half* of the workforce by 2014. They have many wonderful characteristics they are bringing with them: they are natural collaborators; they grew up using technology to communicate, learn, and solve problems; they are curious and have a constant desire to learn. But Baby Boomers and early Gen Xers had years and years of intentional development and mentoring—in progressively more demanding roles—that the inexorable progress of business will not afford to Millennials.

It's not that Millennials are not currently leading: they hold 28 percent of today's managerial positions.[1] It is that the accelerated rate of Baby Boomers' retirement and the insufficient replacement number of Gen Xers will result in Millennials being advanced into senior roles far faster than previous generations.

This book is not specifically targeted at Millennials, however. The principles of *The Lens of Leadership* are timeless and applicable at *all* levels in *any* type of organization. But unless your organization recognizes and acts on the demographic facts, the leaders you will soon begin rapidly to promote *will not be ready to be responsible for the people and roles you are going to give them.*

Lloyd's of London interviewed 500 global CEOs in order to understand and rank business risk factors for their 2011 Risk Index

---

1 Already exceeding the Boomers' number of 23 percent.

report. Of the ninety risks assessed, those CEOs identified "loss of customers" as the number one threat. Number two was "talent and skill shortages." Think of the catastrophic risk choices they had to choose from: terrorism, the interrupted flow of oil and other material inputs, a natural disaster, political instability, and government interference. But the second biggest risk to the 500 largest companies in the world is that their leaders may not be capable of leading or building a talent bench.

Because of this demographically-influenced leadership exodus, the organizations that will dominate the 2020s will be the ones that have built highly skilled and experienced leaders at several levels—even senior directors and vice-presidents—who happen to be in their late twenties and early thirties. If you want to be winning ten years from now, you need to emphasize and accelerate the leadership development of late Gen Xers and Millennials. If you are an ambitious Gen Xer or Millennial, now is your opportunity to *write the history of tomorrow* by learning to serve others, build skills, lead teams, and inspire greatness.

THE QUALITY OF LEADERSHIP MATTERS

In order to develop future leaders, your organization has to *retain* them long enough to do so. An October 2011 Mercer study discovered that Millennials are twice as likely to be looking for another job—even now during this period of extended economic difficulty. Employees who report to managers who are effective at manager-led development deliver *25 percent higher performance*, have a *40 percent higher retention* rate, and have *29 percent higher commitment/engagement* levels.[2] So you have to have a *current* bench of leaders capable of building the Millennials into your future leaders.

---

2 2010 Corporate Executive Board Report on Manager-Led Development

The *Lens of Leadership* will help leaders at *all levels* and their followers to develop into the skilled employees you need them to become in order to remain competitive over the next ten to fifteen years.

THIS BOOK EXPLAINS WHY GREAT LEADERS:

- Act paradoxically as both a leader and a follower at the same time throughout their careers.

- Model the right behaviors every single day, and set the highest bar for themselves.

- Take pride in having led a team to victory, but have the grace to give the credit for that victory to everyone but themselves.

- Have the unshakeable courage to stand alone if necessary to help the team break through barriers.

- Absorb heat from outside the team, not reflect it onto the team.

THIS BOOK IS FOR YOU

- If you are an individual contributor in your organization, this book will get you performing like a superstar by teaching you great "followership."

- If you are an early leader, it will teach you the key fundamental behaviors to master so you are viewed as a leader who is effective beyond your years.

- If you are an experienced or even senior leader, this book includes advanced skills that are effective all the way up into the C-Suite.

- If you have struggled, or your career has stalled a bit, this book will teach you "career recovery" behaviors, including how to communicate your renewed commitment to excellence in an authentic way.

- If you have been denied a promotion, or even lost your job, this book has career-management tools for dealing with life-altering change. It will get you on a new path to career success and happiness.

YOU WILL LEARN:

In the first section, **SERVE**, you will learn that the first important attribute of great leadership is *followership*. All of us are followers no matter what role we are in. And if you are already a leader, you must still exhibit and apply the skills of great followership because leaders are both followers and leaders, *simultaneously*. You will also learn about transitioning to a leadership role and the essential skills of getting more done through others, while maintaining a servant's heart.

In the second section, **BUILD**, you will learn how to manage your own skill development by assertively managing your career. The skills of self-development are important for whatever career stage you are in. You will also learn about essential resources for developing others.

In section three, **INSPIRE**, you will learn to motivate those you lead to help you create a high-performance team by engaging them in a worthy cause. You will also learn to prepare them, and yourself, to be ready for those unexpected moments that define a career and a life.

LET'S GO!

Why should you take this journey with me? I have built and grown early leaders. I have been successful at growing my own career and the careers of others. I have been successful leading in very different sets of circumstances. I have the strategic business experience to influence and coach senior leaders of large enterprises.

Everyone needs advocates and mentors. I want to be your coach. Leadership development is a journey. *Let's get going!*

HOW TO USE THIS BOOK TO IMPROVE YOUR PERFORMANCE AND DELIVER WORLD CLASS RESULTS

This book is structured as a handbook. It is a toolbox that will help you apply its lessons in your daily life to achieve improved performance and deliver better results.

The first tool is called an **Impact Map**.[1] It was developed by Dr. Robert Brinkerhoff, Professor Emeritus at Western Michigan University and an internationally recognized author and leader in training evaluation and effectiveness. His Impact Map process and tool are for both the learner and the learner's supervisor to use. They create alignment—a "line of sight"—between what will be learned in a class, a conference seminar, or by reading a book, and the expected better on-the-job behaviors.

The Impact Map also connects those behaviors to the improved individual and team results the learner should expect to deliver. It explains the positive contribution that those individual and team results will have on the organization's goals and metrics.

An Impact Map also acknowledges that what happens in the learning event is *only the beginning* of converting the new learning into

---

1 Brinkerhoff, Robert O. and Anne M. Apking. *High Impact Learning: Strategies for Leveraging Performance and Business Results from Training Investments.*

improved performance. There also must be several opportunities to practice and *apply* the learning.

The second tool is the **"What? So What? Now What?"** section at the end of each chapter:

"What?" summarizes the key takeaways from the chapter.

"So What?" explains the application and impact of the **"What?"**

"Now What?" is where you should *write out your own customized personal development plan*, including the additional formal learning and social learning you will need from colleagues, teammates, and mentors, and the experiences you will need to convert your "Ah-ha!"s from this book into improved performance and better results.

I have also included a **resource section** at the end of each chapter with some of the best thinking on that chapter's subject. Some of the recommended books are fictional pieces of literature that teach the chapter's lessons in a format outside of the business non-fiction category. These give you the option of blending self-improvement with an exciting tale.

IMPACT: CONVERTING THE READING INTO BETTER RESULTS

I have provided you with an Impact Map worksheet in this section. If you include your manager or a mentor in the creation of your own Impact Map, you will be much more likely to achieve success.

HERE'S HOW IT WORKS:

The most important lessons from this book are in the far left column (A). You and your leader should discuss and come to agreement on which two or three of those lessons, if adopted and applied, would make the biggest impact on your development at this point in your career.

You and your leader should agree on two or three specific situations in which you will apply the lessons you chose from column A. Then in column B, you specifically describe the different behaviors you will demonstrate that people should notice on the job.

To the right, in column C, you and your leader detail the benefit the different behaviors will have on team or unit results in the context of your team's annual initiatives or strategic goals. Describe this benefit in specific, preferably quantifiable, terms of project goals achieved, dollars saved, sales won, or relationships strengthened.

Then, connect your metrics in column C to the broader organizational metrics in D that will be affected—even distantly—by your improved impact on your team's results. Will your improved impact increase the top-line sales number? Will it drive efficiency, quality, or safety metrics? Bring the company closer to achieving an internal employee development goal?

Take the time to connect the lessons in the book (A) to how you learn those lessons to drive results for your organization (D) and you have the action plan for increasing your impact!

AN EXAMPLE

Take a look at the completed Impact Map in Figure 1 on page 14. This person has introduced her manager to this book and to the idea of using an Impact Map as part of her development plan. After reviewing column A and this book's Table of Contents, she and her manager discussed her most important development opportunities for the next twelve to eighteen months. They have decided that taking more initiative and strengthening her change management skills are the two most important competencies for her to work on over the next year.

In column B, she has listed the behaviors that will demonstrate her learning: initiating at least three design modifications to the upper valve housings, including the research and business case development. She will also lead a high-priority, company-wide project (the procurement and installation of a new manufacturing machine) and she will use the Six Sources model (explained in Chapter 15) to manage the change effort.

If she is successful, the valve redesigns will increase quality and reduce costs. The Bryant machine will enable an important new product offering and increase employee occupational safety. These goals for her plant are then connected to the corporate goals they will support.

Only 10 to 15 percent of typical leadership learning gets converted into measurable, improved business results. But Impact Maps clearly connect the learning to behaviors and results. This connection enables support and accountability for both the employee and the manager. *Eighty to ninety percent* of employees and managers who work together to create an effective Impact Map will create measurably improved results.

So now turn to Figure 2 on page 15 and take a shot at filling in *your* Impact Map. Then connect with your supervisor and introduce him or her to the concept. Review column A and the Table of Contents, and create the development plan that will help you deliver better results and grow your career as a teammate and leader.

EXAMPLE IMPACT MAP FOR **THE LENS OF LEADERSHIP**

Knowledge & Skills (A)	On the Job Applications (B)	Job/Team Results (C)	My Organization's Goals (D)
	(My few, most important new behaviors most likely to drive improved team results)	(Team results/metrics expected to be improved by my new behaviors)	(The ones most likely to be impacted by my new behaviors)

Knowledge & Skills (A)	On the Job Applications (B)	Job/Team Results (C)	My Organization's Goals (D)
Earn a reputation for strong leadership at every level through your "followership."	I will initiate at least three design modifications to the upper valve housings.	Our team's quality index should improve above 96.5% and cost should finally break the 9¢ per thousand threshold.	Grow Net Dollar Sales +6.6%
Motivate others by being a sterling personal example of loyalty, integrity, and **initiative**.	I will research and present the business cases to the plant engineer and modify them until they are right for our line.		Blended Op Efficiency/ Quality Rating > 94.75%
Achieve superlative performance by nurturing a network of people who are better than you are.			Deliver $32MM in Profit
Lead change management successfully by earning personal and organizational influence.	I will source the equipment for, and lead the cross implementation of, the Bryant machine.	The Bryant project is a Top-5 company priority. If successful, it will bring us into a new product category and lower manufacturing injury risk by 15–18%.	Achieve 10% of Annual Sales from Products Less Than 3 Yrs. Old.
Become a superior leader by developing a servant's heart.	I will use the Six Sources model and multimedia communication to win early approval and 90% operator qualification by 31 December.		Reportable Injury Rate of <.001 per 1,000 Hours
Develop, market, and "sell" your own authentic leadership brand.			
Increase your team's effectiveness through development and hiring.			
Hold performance and accountability conversations early and often.			
Use power and influence to inspire a high performance team.			
Be skillful in the unexpected, career-defining "moments that count."			

FIGURE 1

Adaptation used with permission of the authors Robert Brinkerhoff & Anne Apking, High Impact Learning, (Basic Books) 2001

YOUR IMPACT MAP FOR THE LENS OF LEADERSHIP

Knowledge & Skills (A)	On the Job Applications (B) (My few, most important new behaviors most likely to drive improved team results)	Job/Team Results (C) (Team results/metrics expected to be improved by my new behaviors)	My Organization's Goals (D) (The ones most likely to be impacted by my new behaviors)
Earn a reputation for strong leadership at every level through your "followership."			+ _____ % Net Sales, Units and/or Share Growth
Motivate others by being a sterling personal example of loyalty, integrity, and initiative.			_____ % of Sales from New Products
Achieve superlative performance by nurturing a network of people who are better than you are.			Achieve _____ % Market Share
Lead change management successfully by earning personal and organizational influence.			Financial: _____ % Profit Margin _____ % Return on Net Assets
Become a superior leader by developing a servant's heart.			Operational: Decrease COGS by _____ %
Develop, market, and "sell" your own authentic leadership brand.			Human Resources: _____ % Internal Promotion Rate for Leadership Roles
Increase your team's effectiveness through development and hiring.			
Hold performance and accountability conversations early and often.			
Use power and influence to inspire a high performance team.			
Be skillful in the unexpected, career-defining "moments that count."			

FIGURE 2

Adaptation used with permission of the authors Robert Brinkerhoff & Anne Apking, High Impact Learning, (Basic Books) 2001

SERVE

PART ONE

FOLLOWING

I love the man that can smile in trouble, that can gather strength from distress, and grow brave by reflection. 'Tis the business of little minds to shrink; but he whose heart is firm, and whose conscience approves his conduct, will pursue his principles unto death.
— Thomas Paine, *The Crisis*, No. 1, 1776

CHAPTER ONE

FOLLOWING IS THE FIRST FORM OF LEADING

Give me a stock clerk with a goal, and I will give you someone who will make history. Give me someone without a goal, and I will give you a stock clerk.
— J.C. Penney

If you believe lack of authority prevents you from leading effectively, it is time to rethink your understanding of leadership.
— Mike Bonem and Roger Patterson, *Leading From the Second Chair*

Just about everybody has a boss. You do. Your boss does. If you work for a company or even a not-for-profit, your most senior leader probably reports to a Board of Directors. Each director is elected or appointed by a collection of shareholders or other stakeholders. If you work in an obvious hierarchy like a factory, the government, or a multinational corporation, then you can see the stack of bosses in the organizational chart. If you are a small business owner competing in a Darwinian market, the customer is your boss. Even the President of the United States, "the most powerful man in the world," has a boss: the American people. He gets daily informal feedback through polls, and he endures what is probably the world's toughest performance review after four years.

Unless you are one of the very rare exceptions (a self-employed visionary inventor, Employee #1 in your own company, or a senior family member in a privately-held business), the journey to great leadership begins—and continues throughout your career—by demonstrating great followership. Great leadership is mastery of the paradoxical dual roles of both leader and follower. The first among these is the follower.

BECOMING A FOLLOWER

The skills of great followership are so important because they teach us a vital first principle of leadership: *service*. Many great, global organizations as diverse as General Electric, the Peace Corps, Procter & Gamble, and the Walt Disney Company have leadership development programs that start with some sort of early process for revealing, then reducing, the natural tendency of people to act in their self-interest *first*, which teaches the cornerstone of camaraderie and sacrifice: that you are part of something larger and more important than yourself.

The most obvious example of this is the military services where, upon your joining, your commanding officer will order your hair cut short, issue you standard uniforms for all occasions, restrict you to various standard behaviors, and work hard to break you down physically, mentally, and emotionally as an individual before building you back up. Military recruits lose their sense of individuality and establish their primary self-identification as being part of their unit through this process. They earn tangible artifacts—like T-shirts, patches, awards, qualifications, and ribbons—through shared trial and experience. They learn self-mastery through service to the greater team. During this time they learn that individual accomplishment is not what is rewarded. They learn that accountability is bigger than just responsibility for self: it is accountability for the success of the whole.

It's not just the military that has this sort of intentional, directed acculturation. In *Built to Last*, Collins and Porras coined the phrase "Cult-like Cultures" to describe one of the indicators that distinguishes a currently-successful firm from a truly visionary company that is likely to deliver long-term, self-sustaining success. Many of these high-performing, long-successful companies have culture-perpetuating tools:

- An ideology with an inspiring affirmation or pledge
- A tendency to hire new people through a tight candidate screening process
- Early employee indoctrination
- Internal "universities"
- On- and off-the-job socialization
- A stated promote-from-within policy
- A unique language and terminology
- Internal mythology and "folk tales" that reinforce what "great" looks like
- A comprehensive reward system that is designed to create full financial and psychological buy-in to the company.

Many hiring, recruiting, and interviewing processes are designed to accomplish this before you even join the company. Instead of shaving your head and teaching you to march, they make sure that the ones coming through the door will be a "fit" using tools like academic tests (e.g., Procter & Gamble's "P&G-MAT"), personality profiling, behavioral interviews, and pre-offer socialization. And great companies work hard to acculturate new employees as they walk in the door for day one: New "cast members" (employees) at Walt Disney, for example, go through a week-long program called "Traditions."

Team members and employees who learn to "follow first," learn to serve the needs of their leaders. Again, this doesn't mean that they are joining a caste system or perpetuating some outdated industrial-age construct. I'm not encouraging followers to act subservient or to treat leaders deferentially. Great followership demonstrates your recognition that leaders need teammates who are aligned with the leader's goals, are ready to go the extra mile to accomplish those goals, and possess enough learning agility to anticipate their leader's needs and fill those gaps without needing to be told to do so. Followership means learning to write with your leader's style, to speak his (or her) mind and represent his interests at meetings he is unable to attend, and to take on thankless tasks if that is what is necessary for the team to accomplish its goals. It requires you to develop the ability to conduct a comprehensive situational assessment *from the leader's perspective*. It may even require you to assume roles and thinking styles that complement the leader's gaps that he or she may not even acknowledge having.

Followership is a constant part of leadership because "everyone has a boss." The earlier and more consistently you demonstrate great followership, the faster your reputation will develop as a "go to" member of your team, and the faster you will earn promotion to the level and the type of work you are passionate about. Before most leaders will promote you or recommend you to join another team within a company, they want to observe you to perform at *that* level in your current role. They want to see your daily professionalism and consistent willingness to go the extra mile to deliver reliably great results. This mindset is not outdated. It is a timeless reality of professional development. This process is "earn your chops," not "wait your turn." It is a willingness to be measured by your performance and results, no matter how early you are in your career. It screams, "I can hunt with the big dogs, and I'm willing to prove it!" in what Dan Pink calls the "Conceptual Age," our current time when innovative ideas that contribute to solving big problems are the coin of the realm.

Great followership begins with fully investing yourself in the ideology of the company or team you have joined. Take the acculturation seriously. Study the behaviors that earn rewards. Listen to the internal mythologies and tease out what behaviors lead to success and which ones lead to failure. What actions are rewarded or punished?

Ask many different leaders what it takes to succeed and compare their answers. There are many different paths to success in any organization. Look at the behavior of all employees—up and down—through The Lens of Leadership: Do they talk about success and failure in terms of leadership of the project or team? How are people held accountable for results? Do leaders talk about what it takes to win, and how winning will specifically be defined? Do they talk about failure with words and tones that convey contempt for losing? Can they explain *why* they expect to win?

Take note of your leaders and others as they communicate and coach. Collect techniques that are consistent with your style, and adapt others that seem to work so they are right for you to use. You are always building your leadership toolbox because "everyone has a boss." And no matter where you are in an organization, you can learn as much from bad leaders as you can from great ones.

GREAT FOLLOWERSHIP ROLES

Great followers see themselves as one of many facilitators for the team, and a great facilitator serves many roles. In their book *Leaping the Abyss: Putting Group Genius to Work*, Chris Peterson and Gayle Pergamit explain that great facilitators wear many hats. One of them is the "valet" hat: learn your leader's presentation style, the voice she writes with, how she builds her stories and designs her PowerPoint slides, and then design the content you create for her with that in mind.

Another is the "Socrates-like mentor" hat: Know your leader's job well enough to stimulate challenging, counterintuitive thinking. Know when to provoke, and when to let it go. Whatever your leader's weaknesses (the methodology of the research, the financials of the project, the "people" aspects of dealing with change, dealing with marketing, etc.), shore them up by becoming *great* at those things. Amplify your leader's strengths, supplement her gaps, and train yourself to think like she thinks.

The "chameleon" hat demonstrates that you know when to be visible, and when to be subtle or even invisible. Remember, great followership is about making your boss look good, not immediately standing out yourself. A follower who earns a reputation for "seeing around corners" and putting the answer to that unanticipated question in the backup slides for the boss will always be a standout, even while "blending in." This may feel like a big risk. Many early-career followers fear having to share credit—or worse, not getting credit—for every little thing they do. By focusing on making your boss look good, you certainly risk being taken advantage of. But a leader who repeatedly exploits your facilitation and gives you inadequate public credit is telling you loudly and clearly that he or she is unworthy of your followership.

Earning what Jack Welch calls the "Pastor/Parent" hat gives followers the opportunity to demonstrate their professional maturity. Welch writes, "Pastors hear the 'sins' and complaints without recrimination. Parents love and

> Like "The Force" in *Star Wars*, the "Pastor/Parent" role has a dark-sided temptation. You must recognize that an enormous trust has been vested in you. Never "borrow" the rank of your boss, and never leverage the trust, the power, the access, or the voice you have earned to serve yourself or manipulate others. Your abuse will be discovered because once you use it successfully, you will continue to use it, but more sloppily, until you destroy the trust. Once your over-step as a consigliore is discovered, it will end your influence, and probably your career in that organization.

nurture, but give coaching fast and straight when you're off-track." Once you have earned the Pastor/Parent trust, you will become a "go-to" influencer with your boss.

I observed one of the best examples of followership I have ever seen when I was shadowing a very young director I was hoping to work for at Newell-Rubbermaid in the early 2000s. I was in a divisional marketing role, and he was the leader of the company's corporate NASCAR program. We were at a dinner hosted by the CEO and his staff for all twenty-five of his division presidents, who were there to network and lobby for resources. At that time, Newell-Rubbermaid was a very political organization, and the CEO, who was a fierce and hot-tempered competitor as far back as his college wrestling days, encouraged that kind of competition between his presidents. It was a business mixer, and each of the division leaders jockeyed for time alone with the CEO to "kiss the ring."

Early in the evening something big came undone, and before we knew it, the CEO and his COO left the gathering angry and in a hurry. We were in a city the whole group was used to gathering in, and the young director I was shadowing knew where the CEO and COO were likely to go to eat their dinner and sort out the problem unobserved by the twenty-five presidents. He confirmed this with a president who was closely connected to the CEO, and over the next few minutes, I heard him demonstrate a deft and exemplary act of followership.

He called the exclusive restaurant and asked for the maître d'. He said, "Two very important, powerful men are on their way to your restaurant, and they are having a very, very bad day. I would like to help you ensure that they have a great experience at your restaurant. I want to make sure they come away having solved their very big problems and enjoyed themselves over a fantastic meal." He told the maître d' insights about the pair's culinary knowledge and preferences, gave him his name and cell phone number, and encouraged him to call if there were any questions or subtleties about the

"What if I have a lousy boss?"

All the more reason to support him or her! You WILL be noticed—and viewed very positively—if you can fill in your leader's "gaps." Think of it as "serving the role, not the person." You are helping to make the team successful, and that is your obligation, whether you like and respect your leader, or not. You can motivate yourself by thinking about the informal leadership skills you are building.

"Won't I be perceived as a brown-noser?"

Not if your behaviors reflect an authentic, genuine desire to serve the team's interests. If your behaviors are supported by that spirit, and you accomplish your work with a high degree of professional maturity, others will see you as taking initiative and leading, not sucking up.

service that the maître d' wanted to know. Then he gave the maître d' his corporate credit card number in order to guarantee the servers a particularly high gratuity if the CEO and COO did not leave enough. Finally, he asked to speak to the restaurant's sommelier, to whom he gave important insights about the CEO's wine knowledge and preferences.

This young director demonstrated exceptional followership skills in "managing up" that evening. He knew his leaders inside out, and wanted only for them to accomplish what they needed to accomplish that night. He asked for no recognition. I doubt the CEO and COO even knew he involved himself. But he anticipated their need, facilitated an exceptional transition from anger to productivity for them, and he worked the crowd of presidents back at the corporate dinner like a diplomat. He did it for all the right reasons, and for the benefit of all, even those who never knew they were benefitting.

If you can follow by being a facilitator, valet, consultant, and Pastor/Parent, you will be leading through your followership. Leading as a follower is a fine line to walk. Like any professional skill, it takes some time and trials to master, but the best leaders want an army of this kind of follower because they are the ones demonstrating the aptitude and self-development skills to become the next generation of leaders.

There are many benefits that result from developing your followership skills. Early in your career you might lack the perspective necessary to recognize the value of the camaraderie developed through trials endured with others. But the bonds you form with peers and mentors during these formative professional years will serve you throughout your career.

You will realize that your early roles provide you with a "leadership laboratory" where you can experiment with various techniques of execution and motivation. As an effective follower, you should volunteer for leadership roles (on project teams, for example) early and frequently. You will develop more tools for your leadership "toolbox" earlier and faster as a result.

You will also learn to push the boundaries of your authority, and you will earn a reputation for being highly accountable. Acting like an entrepreneur and "owning your business" will teach you to set the course for things within your control and not let your project or team become victims of circumstance. Learning to subordinate your will to the team's needs and the leader's direction will demonstrate your professional maturity at a time when others may be acting more selfishly. This maturity will be apparent to, and valued by, the leaders around you.

Finally, as a follower you should develop a habit of looking at your career through The Lens of Leadership: How did leadership skills contribute to the success or failure of your projects, teams, and interactions? Be observant, and connect every result—be it a large or small outcome—to the ultimate accountability that the leader has and the role he or she plays for and with the team. Collect these experiences and commit to best-practice behaviors when *you* have the opportunity to be a leader. And remember, no matter who you are, you are simultaneously a follower and a leader. The natural tendency is to focus on the skills needed to be a good leader. Recognizing the value of being a good follower will make a good leader *great*.

Summary & Exercise:
Chapter 1—Following is the First Form of Leading

WHAT?—SO WHAT?—NOW WHAT?

What? Great leadership begins with great followership. Everyone is simultaneously in the roles of both leader and follower, and both of these roles are servant roles.

So What? You must recognize and differentiate between your obligations as a follower and a leader. You must develop the skills necessary to be successful in these paradoxically simultaneous roles. Knowing how to serve others up, down, and sideways will earn you a reputation as a powerful asset to any team.

Now What?

I will study _____

_____ to learn more about followership.

I will reach out to _____

_____ in order to seek more insight, guidance, and advice.

I will ask _____ to hold me accountable for _____

_____.

And I will _____

_____

_____

_____ in order to create an experience with elements/competencies that I have not yet adequately developed by *(date)* _____.

ADDITIONAL RESOURCES FOR YOUR "NOW WHAT?" JOURNEY:

Carnegie, Dale. *How to Win Friends and Influence People.*

Chaleff, Ira. *The Courageous Follower: Standing Up to and for Our Leaders.*

Covey, Stephen R. *The 7 Habits of Highly Effective People.*

Hughes, Richard, Robert Ginnett, and Gordon Curphy. *Leadership: Enhancing the Lessons of Experience.* (7th ed.)

Maister, David H., Charles H. Green, and Robert M. Galford. *The Trusted Advisor.*

Pink, Daniel H. *The Adventures of Johnny Bunko: The Last Career Guide You'll Ever Need.*

Riggio, Ronald E., Ira Chaleff, and Jean Lipman-Blumen, eds. *The Art of Followership: How Great Followers Create Great Leaders and Organizations.*

Tulgan, Bruce. *It's Okay to Manage Your Boss: The Step-by-Step Program for Making the Best of Your Most Important Relationship at Work.*

CHAPTER TWO

BEING INTENSELY LOYAL

To my country: May she ever be right. But right or wrong, my country.
— Commodore Stephen Decatur's society toast

*Many persons have a wrong idea of what constitutes true happiness. It is
not attained through self-gratification, but through loyalty
to a worthy purpose.*
— Helen Keller

Loyalty is one of the longest levers you can pull in your follower role; therefore, it is one of your most powerful tools. Loyalty is important for leaders to earn, and vital for followers to demonstrate. It should be an expectation you set for yourself, and that your leader sets for the whole team. On the best teams, it is a self-monitoring process: the team members demand it from one another at all times.

Loyalty is putting something *else* before your own self-interests. One of the most frequent and important tests of loyalty is when you personally disagree with your leader's choice or decision, yet are expected to execute it yourself and communicate that decision to others who will also act to "make it happen." Such moments can be career crossroads for you.

I believe that loyalty is a commitment to the leader's decision even when a decision didn't go your way. A skilled, well-respected leader will not use consensus as a decision-making tool, and it should not be expected from a wise follower. On the best, most effective teams, all members have the right to *be heard*, but not to be the decision-maker. There can be only be one decision-maker, and heavy is the weight of that responsibility for the one who will be held accountable for that decision's outcome.

Stuart Landersman's excellent leadership fable, "The Damn Exec!" tells the tale of decision-making and loyalty aboard a Navy ship in port. The captain makes a simple, weather-based decision about the crew's uniform of the day, and passes it down through the "exec" (number two officer, akin to a COO). The decision is not very popular because it results in some inconvenience for the crew.

One of the officers receiving the decision from the exec, not wanting to be blamed for the inconvenience, passes the decision down to his people by telling his direct reports, "The exec wants you to wear…." It then continues being passed throughout that officer's team as being the lousy decision of "the damn exec."

Later in the fable, the captain overhears junior sailors grumbling about the "damn exec's" decision, and he knows he has got loyalty trouble aboard his ship. He goes on to teach his officers that you know the level at which loyalty breaks down by who is blamed as the decision gets passed. The fact that the "damn exec" is the one taking the heat means that loyalty broke down at the level below the exec.

While it is a military fable, its lesson is important for all organizations: once decisions are made, leaders at all levels demonstrate loyalty by communicating those decisions as if they were their own. If the "rumor mill" is rife with grumblings about the "damn manufacturing manager's" decision, then the director of manufacturing knows that her manufacturing manager has got at least one direct report who isn't on-board with the team.

I am surprised by how many leader/followers make a habit of passing on unpopular decisions by transferring ownership of that decision to someone else, and then miss the fact that they are robbing themselves of their own influence and diminishing their team's respect for them. If you consistently pass on decisions by saying, "So-and-so says we have to…," then eventually, your team members will think to themselves, "What do we need *this* clown for? How ineffective a leader is he that he can't ever change the mind of *his* boss before a bad decision is made? If I had his job, I would be more effective." Thus begins the erosion of your influence.

Retired General Colin Powell explains the importance of dialogue before, and loyalty after, the decision this way: "When we are debating an issue, loyalty means giving me your honest opinion, whether you think I'll like it or not. Disagreement, at this stage, stimulates me. But once a decision has been made, the debate ends. From that point on, loyalty means executing the decision as if it were your own."

To avoid reducing your personal effectiveness and lowering others' estimation of your leadership and loyalty, pass on decisions as though they are your own. "Here's how we're going to move forward…" is a great transition statement in front of a team. If complaining starts, nip it in the bud early by saying, "This isn't going to be easy, and we will need everyone's input to make it successful. Let's get talking about how we can make this work effectively." If your idea didn't carry the day back in the dialogue phase, then resolve to bring a more complete and persuasive argument next time!

When conflicts do arise, deal with them at the lowest level possible. Nobody wins when people engage in the game of "my boss is bigger than your boss." It wastes time, and it makes both people look foolish, weak, and incapable of working as a team. Instead, bring your facts to the table, along with a mindset that what you really want is what's best for the organization at a level or two above you.

As a brand manager and project leader, I have had plenty of occasions where I would have liked to leverage the rank or power of my leader in order to trump a colleague who was causing delay to my project, or just wouldn't "get with the program." However, my career and professional relationships have benefited a great deal from something I learned from Mark Clemente, now a senior operations leader at The Boeing Company. Once when I was feeling like it was me against a peer from another team inside our organization, Mark said, "You know, there's really never an excuse for getting yourself stuck in an 'Us versus Them' mindset, Cory. Even in a steeply hierarchical organization, once you get one level—never more than two levels—above you, there is no 'them.' It's all 'us!' You'll always seize the moral high ground when you are the one professionally mature and organizationally savvy enough to bring that spirit to the conversation."

KEEP THE FAITH

If you ever find yourself struggling to maintain your own loyalty because of a consistent stream of decisions with which you disagree, or because you lack sufficient understanding or perspective to judge whether the decisions being made are the right ones or not, adopt a mindset of "keep the faith."

A lot of us have heard this phrase, but it, too, can lead to negative thoughts and even cynicism if not fully understood. I learned its power when I was in prisoner-of-war training (called "*SERE*," or "Survival, Evasion, Resistance, and Escape") after earning my wings as a Naval Flight Officer.

Article IV of the Code of Conduct for U.S. military members reminds us that, "If I become a prisoner of war, I will keep faith with my fellow prisoners. I will give no information nor take part in any action which might be harmful to my comrades." *SERE* training begins in a classroom, where soldiers, sailors, airmen, and Marines memorize the Code of Conduct. I "knew" the Code from as far back as Plebe (freshman) Year at the Naval Academy, and could recite it verbatim. But the lessons with the biggest impact come from actual experiences.

There comes a time in *SERE* training after the "evasion" phase when you have been "captured"

> Loyalty is a powerful force. It will earn you respect, enhance your reputation throughout the organization, and expand your influence over time. Loyalty, however, should never come before integrity and ethics. You and your team members have been hired for your discernment and ethical judgment as well as your skills. You should never follow "blindly." We will explore this potential conflict in the next chapter.

and have spent what seems like a long time in a small, cold prison cell when you are removed for various "interrogations." This is to give you a chance to practice the resistance techniques you would use if you were really captured in time of war. One of the most dispiriting moments for me was during an interrogation session when I was shown photographs of some of my classmates—men and women I *knew* to be of high character and commitment, physically and mentally strong, and well-trained—in situations that made me doubt their commitment. There they were in front of a steaming bowl of soup, or holding a signed confession admitting that they were "war criminals," or sitting in front of a warm fire chatting with this "enemy" camp's commandant. How deflating. It was a low point in my training, and made me question my commitment and ability to continue to withstand the continued privation and physical discomfort while my classmates had apparently given in. Luckily, welling up from somewhere deep in my weary mind, Article IV of the Code of Conduct reminded me to "keep faith with my fellow prisoners."

It was at one of my next "interrogations" that I discovered the truth: My head was covered with a sack and I was led out of my cell into a room where I was forced into a chair, and my hands were placed in front of me. Before I knew it, the hood was pulled off, a momentary bright light blinded me, and the hood was placed back over my head. No questions were asked and no benefits offered. I wasn't sure what had just happened, but I knew that was not the worst "interrogation" I had experienced. Maybe something went wrong in another part of the camp and they needed to get me back to my cell to focus on someone else?

It wasn't until days later, when I was clean-shaven and well-rested back in a classroom environment, that I learned the power of "keep the faith." During my one-on-one debriefing, I was shown a picture of me with my hands resting on a signed confession admitting I was a "war criminal," which was used to dispirit classmates who followed me through the process.

That experience has buoyed my spirits over the years when I have questioned decisions of leaders over me, or I have questioned the motives of colleagues when I lacked as much information as I wanted. When you are tempted to start passing down decisions as someone else's, or start to wonder whether "they" even understand the business realities at your level, remember to "keep the faith." Remain loyal to the decision-makers, and seek out more complete information until you understand the whole situation better. Even if you are still dissatisfied after you seek out more information, remain loyal to those you work for and with. Your influence will increase, and you will have earned the opportunity to make those decisions yourself someday.

If loyalty within a team is high, it is because the leader and the team as a whole all monitor and hold each other accountable for remaining loyal. If your team members lack loyalty to decision-makers, escalate conflict too quickly, or lack faith in each other's skills and good intentions, then step up and suggest that the team or the leader re-examine things through The Lens of Leadership.

Summary & Exercise: Chapter 2—Being Intensely Loyal

WHAT?—SO WHAT?—NOW WHAT?

What? Loyalty is one of the most powerful levers you have in your follower role. It is built when teammates pass on decisions with an ownership mentality. It is enhanced when conflicts are resolved face-to-face at the lowest level possible. Loyalty becomes a strong cement that bonds a team when teammates "keep the faith" and trust, often in the face of less information than they would like, in the competence and good intentions of other teammates and leaders.

So What? You must examine the state of loyalty on your team. If decisions are passed on like the "damn exec!", if teammates avoid conflicts face-to-face, and then escalate them to leaders, or if cynicism exists about team member competencies and intentions, then you must raise the conversation and confront this poisonous, damaging condition. You can be successful helping your team improve results by increasing loyalty and engagement.

Now What?

I will study _____
_____ to learn more about the
power of loyalty.

I will reach out to _____
_____ in order to seek more
insight, guidance, and advice.

I will ask _____ to hold me
accountable for _____
_____.

And I will _____

_____

_____

_____ in order to create an experience with elements/competencies that I have not yet adequately developed by *(date)* _____.

ADDITIONAL RESOURCES FOR YOUR "NOW WHAT?" JOURNEY:

Dickens, Charles. *Great Expectations.*

Felten, Eric. *Loyalty: The Vexing Virtue.*

Keiningham, Timothy, Lerzan Aksoy, and Luke Williams. *Why Loyalty Matters.*

Landersman, Stuart D. "The Damn Exec!" *Proceedings Magazine.* (Jan. 1965)

Patterson, Kerry, Joseph Grenny, Ron McMillan, and Al Switzler. *Crucial Conversations, Tools for Talking When Stakes Are High.*

Tolkien, J.R.R. *The Fellowship of the Ring.*

White. E.B. *Charlotte's Web.*

CHAPTER THREE

LIVING WITH INTEGRITY

Character cannot be summoned at the moment of crisis if it has been squandered by years of compromise and rationalization. The only testing ground for the heroic is the mundane. The only preparation for that one profound decision that can change a life, or even a nation, is those hundreds of half-conscious, self-defining, seemingly insignificant decisions made in private. Habit is the daily battleground of character.
— Dan Coats, former U.S. Senator

Trust cannot be surged.
— Admiral Gary Roughead, Chief of Naval Operations, referring to the strategic impact of long-term allied relationships

One of the hardest letters I have ever had to write was to the Honor Board at the Naval Academy in the spring of my senior year. A professor had accused a classmate of cheating on his senior project. This was not just any classmate—he was like a *brother* to me. We had spent three years as company mates. I had hosted him in my hometown. We had traveled together during school breaks. We had worshipped cross-culturally together. We had triumphed and struggled together academically and athletically.

I had no knowledge of the details of the case and had not been involved in the board's proceedings, but I was a fourth-year "striper"— a high-ranking student leader—and my classmate had asked me to write to the board as a character reference for him. I wrote chapter and verse about my personal and professional experiences with my friend, and how I had always observed him acting with exceptionally high character. But I also had to write these words: "If the Board should find him in violation of the Honor Concept, [my friend] knows how strongly I believe that Midshipmen convicted of an honor violation should be separated from the Naval Academy." I believed my honor required me to be clear to my friend and to the board about my faith in the justice of the system.[1] I also did not want even the *appearance* of inconsistency between the messages I conveyed as a leader and what I conveyed as the friend of someone before the Honor Board.

The Naval Academy's Honor Concept was written by midshipmen from the Class of 1951[2]: "A Midshipman does not lie, cheat, or steal." The Military Academy at West Point has its Honor Code that reads slightly differently: "A cadet does not lie, cheat, or steal, *nor tolerate those who do.*" There are many civilian colleges and universities that have similar honor statements that students sign, and some also have student-led boards that administer the enforcement of the honor program. The world is an imperfect place filled with imperfect people. Why is "honor" such a big deal? Because organizations are filled with people who make big decisions every single day. Regardless of whether they work in business, the military, the clergy, journalism, law, medicine, a not-for-profit, or in socially-mo-

---

1 The years, however, have taught me that ideal systems overseen by human beings can still fail to deliver justice.

2 Led by two students who went on to make other great contributions to the world: H. Ross Perot and William P. Lawrence.

tivated "cause" organizations, those decisions dramatically impact the current and future lives of others. They affect peoples' careers, their ability to provide for their family, and their financial futures. Unknowable triumphs and tragedies lie in peoples' futures; so, to-day—as followers, and leaders, and "deciders" of matters large and small—you are morally obligated to act with integrity.

DO THE RIGHT THING

First, let me be clear that I am not intending to position myself as holier-than-thou. My reason for including this chapter is to emphasize the importance of having a personal reputation for integrity, ethics, and character as both a follower and a leader. Today's headlines are too full of people who have selfishly compromised their integrity to ruinous effect on the lives of others. This subject should be talked about frequently by leaders at all levels throughout every organization. It is the number one enculturation topic that should be covered with people new to the organization, and it is the number one ongoing conversation that organizations should be having with long-tenured members.

The simple definition I have come to use is: *"Integrity is doing the right thing even when nobody else is watching."*

Simple, but not always easy to live up to, right? And what you think is the "right thing" to do may be very different from what someone else in your organization—perhaps on the other side of the world—believes the "right thing" is. That is why these conversations should be happening constantly.

Why do the Naval Academy and West Point put so much emphasis on honor? Why do they spend so much time and so much money teaching the principles and applied philosophies of character? Why do they create—and then monitor each student's decision-making in—thousands of "gray" situations over four years, all while under the pressures of time, a significant academic load, and physical exhaustion? Because they believe that if a student will compromise his integrity on something "small," like cheating on a chemistry test, or lying about whether he performed a certain undesirable task, then he is certainly unworthy of his nation's trust on "big" things like whether the criteria for engagement were fully met before firing a missile into a target, or completing the scheduled maintenance on nuclear-tipped missiles. *Big character flaws reveal themselves through everyday actions.*

Every military officer's commission cites the "special trust and confidence" that America is placing in the personal honor and trustworthiness of that new officer. Your organization is placing a "special trust and confidence" in *your* personal honor and trustworthiness as well.

> **"Cory, in the last chapter, didn't you write to be loyal to my leader and my colleagues?"**
>
> Not blindly so. Unfortunately, life will test your integrity regularly. You must decide for yourself to what and whom you will remain loyal. Use your personal beliefs and your organization's values as yardsticks. When you find your integrity tested by a leader, a colleague, or even a friend, you can't go wrong remaining committed to time-tested guiding principles that connect you to higher loyalties.

HIGH INTEGRITY LEADS TO HIGH TRUST

When any team or organization acts with integrity consistently, the members of that team learn that they can depend on each other to live up to promises and to deliver against expectations. That builds a trust among the team's members that becomes self-perpetuating and reinforcing, as long as the trust is continuously nurtured and earned. The more the trust is extended and delivered upon, the more it is reinforced, and thereby, earns even *more* trust.

The American political economist Francis Fukuyama is quoted in Stephen M.R. Covey's book *The Speed of Trust* as saying, "Widespread distrust in a society…imposes a kind of tax on all forms of economic activity, a tax that high-trust societies do not have to pay." A company with low trust has volumes of oversight policies and structures in place, theoretically, to prevent people from doing the things that damage trust. There are long lists of "approvers" that slow down the capital process. There are several layers of management to approve the sales and marketing programs that customers may take advantage of. There are redundant systems and armies of lawyers and accountants to cover all of the bases.

But this high-control environment actually robs individuals of their opportunities to *demonstrate* integrity. It is a false economy to believe that high levels of control increase organizational integrity. Evidence of that truth abounds in daily news stories. When those situations get analyzed in board rooms and in the press, they are often covered as *process failures*, not as failures of human integrity. "If only there had been more *oversight*," then the situation would have been avoided. No! If only the human beings surrounding the human beings making the ignoble decisions had shown the integrity to speak up, the publically-embarrassing event that hurt the organization, its business, its investors, its people, and its reputation, may have been avoided.

To create a high-trust environment, people have to be honest, honorable, and of high character. But that is not enough. It is not just about honesty and confronting behaviors that lack integrity. If people are unskilled at their jobs or lack fundamental tools like quality control processes, then trust is damaged because the *results* are not earning trust. People must be well-trained and equipped in order to earn the trust of their customers, regardless of whether they are internal or external.

It takes both integrity *and* results to become a high-trust team. High-trust teams live with a different operating model than low trust teams. Instead of their efforts being weighed down by the "tax" of low trust, they operate very efficiently and effectively by earning what Covey calls the "dividend of high-trust." Those high-trust teams deliver results faster, and they deliver *better* results because there are fewer constraints and controls in place that slow things down and impede the progress of the team.

Because they know they can depend on people to do the right thing (even when nobody is watching), and because they know their teammates are well-equipped and are great at their jobs, these high trust teams are the ones that will outperform their competitors.[3]

WHAT YOU MUST DO

How can you help build a high-trust team? There are three things you must do to contribute to your organization's collective level of integrity: *teach*, *model*, and *reinforce*.

Teach

People in your organization can be different in many ways. While none of those differences justify dishonorable or dishonest behavior, people come to the workplace with different ideas about right and wrong. You should make a deliberate effort to start engaging conversations about integrity, ethics, and character by using behaviorally-specific examples and stories. Leaders from throughout the company—not just from the Ethics Council or from Human Resources—should be seizing on teachable moments that appear every day in popular business and news media. They should jumpstart conversations that explain the company values and give examples of behaviors that demonstrate when those values are being lived or not lived.

The focus should not be on why actions are "against policy" or "will get you in trouble." People should be discussing the *natural* consequences of dishonest behavior. Natural consequences are what will *inevitably* happen to safety, quality, efficiencies, and the spirit of teamwork and team "trust" as a result of people selfishly engaging in

---

3 More on this topic in Chapter 21 on building a high-performance team.

unethical conduct, even if the news of it never gets outside the organization. Remember, it's not just about being honest. Competency plays a big role in creating high-trust environments. Leaders should be discussing (and enabling) excellence in performance and people development so high-performance expectations are being delivered with high integrity.

If those teaching conversations are not happening, then you as a follower should take the initiative to start them. When you hear or read about dishonest or unethical behaviors in other organizations, strike up "water cooler" conversations about whether that kind of behavior—low ethics or low performance—could ever happen "here." Wonder aloud, "How would you keep from being tempted?" or "What should we be doing to get better at our jobs?" Those kinds of thought-provoking questions can start the conversation and create an environment where "right" behaviors are taught through the example of others. People ask me whether integrity can be developed, or whether people just "have it" or don't. My answer is that conversations like I have described are *absolutely essential* in developing a higher level of integrity in any organization.

Model

Teaching is important, but "walking the talk" is vital. Nothing will breed cynicism and kill high-trust faster than being an organization that puts its "values" up on the wall, but has leaders and teammates whose behaviors blatantly contradict those values.

The fast-food chain Chick-fil-A models two of its owners' values of "Faith" and "Family" by remaining closed on Sundays, one of the highest-revenue days of the week for quick-service restaurants. This decision sends a powerful signal to all of the company's associates by putting personal rest, contemplation, and family time before another day of profits. The company acts consistently with its values, and its employees and customers reward it as a result.

Hypocrisy can kill a high-integrity environment. The power of modeling is driven by *consistency*. You and all of your teammates consistently need to demonstrate *all* of the behaviors of your organization's culture, not just the ones about honesty. That may mean flying on economy airline tickets because it is a financial expectation. It may mean managing your hotel and meal expenses in ways that are Spartan in order to be consistent across the organization. These behaviors will help prevent perceptions of unfairness and inconsistency from surfacing. You can also demonstrate high integrity by subjecting your work to the scrutiny of others before presenting it to leaders. Taking ownership for your deliverables demonstrates high *competence* integrity.

Reinforce

In order to reinforce your organization's commitment to excellence and integrity, you must be prepared to *celebrate the heroes* and *separate the violators*.

When somebody lives out one of your values or does the "right thing," especially when it was hard, you have to celebrate that person. Tell his or her story far and wide. Put it on your organization's internal home page. Write about it in your company newsletter. Get the word out that doing the right thing—whether it is about results or character—is valued and will be celebrated!

And when someone repeatedly misses the mark—especially with values violations—that person must be separated from the team, and the separation should be communicated to the entire organization. It must be done delicately and respectfully, but it *must* be done. Communicating about the separation accomplishes three important things: it reinforces the *importance* of the values, it demonstrates the organization's *commitment* to those values, and it *reduces cynicism* and misinformation that may come from people not understanding what happened.

I know of a company where a vice-president was separated for repeated values violations. It was the right thing for the leadership to do, and each functional head went to his or her direct reports and told them the same story, instructing them to tell their direct reports until it had filtered down to the whole organization. "So-and-so is a good person. He really delivered results for us for a long time. But he cannot be one of us anymore because he could not live our values. And we know that because several people from across the company had the courage to step up to risky conversations about those behaviors. They did exactly the right thing." That was a powerful step in reinforcing behaviors and demonstrating transparency across that company.

Your organization has a lot at stake. Each member of it has responsibilities that affect people's lives in important ways. Your team's collective integrity and character will affect business results and the workplace's culture. Do not underestimate the negative impact of Francis Fukuyama's low-trust "tax." The systems and behaviors of a low-trust team are a ball and chain around the legs of your business. Great followers and great leaders understand that *they* are accountable for the ethical culture of their team. By viewing results and character through The Lens of Leadership, they will take action to *teach*, *model*, and *reinforce* the behaviors that drive that culture.

Summary & Exercise: Chapter 3—Living With Integrity

WHAT?—SO WHAT?—NOW WHAT?

What? Integrity is doing the right thing, even when nobody is watching. Your organization's reputation and success depend upon *your* actions. High integrity leads to high trust, and high trust is built upon competence as well as character.

So What? You make decisions that affect people's lives. You must, therefore, teach, model, and reinforce ethical behaviors—whether you are a follower or a leader—in order to create a high-trust, high-performance team.

Now What?

I will study _____

_____ to learn more about the individual and organizational benefits of integrity, ethics, and character.

I will reach out to _____

_____ in order to seek more insight, guidance, and advice.

I will ask _____ to hold me accountable for _____

_____.

And I will _____

_____ in order to create an experience with elements/competencies that I have not yet adequately developed by *(date)* _____.

ADDITIONAL RESOURCES FOR YOUR "NOW WHAT?" JOURNEY:

Bennett, William J. *The Book of Virtues.*

Chanski, Christopher J. *Principled Performance from the Mailroom to the Boardroom.*

Covey, Stephen M.R. *The SPEED of Trust: The One Thing That Changes Everything.*

Covey, Stephen M.R. *Smart Trust: Creating Prosperity, Energy, and Joy in a Low-Trust World.*

Geisler, Norman L. *Integrity at Work: Finding Your Ethical Compass in a Post-Enron World.*

Krulak, Charles. "The Eagle and the Wolf." (Google It)

Maxwell, John C. *There's No Such Thing As "Business" Ethics: There's Only One Rule For Making Decisions.*

Simons, Tony. *The Integrity Dividend: Leading by the Power of Your Word.*

Sommers, Christina Hoff and Fred Sommers. *Vice and Virtue in Everyday Life.*

CHAPTER FOUR

MAKING IT HAPPEN

To reach an intended port, we must sail sometimes with the wind, and sometimes against it—but we must sail, and not drift, nor lie at anchor.
— Oliver Wendell Holmes Sr., American physician and writer

It's easy to drift
when the current is swift,
and lie in your boat and dream;
but according to Nature's plan,
it takes a real man,
to paddle his boat upstream.
— Charlie Wintermeyer, a family friend

The first thing I was issued at the Naval Academy was given to me before I had even officially joined the Navy. It was a copy of Elbert Hubbard's *A Message to Garcia* that was sitting on the unmade bunk I was to sleep on the night before I took my oath as a Midshipman.

A *Message to Garcia* is a powerful fable on initiative, resourcefulness, and self-reliance. It was written in 1899 about America's early involvement in what would become the Spanish-American War. In it, the narrator tells the story of U.S. Army First Lieutenant Andrew Rowan and his limitless sense of initiative and indomitable "can-do" attitude. Rowan independently finds his way across hostile seas, establishes relations with the anti-Spanish insurgency, and single-handedly carries President McKinley's offer of military assistance to the Cuban rebel general Calixto Garcia. Rowan asks no questions of the President, and leaves McKinley without doubt that he will succeed, or perish trying.

Hubbard's article became so popular that he reprinted the tale pamphlet-style and sold it by the thousands to companies. The pamphlets were distributed a hundred years ago to turn-of-the-century workers in hopes they would learn to demonstrate initiative, be a low-needs follower, and relentlessly deliver on expectations.[1]

Hubbard concluded his piece by emphasizing that an employee like this, "never gets 'laid off,' nor has to go on a strike for higher wages. Civilization is one long anxious search for just such individuals. Anything such a man asks shall be granted; his kind is so rare that no employer can afford to let him go. He is wanted in every city, town, and village, in every office, shop, store, and factory. The world cries out for such: he is needed, and needed badly—the one who can carry A Message to Garcia."

A *Message to Garcia* is sometimes misinterpreted because Hubbard used contemporary industrial language to tell his tale. Many modern readers miss the fable's timeless, indispensable lessons because of his directness. It is a fact of real life, however, that someone who accepts full responsibility for the accomplishment of a task is always preferred by a strong leader over somebody who needs constant care and feeding to get the task done. The job of any modern leader is to accomplish a lot through delegation to strong team members. Strong leaders want goals accomplished without having to tell fol-

1 If you are a Millennial reading this book, you can take comfort in knowing that every generation's senior leaders doubt the work ethic of the incoming generation. You just happen to be in the spotlight this decade. Be assured that your time to doubt the commitment and work ethic of some unnamed future working generation is still to come.

lowers *how* to get it done. In order for that to happen, they require highly skilled, highly empowered, autonomous team members who *consistently demonstrate initiative, are "low-needs" followers,* and *deliver relentlessly on expectations.*

CONSISTENTLY DEMONSTRATE INITIATIVE

Be a person of action. Anticipate the needs of the situation, the project, the team, and the leader. Anticipating doesn't mean becoming "political," a "suck-up," or as my grandfather used to say, an "apple-polisher." It *does* mean that if you see a void—some task not being done, a pitfall that has not been planned for, a need not being fulfilled—then be the one who addresses that gap.

Developing a reputation as someone who regularly takes on extra work before it is assigned, who delivers an answer before the question has been asked, and who helps others accomplish their tasks without the need for public recognition will be the single biggest "booster" you can give to your career, no matter what career stage you are in. No need for recognition exists in these instances because the word will get out. Leaders, teams, and organizations just *know* who the "go-to" people are. Do not, however, do the work of others. That is political, and it is bad teamwork. Instead, be the one who *helps* when others need it.

"What am *I* supposed to do?" you may ask. "I don't have the power to take the initiative." Best-selling author and project management expert Neal Whitten will ask a seminar audience or group that he is training, "When was the last time your boss sat you down—or maybe just pointed his finger in your face—and told you that you had exceeded your personal authority?" Neal gives them a few seconds to ponder, and then he continues, "Hold up your hand if you have been coached in the last few months that you just didn't have the right to make a particular decision that you made...that you had *really* exceeded a boundary?" He'll ask, "Three months? Six months? Who's heard that within the last year?" Invariably, almost no hands will go up, even in large public events. Then he delivers a pretty stern admonishment: "If you can't remember the last time you were corrected for 'exceeding your authority,' then I don't want to hear you complain about not having enough personal power or authority. You're not even pushing the boundaries on the power you *do* have."

Don't believe your own stories that you are not empowered enough, or you lack the authority to take the initiative. Push those bounds. Ask for a little forgiveness instead of permission. Do not wait around for someone *else* to "do something." *You* make it happen!

BE A "LOW-NEEDS" FOLLOWER

Nobody likes an overly "needy" teammate. Followers have enough to do without tying up loose ends for their leader, and leaders definitely do not need the extra burden of verifying the work of those they lead. "High-maintenance" followers have a hard time shaking that reputation once word is on the street that so-and-so needs a lot of handholding to get the job done or has a way of letting his personal life complicate or interfere with his professional life.

Just to be clear, I am not saying that you should not occasionally ask for help from your leader, a mentor, or teammates. When you *do* ask for help, start with your teammates. Treat their time as a resource as valuable as your own, and keep communication lines open with them. If you worry that you are requiring more help from them than you expected, ask them what you need to do to become more capable of doing the work yourself. Your peers or teammates will be your best early-warning system of whether you are becoming a burden. Also, ask your leader for his perspective on team priorities to make sure you are concentrating on "the right stuff."

We all have events in our personal lives that affect our work. The best followers have a way of minimizing the impact of their personal life on work. I don't mean to minimize the important role that workplace friends can have in helping you through (and even celebrating!) certain life events. I do want you to be regularly self-reflective on whether or not you are contributing to or taxing the supportive environment of your team. Are you asking more from your leader than you are giving? The best followers are not a burden to their leader. They go out of their way to lighten his or her load.

DELIVER RELENTLESSLY ON EXPECTATIONS

The most important thing for you to do in your role as a follower is to…"do!" In *Execution: The Discipline of Getting Things Done*, Larry Bossidy and Ram Charan teach that, "Execution is *the* job of the business leader." Your reputation for being someone who will regularly break through walls and get over all hurdles to exceed expectations of timing and quality will be one early indicator of your future effectiveness as a leader. This reputation will be one of the earliest ways to differentiate yourself from your peers. Here are some ways to earn that reputation:

Pay attention to details. It has been my observation that people who are attentive to details in managing their daily projects and events will be the most successful.

Be punctual (even when others are not). Be a couple of minutes early to each meeting.[2] Deliver on your timeline commitments. Encourage others to do the same.

Be passionate. People will listen more attentively to someone demonstrating conviction. So often the workplace can become a place where people just "show up." Be someone who believes in what he is doing and saying, and communicate why.

Be intellectually curious. Ask a lot of questions. Offer to play the role of "Devil's Advocate" on your team. Read a lot of books. Become a voracious learner. It is in your organization's best interest for everyone to be reading, growing intellectually, and challenging each other by asking lots of questions.

If you subscribe to the Apollo 13 motto of "Failure is not an option" in your quest to deliver relentlessly on expectations, you will

---

2 Bring some additional work you can be doing in case others are not on time.

also have to earn a reputation as someone who is resourceful and creative in her problem-solving.

CAVEAT EMPTOR: ROWAN'S PARADOX

In this same chapter, which I began by extolling the virtues of Lieutenant Rowan's "no-questions, get-it-done" sense of follower-ship, I am also going to encourage you, in today's modern and collaborative workplace, to reach out to others.

There is a big difference between being an independent self-starter, and being too stubborn to know when to ask for help. Explore and decide for yourself where the appropriate balance between independence and collaboration is within the context of your corporate culture and immediate team dynamics. Do not take *A Message to Garcia* too literally. You do not want to work beyond the point of diminishing return on your independence just because you would not ask for some help getting over the learning curve. By all means, collaborate, but earn a reputation for being self-reliant and knocking down brick walls to deliver your *Message to Garcia*.

Also, do not become overzealous. *How* you "make it happen" is very important. Rowan collaborated with British and Jamaican sailors to get to Cuba, and with ruthless Cuban rebels to earn an audience with General Garcia. He acted as a diplomat throughout his journey, connecting his goal to theirs by highlighting a mutual purpose. The way you go about being "relentless" in your delivery will determine whether your reputation is improved or diminished. As Dale Carnegie wrote in his classic *How to Win Friends and Influence People*, "My popularity, my happiness, and sense of self-worth depend to no small extent upon my skill in dealing with people." Your reputation and ability to deliver unexpectedly superior results in the face of adversity will depend on your deft, light touch as you navigate through waters filled with messy, fallible human beings. Do not leave damaged people in your wake.

WHAT ABOUT DIFFERENCES AMONG PEERS?

Inevitably, you will run into situations where you have differences of opinion with people over whom you have no authority. Commit to resolve the disagreement at the lowest level possible. Don't immediately escalate the problem in a game of "My Boss Is Bigger Than Your Boss." Successful resolution can require significant cooperation between you and your colleague, and your leaders have enough on their plates without regularly having to play umpire. Make sure your conversations are about the project, and not personalities. Focus on your mutual, common interest (brainstorm one together, if you have to), not just on the *positions* you have each staked out. Make sure you are not so invested in your position or opinion that you might be reluctant to change it because of pride.

Once you both have made a good faith effort to find agreement, and you realize that the problem cannot be resolved at your level, do what Neal Whitten calls, "escalate to closure." Within two working days of realizing you are "stuck," schedule an escalation meeting with both leaders. Whitten writes, "In most cases, neither party is 'wrong.' Both are correct from their point of view. Often people with broader responsibility are required to weigh the options more objectively and resolve the issue." It's better to save time and get resolution faster, rather than making your project pay what I call the "Opportunity Cost of Indecision."

MAKE IT HAPPEN

Looking at initiative through The Lens of Leadership, it will become clear that many successes and failures are a result of the authority and autonomy delegated, and the responsibilities that followers are willing to take on. Rowan's success was critically enabled by his assumption of accountability for the mission. If he had just been "following orders," it is very likely one of the many hurdles would have tripped him up.

A Message to Garcia also contains a powerful lesson for *leaders*. Just as Rowan does not ask, "Where is [Garcia] at?" or "How can I find him?" (he just sets off to accomplish the task), neither does President McKinley direct Rowan in how he should do so. This story compels leaders to create an environment of empowerment where the Rowans of the workplace can carry their letters to Garcia without being micro-managed.

Sitting on my bed that night before joining the Navy, I didn't know much about the history of the Spanish-American War, nor about the terrain of Cuba, nor what the word "perihelion" meant. It was, however, crystal clear to this Midwestern youngster that if I were going to be successful in life, I had better be prepared *to consistently demonstrate initiative, be a low-needs follower, and deliver relentlessly on expectations,* without fail.

That early lesson in followership has made all of the difference in my life, and it will in yours as well.

Summary & Exercise: Chapter 4—Making It Happen!

WHAT?—SO WHAT?—NOW WHAT?

What? Leaders and teams need teammates who are highly-skilled, highly empowered, and autonomous. Most people vastly underestimate the power they already have. The best followers consistently demonstrate initiative; they are "low-needs" followers; and they deliver relentlessly on expectations.

So What? You must dig down deep inside of yourself and decide whether or not you will work to grow the sense of initiative that Rowan demonstrates in *A Message to Garcia* to earn the reputation as a reliable, "go-to" teammate in your follower role. You will build your career as a leader upon this foundation.

Now What?

I will study _____

_____ to learn more about

initiative, resourcefulness, and self-reliance.

I will reach out to _____

_____ in order to seek more

insight, guidance, and advice.

I will ask _____ to hold me

accountable for _____

_____.

And I will _____

_____

_____

_____ in order to create an experience with

elements/competencies that I have not yet adequately developed by

(date) _____.

ADDITIONAL RESOURCES FOR YOUR "NOW WHAT?" JOURNEY:

Allen, David. *Getting Things Done: The Art of Stress-Free Productivity.*

Blanchard, Ken, Susan Fowler, and Laurence Hawkins. *Self-Leadership and the One Minute Manager: Increasing Effectiveness Through Situational Self Leadership.*

Carnegie, Dale. *How to Win Friends and Influence People.*

Charan, Ram and Larry Bossidy. *Execution.*

Covey, Stephen R. *The 7 Habits of Highly Effective People.*

Heinlein, Robert A. *Starship Troopers.*

Hubbard, Elbert. *A Message to Garcia.*

Manas, Jerry. *Napoleon on Project Management: Timeless Lessons in Planning, Execution, and Leadership.*

McChesney, Chris et al. *The 4 Disciplines of Execution: Achieving Your Wildly Important Goals.*

Nelson, Bob. *1001 Ways to Take Initiative at Work.*

Whitten, Neal. *Neal Whitten's No-Nonsense Advice for Successful Projects.*

CHAPTER FIVE

ACTING WITH PROFESSIONALISM

You can't build a reputation on what you are going to do.
— Henry Ford

So live that those who know the most about you have the greatest confidence in you.
– A handwritten quote beneath a photo of my grandfather, Lowell H. Bouck

I was on summer training after my Plebe (freshman) year at the Naval Academy aboard *USS New Orleans,* an amphibious assault ship, in the middle of the South China Sea when I got one of my most valuable pieces of mentoring: "Set a sterling example, and keep your reputation shiny, just like this brass." A navy enlisted man was teaching me to shine the ornamental brass on the ship's bridge up to fleet standards. He was also advising me with a perfect metaphor for how professionals act and manage their careers.

I have a piece of distinctly-unattractive art on the wall near my desk that holds another great piece of wisdom I received early in my career. In the frame is the torn-off cover of a Navy standard-issue blue folder.

I laminated it at some point to protect the yellow sticky note on it that has these words: "*Be Productive. Be Innovative. Be the Expert. Be Polite.*"

That sticky note was written in passing by a squadron mate named Terry Mentzos as his way of welcoming me as the new rookie to Patrol Squadron 45 in Jacksonville, Florida. Arriving as the "nugget" to an environment as tight as a naval aviation squadron can make you feel a little bit like you are landing on the island in *Lord of the Flies*. Terry was just glad not to be a nugget anymore, and he scribbled off the note as a way of mentoring me without investing too much in me, at least without my earning it first. It was and is timeless, pure, career-management gold.

BE PRODUCTIVE

Whatever you do for a living, you are producing *something*. It may be as tangible as a product you can hold, eat, watch, or use to save a life. Or maybe it is intangible, like an emotion resulting from your performance as an actor or as a Good Samaritan. Maybe you create an experience for others to enjoy. There are a million ways to earn a living in this world. Whatever the business model of your organization is, Be Productive at it!

Develop a reputation as a high-quality, high-volume producer of the goods or services your team is charged with creating. No matter what career stage you are in, consistently generate more than others. Don't shy away from trying to be "the best." Many teams will have incentives geared toward high producers, but even if yours doesn't, produce anyway! You will earn a reputation as a "go-to" person when the chips are down and short-notice results are needed. Be someone who helps solve the problems of others.

What if you work in an environment where standing out is *not* rewarded? What if your desire and ability to cheerfully produce more than others earns you the burden of negative peer pressure? Then you must evaluate your circumstances through The Lens of Leadership: are you holding yourself accountable for living and working in circumstances that are consistent with your authentic self? I wrote in Chapter 3 about integrity. Integrity also means being true to yourself. It's hard to work in an environment that asks you to be someone different than whom you are. Start right now developing a plan to get you into a role where you can be productive, and through your healthy competitive spirit, inspire others to elevate their game as well.

> "Professionalism" as a follower means making your boss look great. I don't mean for you to become obsequious or submissive. What I do mean is that leaders want followers who work hard to deliver a little bit more than required. And if you are serving the needs of your leader, you will also be serving the needs of your team.

Put a lot of pride into your work, no matter what the work is. In his autobiography *My American Journey*, General Colin Powell tells the story of the summer during high school that he spent mopping floors at a local bottling plant. "It could be godawful work, as it was the day fifty cases of Pepsi-Cola bottles came crashing down from a forklift and flooded the floor with sticky soda pop. But if that's what it took to earn $65 a week, I'd do it. I'd mop the place until it glowed in the dark. Whatever the job required, I soon mastered it." At the end of the summer, the foreman told Powell, "You mopped pretty good. Come back next summer and I'll have a job for you." Powell replied, "Not behind a mop." Powell wanted to work on a bottling machine, but those were manned mostly by white men. The next summer, Powell ran a bottling machine and was promoted to deputy shift leader. "I had learned a valuable lesson: all work is honorable. Always do your best, because someone is watching."

Do you hate where you are at or what you are doing? Work even harder to deliver excellent results. Few people will promote or recommend to others someone who is mediocre. Someone who is candidly interested in another role, team, or type of profession, *and* delivers greatness where he is, however, will find mentors and leaders willing to help him navigate those transitional waters successfully.

When working on something that will end up in front of anyone, not just your boss, bring that person *answers*, not just more questions. Bring him or her two or three well-researched options, and also have a strong recommendation. Leaders are looking for people with strong critical thinking skills, the ability to think logically, and to solve problems. Sometimes, it's hard to remove personal preferences or agendas from business situations. I encourage you to listen to "the data," then apply equal amounts of experience and common sense as a brain-check. It is important to make *rational* decisions at work, so when speaking, don't say, "I feel…" because it communicates less forethought and commitment to an idea than "I think…" or "I believe…." You can demonstrate even more decisiveness by being purely declarative: "We should…." When emotion *should* play into your recommendation, be clear to distinguish between what your brain is telling you, and what your heart or gut is telling you. This difference will add the right texture to your answer and demonstrate a high degree of professional judgment and maturity.

Learn to communicate with your boss' voice if you create documents and presentations for her. Read what she has written. Watch her previous presentations. Notice her writing and speaking styles. Watch for trends in how she builds an argument and arrives at her conclusions. Then work hard to make what you create for her in a voice that is authentic to hers. This talent is the great speechwriter's gift. It shows a strong ability to pay attention to details, and it demonstrates your absolute commitment to delivering greatness in a way that makes her successful in the most value-added way for the organization.

BE INNOVATIVE

The world has never required us to be more innovative. The rate of change of complexity—and therefore the need for adaptation—is exponential today, and in order to remain viable for the future, we and our work must develop truly new insights and solutions. Your professional goal should be to leave every role changed in some way, and better off than you found it. That will require innovation.

Innovation occurs along a continuum. At one end is what I call a Continuous Improvement (CI) mindset. At the other is what I call Breakthrough Innovation (BI). Different people tend to operate in one area on that continuum throughout their professional lives. People who tend to be CI-oriented will adapt what "is" and make it the best it can possibly be. People on the BI part of the continuum can ignore what "is" (they may even have contempt for the *status quo*) and work to create what "ought to be." Forcing someone to work at one end of a scale that is opposite to his or her natural inclination causes great stress and may lead to burnout. That is not to say that different people cannot learn different techniques of creative problem-solving. Great teams, however, need to be well-balanced with members from all along the continuum, so forcing someone to be different than he really is will not be nearly as effective as building a team that represents both mindsets well.

Your leaders need creative people who can "see around corners." These "seers" are incredibly valuable teammates, but they are hardly Nostradamus. You can "see around corners" yourself by running several problem scenarios and creating "If-Then" solutions for the most likely ones. You can also start studying the problem from the perspective of a leader who is a couple of levels above you. If you are studying competitive products, expand out to adjacent categories. If you are studying a problem within your industry, then search for how a different industry solved a similarly-constituted problem. Need to know what your competitor will do next? Create a war-gaming environment throughout your team and convene an adversary council to work through the "What if?" scenarios. These are all ways you can add value through innovation and enhance the way you and others around you think and solve problems.

The innovation might just be to bring an overwhelming likelihood of victory with you to the arena. I once worked with a battle fleet commander whose maxim was, "I always bring a shotgun to a knife fight." Perhaps you will create a more comprehensive, multimedia, multi-targeted marketing campaign than ever before. Or maybe you will develop a way to add so many features affordably to the new version of your product that it will leapfrog the established leader. Whatever your work is, do it with an innovative mind.

BE THE EXPERT

There just is no substitute for having an incredible amount of competence in your daily work. Nothing will set you apart earlier or more obviously than your quick, deep knowledge of the functional underpinnings of your job or profession. And nothing will hurt your career more—or damage your influence more quickly—than an obvious lack of that knowledge and those skills.

Competence can only be earned through study and application. No matter your disadvantages, let nothing come between you and quickly earning a reputation as the go-to person for knowledge and information. If training roles exist within your type of work, rise quickly to the level of teaching others. This ability demonstrates job mastery and will expose you to situations not covered by "the book." Teaching will further increase your knowledge base, and will also earn you opportunities for peer leadership roles.

Leading peers is the hardest of all forms of leadership because you can't rely on formal authority. Without an obvious difference in seniority or tenure, you are forced to lead and "win" through superior knowledge, ideas, and your ability to form mutually-supportive relationships. Peer leadership begets opportunities to lead and teach larger groups, which further increases your ability to influence. Manage those relationships carefully. Your desire for peer leadership should be rooted in your honest desire to see the group succeed.

Your expertise will also lead to opportunities to share your knowledge with more senior leaders, either because they are "rusty" and need to be brought back up to speed, or because your competence is so high that you are bringing truly new, fresh thinking to the conversation. Either way, it is an opportunity to demonstrate great leadership through your skills of followership. Your expertise will result in you taking on higher levels of risk and responsibility, as well. Additional responsibility must be treated as a sacred trust because of the increasing consequences of failure.

The final step in my becoming a fully-qualified aviation navigator was demonstrating that I could safely and accurately guide my airplane from Jacksonville, Florida across 2,400 miles of the Atlantic Ocean at night using only celestial navigation—the stars and planets. We would be flying to the Azores, a small archipelago 900 miles west of Portugal. In the mid-1990s, I was going to fly for eight hours looking for one small island using the same techniques that Christopher Columbus used in the fifteenth century! The reason for this test was that the Navy was about to frequently entrust me with the lives of eleven other crewmen across vast expanses of open water. This was before the Global Positioning System (GPS) was prevalent and reliable, and nobody wanted to be the navigator whose crew got lost, ran out of gas, and ditched in the ocean after his primary navigation tools failed. Not only did I succeed in finding the Azores, but I went on to develop a reputation for excellence that earned me the opportunity to become a navigator trainer. I adapted my skills when

GPS was introduced and earned the highest accuracy scores for weapons placement in squadron history during the next evaluation.

Your followership reputation as an expert will carry you a long way toward earning the roles you want to achieve. The way you communicate your expertise will help. It can also hurt, however, if not done wisely. One of the first things you learn as a follower at the Naval Academy is your "Five Basic Responses." Any question you are asked can be answered only by one of the "Five Basic Responses," which are: 1) "Yes, sir." 2) "No, sir." 3) "Aye, Aye, sir." (if an order has been given and understood) 4) The correct answer (if a knowledge question has been asked, and the answer is known) or 5) "I'll find out, sir."

Sounds pretty rigid, right? But these responses contain invaluable lessons for all followers:

- Be decisive between "Yes" and "No." Nobody likes "maybe."
- Deliver an answer with accuracy and brevity.
- Communicate that you accept accountability for performing the task: "I understand, and I am *willing and able* to carry out the task."
- Never try to "B.S." your way through an answer. Instead, communicate that you will find out or confirm the correct answer and will do so quickly. The way you answer questions is a constant test of your integrity.

My father used to be relentless about keeping all of the knives in our house and his pocketknife incredibly sharp. As he was sharpening a blade, he would say, "There's nothing more useless than a dull knife. You can't depend on it. It won't work when you need it, and it will do more damage—ripping and tearing—than actual cutting." He was honing a blade, but he was also using it a thousand times as a metaphor to remind me always to keep my professional "knife"—

my knowledge and set of skills—sharp and ready to perform at the highest level so I could be an expert.

BE POLITE

Many ways exist to be impolite. I believe much of what gets described as a "lack of professionalism" in the workplace boils down to bad manners. We can all compete vigorously, disagree wholeheartedly, and cling tenaciously to our ideas and the projects we believe in while still maintaining the manners we require of a third grader.

"Professional immaturity" is what project management expert Neal Whitten blames as the biggest reason for the lack of proper behavior in the workplace. These behaviors are "disruptive, destructive, and otherwise void of benefit in a business environment. Professional immaturity often manifests itself through behaviors such as weak personal initiative, weak accountability, self-absorption, and low awareness of the impact of one's own behavior." He writes that professional immaturity includes behaviors like having to be asked to put in extra hours to complete a job, expecting others to initiate needed changes in areas that affect their work output, bringing problems to light without offering any solutions, failing to live up to commitments, failing to take the initiative to solve problems, and acting out with sarcasm or cynicism.

People who regularly demonstrate these kinds of behaviors fail to recognize that not only are they less likely to grow friendships and essential mentoring relationships at work, but their behaviors will ensure that their bad reputation precedes them as they move through project teams and across functions. Professional immaturity will hurt your career.

In your follower role, no matter what career stage you are in, your reputation will precede you. In today's hyper-connected world, anyone can learn about your work and personal histories, habits and musings, and whom you associate with by calling up Google.

Therefore, it only makes sense to live both your professional and your personal life authentically and consistently with a high degree of professionalism. A great question to ask yourself before sending that email, or posting that thought on Facebook is, "How would I feel if this ended up on the front page of *The Wall Street Journal*, above the fold, with one of those dot-matrix photos of my face next to it?" If the answer is, "This will enhance both my professional and personal reputations," then by all means, click "Send."

Arrogance is another way we can be impolite. Early in someone's career, arrogance is likely to be seen as overconfidence. At best, it conveys a lack of self-awareness of one's own limitations. At worst, if not corrected quickly, it can grow into hubris, which will keep you blind to the damage you are doing to yourself, even as you believe you are paving your own way to success.

The Superintendent at the Naval Academy when I returned as an instructor was Vice Admiral Charles Larson. Admiral Larson had been brought back for a second time as "the Supe" to repair damage done to the Academy's reputation by a large cheating scandal. One of the first things Admiral Larson determined was that a spirit of arrogance existed among the midshipmen—that some felt entitled to "take the easy way" when they could because of the otherwise demanding and Spartan life they were living. He would have none of that spirit. He knew how damaging self-rationalizing arrogance of that sort is in any organization, and how unacceptable it is at an organization entrusted with America's "special trust and confidence." That kind of arrogance *inevitably* becomes hubris. Tolerated that early in an officer's career, it will grow to damage morale, good order, and discipline. That kind of conceit can irreparably damage an officer's credibility and reputation, rendering his leadership ineffective, thereby weakening his unit's ability to carry out its mission.

To eliminate arrogant behavior, Admiral Larson instituted his "excellence without arrogance" campaign. It was tremendously effective, and over the next few years, a dramatic change happened in the spirit of the Brigade of Midshipmen. Bad apples still exist in any large group, but at the Naval Academy, they no longer excuse arrogant behavior as an "earned privilege" of high achievers. Humility cannot be a way of behaving or acting: it is a condition of being, reflective of the way you truly see others and your role in serving them. Leadership is noble because it is a privilege granted by others; a privilege for which we should be grateful.

One of my favorite historical examples of someone's leadership that was improved by others confronting their hubris is from one of America's early presidents. John Quincy Adams was the son of founding father and second U.S. President John Adams and his eloquent wife, Abigail. John Quincy studied throughout Europe during his youth, but he returned to the United States to attend Harvard while his parents remained behind because his father was U.S. Ambassador to the Court of St. James in London.

John Quincy's mother, Abigail, received many letters from Massachusetts indicating that he was a little over-enamored with himself and had become quite boastful, and that it was tarnishing the Adams family name. She wrote to her son:

> If you are conscious to yourself that you possess more knowledge upon some subjects than others of your standing, reflect that you have had greater opportunities of seeing the world and obtaining knowledge of mankind than any of your contemporaries. That you have never wanted a book, but it has been supplied to you. That your whole time has been spent in the company of men of literature and science. How unpardonable would it have been in you to have turned out a blockhead.

Being a "blockhead" is always unprofessional. Make sure you have people you trust who will help you remain self-aware.

The final differentiating behavior of polite followers and leaders is conflict management. The best leaders develop conflict management skills while they are still followers. These skills, when developed completely and used deftly, will break you out of the pack of your peers. No matter the situation—conflict up, down, or sideways—you will be more effective if you are able to seek objectivity in conflict, and see conflict as an opportunity to get the best out of people.

I want to be clear about what I mean by "conflict." I don't mean open arguments because they often are driven by ego, by unflattering emotions like pride, and by dark motives like overzealousness. Healthy conflict is unfiltered debate: 100 percent candid and 100 percent respectful. Teams that nurture an environment where everyone's opinion is valued and everyone has the right to be heard will generate more and better ideas. The ability to engage in healthy group conflict requires that the whole team, not just the leader, be responsible for policing when the line has been crossed from "healthy" over to "destructive." A self-monitoring and self-correcting team will always be more successful than a team that devolves into personal attacks and "let-me-show-the-room-how smart-I-am" behavior. If you can be a cheerleader for healthy conflict in your teams and in your one-on-one relationships, you will be much more successful than your peers.

Be highly professional in all things. My squadron mate Terry's advice is easy to remember and the best career advice I have ever received: Be Productive. Be Innovative. Be the Expert. Be Polite. By looking at professionalism through The Lens of Leadership, you will be more likely to hold yourself and others accountable to higher standards of conduct and performance. The reputation you will earn will lead to you achieving your goals more quickly, and afford you greater opportunities to influence others.

Summary & Exercise: Chapter 5—Acting with Professionalism

WHAT?—SO WHAT?—NOW WHAT?

What? Be Productive. Be Innovative. Be the Expert. Be Polite.

So What? You must work harder than your peers to earn a reputation for being highly professional. This work includes becoming an expert beyond your years at your craft, "seeing around corners" to be ready for future challenges, communicating effectively, and working to achieve "excellence without arrogance."

Now What?

I will study _____

_____ to learn more about career professionalism.

I will reach out to _____

_____ in order to seek more insight, guidance, and advice.

I will ask _____ to hold me accountable for _____

_____.

And I will _____

_____

_____

_____ in order to create an experience with elements/competencies that I have not yet adequately developed by *(date)* _____.

ADDITIONAL RESOURCES FOR YOUR "NOW WHAT?" JOURNEY:

Charan, Ram. *Know-How: The 8 Skills That Separate People Who Perform from Those Who Don't.*

Kirton, Michael. *The Kirton Adaption-Innovation Inventory.* (www. kaicentre.com)

Lencioni, Patrick. *The Five Dysfunctions of a Team.*

Patterson, Kerry, Joseph Grenny, Ron McMillan, and Al Switzler. *Crucial Confrontations: Tools for Resolving Broken Promises, Violated Expectations, and Bad Behavior.*

Shaw, Peter J.A. *Making Difficult Decisions: How to be decisive and get the business done.*

Whitten, Neal. *Neal Whitten's No-Nonsense Advice for Successful Projects.*

Whitten, Neal. *Neal Whitten's Let's Talk!—More No-Nonsense Advice for Project Success.*

PART TWO

SERVING THROUGH LEADERSHIP

Life is tough. Wear a cup.
— Dennis Miller

CHAPTER SIX

LEADING IS NOBLE

The general's reward is not a bigger tent, but command.
"Command." Silliness to a banker or a lawyer, but a goal worth
dying for to a Midshipman.
— James Webb, *A Sense of Honor*

When you get your first promotion, and you go from being an individual
contributor to a leader, it's not about you anymore. It's about them.
— Jack Welch

Congratulations! You've just made the biggest professional transition you will make in your career by going from being a follower—a "doer"—to being someone who leads by getting a lot more done through others. It feels pretty good, doesn't it? Enjoy the moment… but not for too long. There is work to be done, and *you* are going to be held accountable for it. And now, not only is there work that you are responsible for measuring, managing, and improving, but you also have the careers and livelihood of others depending on your wisdom, guidance, and judgment. Welcome to leadership! It is simultaneously thrilling and a little bit humbling. Or at least it should be.

WHY LEAD?

Leading others is a worthy endeavor. When I resigned my commission as a naval officer, I considered my own self-identity: How would I replace the worthiness and nobility I felt as a military leader? There is something very satisfying about putting on a uniform and saluting our flag and other military members. How would I replace *that* as a civilian businessman?

I discovered the answer years later: *all* leadership is noble. The act of leading, done well, improves the material and emotional welfare of others. It is a noble act, worthy of pride and respect.

Sometimes, the noble role of leadership comes with additional benefits, but more often than not, leadership comes with responsibilities that require you to give more of yourself than the material value of the incremental benefits you receive. The best leaders are the ones who consider that accounting and choose to lead anyway.

IT IS NOT ABOUT RANK OR POWER

This chapter's introductory quote from *A Sense of Honor* illustrates the spirit with which the best leaders approach their obligations. Inherent in that quote is the desire and self-confidence to assume responsibility for greater works accomplished through collaboration with others. Beware the leader who is motivated primarily by "the bigger tent." It is seductive, and his or her motivation can become selfish.

I was lucky enough to spend some of the summer between my Naval Academy freshman and sophomore years attached to a Marine Corps expeditionary unit[1] in the jungles of Thailand on a cooperative war game exercise. This exercise was my first exposure to real Marines, and to "real" fake combat. It was a lot of fun, and because I was a Midshipman, I got to do some things that a typical Marine might not. A group of midshipmen were being welcomed

---

1 About 2,200 Marines.

into a headquarters camp by a full colonel. In the field, a colonel is quite like a god, but it was an informal gathering where a senior officer took a few minutes to be a role model and recruiter in front of potential future Marine officers.

Before dismissing us, he asked whether we had any questions. One of us asked, "Colonel, you're not wearing any rank on your uniform.[2] How do people know who you are and how to treat you?" It was a fair question for somebody who had just come out of the disciplined rigors and ideal environment of Plebe (freshman) year. The colonel didn't even pause to think. He immediately replied, "Son, if anyone out here doesn't know I'm the Colonel after about two minutes of talking with me, then I need to go back to school." It was a lesson that has stayed with me ever since: You shouldn't need your formal authority to get things done. Your ability to influence groups should be irrespective of the "stripes" you wear on your shoulders.

This spirit requires humility and a habit of self-reflection. It requires leaders to seek feedback about arrogance, aloofness, and being out-of-touch. This discipline of seeking transparent self-awareness requires a high emotional intelligence quotient. "E.Q." is a concept popularized by Daniel Goleman in the mid-1990s, but the best description I have seen is from the international E.Q. expert and trainer, Adele Lynn. Adele says that someone with a high E.Q. has, "Regular success at managing themselves and their relationships with others so that they live out their intentions and values."

Becoming a leader is a transition to a certain alienation from your previous peers. You may now be responsible for the performance results, career development, and salaries and benefits of a group of employees who were very recently your happy hour pals. In a world of constrained resources and hard decisions, it's "lonely at the top."

---

2 A common practice in the field, where snipers target senior officers.

TAKE CARE OF YOUR PEOPLE

You would think the "take care of your people" principle would be self-evident, but without specific actions, it becomes a trite cliché. How does one "take care" of his or her people? First, get to know them *completely*, as, what Stephen Covey calls, "whole people."

To fulfill their obligations, your people bring their bodies and minds to work. Leaders can "rent" those. As long as the organizational "thank you note" keeps showing up in their bank account every two weeks, they'll keep schlepping their physical and mental skills to your workplace. But people also have hearts and dreams. If you can discover what it is they care about and hope to become, you will unleash extra effort that you cannot buy—it can only be donated. It is discretionary. By getting to know them as "whole people," you will earn a higher level of engagement, unleash creativity, and build morale that will deliver superior results.

What role do their families play in their career decisions? If they have children, what activities are they involved in? Do they go to church? What do they like to do on vacation? What do they value in the world? What are their "gifts" beyond spreadsheets and PowerPoint? In today's detached world where there is often a distinct-but-unspoken line between "work" and "not work," many leaders are hesitant to ask such questions from fear of being perceived as intrusive and crossing that line.

Nonsense! The best leaders know their people wholly, and use that knowledge to modify the levers they pull in order to earn more full engagement, and deliver a more meaningful work experience for the people they lead. This process requires authenticity, and commitment; it cannot be achieved during one long lunch. It is an ongoing commitment and a mindset, not an isolated or even occasional act. It requires extra discipline and time, but the best leaders treat it like an investment. It will pay dividends that exceed the opportunity cost of the time spent.

CREATE A LEADERSHIP LABORATORY

People need the opportunity to practice new skills like decision-making, public presentations, influencing, and negotiating for resources. People will be less likely to practice these things if they only get the chance to do so in very public or high-risk environments. As a leader, you have to delegate tasks and create situations in which your teammates can practice safely, in a low-risk situation. You need to create a laboratory within your team.

Create professionally "safe" circumstances where your teammates can experiment with new solutions, styles, and skills, so if they "bomb," few (if any) people will even know, and everybody's reputation will be protected. Be clear about which tasks and places are "lab" and which are real-world so no embarrassing misunderstandings arise. If you can give your teammates a lab in which to experiment, they will grow more skills more quickly than their peers, and you will increase your own reputation as a talent-builder.

LEADING MILLENNIALS

I was a brand manager before the rise of social media. The word-of-mouth radio advertising pioneer Alan Varnson was seeing the future when he told me, "An ad is like walking into a crowded room and shouting '*I KNOW WHAT YOUR FAVORITE SONG IS, AND I'M GOING TO SING IT TO YOU!*' Today, consumers want to be asked, 'What is your favorite song? Will you sing it for me? Now, can I tell you about my favorite song?'"

That is the same deft touch required for leading Millennials. They want to be involved in the decisions that affect their daily work, almost to the point of self-determination. They want to be consulted and have a voice. They want to please, and to receive frequent praise for that effort. They want to be won over as true believers in a cause that is just, and contribute directly to the organization's noble purpose.

Not every teammate will need or want all of that, but in order to deliver it for those who do, you will have to get to know them as whole people. It is a good practice to treat all of them this way, and get them aligned, so you can earn the engagement they can only volunteer.

To become a leader is to join a group that has an immense capacity to do good with and for people. Only a handful of behaviors are necessary to set you apart as a good, if not great, leader. They are simple. But "simple" does not mean "easy." They require discipline and the development of habit patterns that are *different* than the ones you had as an individual contributor. Your growth as a leader is a journey, and early in that journey you may lack perspective. By looking at your role through The Lens of Leadership, you will develop the essential spirit of a servant leader, accountable not just for business results, but also for the growth of the skills and careers of those you lead.

It is a sobering responsibility, but there is no joy like that of delivering the announcement that one of your team members has achieved her own great career milestone. There is nobility in that for the leader and the led. Be noble.

Summary & Exercise: Chapter 6—Leading is Noble

WHAT?—SO WHAT?—NOW WHAT?

__What?__ Being promoted to a leadership role is noble, thrilling, and satisfying. The best leaders know that in order to earn the nobility, you have the obligation to deliver better business results by serving the best interests of those you lead. To achieve that, you must get to know your team members as "whole people." You must discover what they care about, and what they hope to become. That will require earning their trust and confidence.

__So What?__ Now you are a formal leader. If you are to be well-esteemed, you must develop a holistic rapport with all of your team members, not just your direct reports. Your actions must consistently demonstrate that you have the heart of a servant. That mindset is the single most powerful tool you have in your leadership arsenal.

Now What?

I will study _____

_____ to learn more about skills for early leaders.

I will reach out to _____

_____ in order to seek more insight, guidance, and advice.

I will ask _____ to hold me accountable for _____.

And I will _____

_____

_____ in order to create an experience with elements/competencies that I have not yet adequately developed by _(date)_ _____.

ADDITIONAL RESOURCES FOR YOUR "NOW WHAT?" JOURNEY:

The Arbinger Institute. *Leadership and Self-Deception.*

Bennis, Warren. *On Becoming a Leader.*

Eichinger, Robert W. *100 Things You Need to Know: Best Practices for Managers and HR.*

Eikenberry, Kevin. *From Bud to Boss: Secrets to a Successful Transition to Remarkable Leadership.*

Goleman, Daniel. *Emotional Intelligence: Why It Can Matter More Than IQ.*

Hughes, Richard, Robert Ginnett, and Gordon Curphy. *Leadership: Enhancing the Lessons of Experience.* (7th ed.)

Keith, Kent. *Anyway: The Paradoxical Commandments.*

Kouzes, James M. and Barry Z. Posner. *The Leadership Challenge.* (4th ed.)

Lynn, Adele. *The Emotional Intelligence Activity Book.*

Tulgan, Bruce. *It's Okay to Be the Boss: The Step-by-Step Guide to Becoming the Manager Your Employees Need.*

Watkins, Michael. *The First 90 Days: Critical Success Strategies for New Leaders at All Levels.*

CHAPTER SEVEN

ACTING LIKE A LEADER: WHAT GREAT LEADERS *DO*

Leaders love the mess. In selecting leaders, we must be assiduously on the lookout for those who get their jollies in the face of madness... in the face of chaos that causes others to waffle or fold.
— Tom Peters

Being a truly world class leader means having the ability to coach world-class caliber people to become even better.
— Ralph C. Stayer, CEO of Johnsonville Sausage

It is interesting to engage great leaders in discussions about when they first realized they were "leaders." Many will tell you that, as early as their mid-teens, they just frequently seemed to "end up" in leadership roles. Assuming these roles is almost always unintentional in naturally-inclined leaders. It was for me. Starting even before high school, I was either volunteering or being chosen by peers or teachers to be "the leader." I didn't think much of it then. I was just happy to be out front and "leading," whatever that meant. The benefits seemed obvious: visibility (perceived as popularity), influence, the opportunity to make decisions, and the chance to be exposed to—and to learn from—more experienced leaders while I was incredibly young.

Having had that early set of experiences and mindset, I found myself, when I was a naval officer years later, as someone who subscribed to the "Great Person" theory of leadership: that the best leaders are "born with it," whatever "it" is. Some call it "charisma." Others refer to it as someone's ability to inspire or rally others to their opinion or cause. Those of us[1] with "it" were well-blessed; those without "it" were destined to work always in the shadow of the others. This mindset is arrogant, narrow, and incorrect. Great leadership delivers great results. Great results are the product of daily behaviors, not a result of a persuasive personality. Behaviors can be studied and learned, and can, therefore, be practiced and made a habit by anyone willing to stretch himself without becoming inauthentic to whom he really is.

I first became aware that I had fallen prey to the Great Person theory as a leadership instructor at the Naval Academy while preparing for a module on introversion and extroversion in leaders. Both military and civilian research had concluded that extroverts tend to gain power and influence early in their careers through charisma and outgoing personalities, but in general, the most successful senior leaders (CEOs, admirals, and generals) tended to be at least mild introverts.

There comes a point in a leadership career where charisma and extroversion can become career detriments if the leader has a low E.Q., low self-awareness, and lacks a candid feedback loop (either through friends, family, and colleagues who can provide it, or by being a high self-monitor). That leader will probably hit a career ceiling because of emotional or charismatic reactions that reveal too much "personality" and not enough depth and professional maturity.

---

1 I, of course, considered myself as having "it."

Introverts tend to walk the opposite path. They must, of course, achieve excellent professional competency early in their careers. Then they have to remain at it long enough for their domain expertise and consistent excellence to speak loudly for them. Their careers tend to "break out" from the pack later, when their sober judgment and steady, dependable demeanor carry them successfully through many "sticky" moments. This behavior sets them apart from the over-emotional, quick-tempered responses of their extroverted peers. Jim Collins' research in *Good to Great* gave name to leaders with the attributes of great leadership that deliver the best results. His "Level Five" leaders led their companies from "good to great" with "a combination of selfless humility and tenacious, dogged pragmatism," regardless of whether they were introverted or extroverted.

What does this information mean to you? Whether you are an extrovert, worried that you may flame out mid-career because of your "charisma," or an introvert who worries that you may not be recognized early enough to leverage your even keel, there is great news! The best leaders—regardless of their personality—develop and demonstrate specific behaviors throughout their careers to expand their capacity to influence others, moderate their own natural disposition, and keep them very self-aware of their impact on others. You can learn and practice those behaviors to ensure that you will be effective all along your leadership journey.

RESEARCHING LEADERSHIP BEST PRACTICES

My former colleague at Johnsonville Sausage, Tim Ahrens, and I studied the best behavioral literature on leadership and conducted our own internal research to see whether we might be able to identify, and then measure, the best leaders within Johnsonville. We wondered whether the leadership behaviors that led to success in a mid-size, privately-held company might differ from the environments studied by most of the popular literature.

We began by identifying three tiers of leaders within Johnsonville using a combination of quantitative and qualitative measures of effectiveness. We recorded several typical corporate performance metrics. We determined each coach's Net Promoter Score using Fred Reichheld's[2] excellent "likely-to-be-recommended-by-others" methodology. We also measured each coach's ability to engage, respectfully but candidly, in what our colleagues and role-models at VitalSmarts, Inc., call "Crucial Conversations." The final component of great leadership we measured was talent management. Who were the leaders who built future leaders?

As part of identifying and bucketing Johnsonville's leaders, we also determined whom the "influencers" were within Johnsonville: who were the "go-to" people whom other members[3] sought out regardless of their formal authority or professional expertise?

Once we determined who fit in to each of the three normally-distributed tiers, we conducted rounds of interviews to measure the habits and behaviors of leaders from within the three tiers in hopes of finding a clear connection between certain behaviors and better quantitative and qualitative performance results. What we found is a recipe for all leaders to be successful throughout the various stages of their careers.

WHAT WE FOUND

The best leaders have a larger, broader "leadership toolbox" than other leaders, and they are constantly and intentionally acquiring new tools. Not only do they have more tools to choose from, but they have experimented with each one so they know exactly when the right tool is "the right tool."

The toolbox of the best leaders has four compartments: *Power and Influence, Network, Daily Behaviors*, and *Congruence*.

2 Bain & Company's customer satisfaction and loyalty Fellow.
3 All employees at Johnsonville are called "members."

Power and Influence

We examined 750 qualitative behavioral descriptors that we collected on coaches from their members by using five different evaluation tools: The Center for Creative Leadership's (CCL's) classic models of power and of influence; Korn-Ferry's Lominger Competency Model (created by Michael Lombardo and Robert Eichinger); simple theme-based word cues (e.g., "People Skills," "Relationship/ Trust," "Experience," "Resource Acquisition," "Functional Job Skills"); and VitalSmarts, Inc.'s Six-Sources of Influence model. The team took the 750 descriptors and "bucketed" them according to their assigned model. We were looking to see which few of the particular tools within each of the models would become the obvious levers the top-tier leaders chose to use as their "go-to" skill—a few "silver bullets" they could use when needed.

What we found, in all five examinations, was that the differentiator between the best leaders and the rest was the broad and situationally-appropriate use of *all* of the levers. We didn't find any "silver bullets." We found leaders with the skills, discipline, and judgment to apply each of them appropriately to different situations. I'll use CCL's models to illustrate:

When the situation required compliance, the best leaders would appropriately apply several of the following:

- use their power as experienced experts
- use the power their members would grant them based on their relationships
- use their abilities to grant and withhold rewards
- use (although rarely) the legitimate powers given them by virtue of their roles

When power would be too heavy a tool, the best leaders influenced their teams to gain commitment using *a variety of tactics*, including several of the following:

- rational persuasion with their analytical teammates

- consultation and even ingratiation with their more collaborative teammates
- coalition tactics
- an exchange relationship with their transactional peers
- inspirational *and* personal appeals with people for whom it was appropriate, given the conditions

We found the same results with the competency-based, the theme-based, and the Six-Sources models: the best leaders' behaviors around power and influence were broad and varied. The middle ranked tier of leaders tended to use only two or three levers, and the lowest-scoring leaders tended to be "one-trick ponies," resorting to, generally, one of two tools: a hammer or a pulley.

Network

The best leaders had professional and personal networks that were different than the other leaders in both scale and scope. They leveraged personal relationships that went back to college and even high school. They can and do reach out to sorority sisters, athletic teammates, or friends from extra-curricular activities when those people can help them solve business challenges. They will also connect people from throughout their network with each other, when they know those relationships could turn out to be mutually beneficial. They are happy to take the time to listen to needs from throughout their network, and then spend a little time connecting people with others—or tools—that could solve problems.

The best leaders are generous with their time because they view the time it takes to connect these people as a "professionally-social investment"—an investment in their own future. They have found that enough of these people will return the favor in the future, thus earning them a suitable return on the investment of their time. This practice was an essential habit of the best leaders even before Facebook, LinkedIn, and other social connection sites made it easy and intuitive to do so. Wise leaders dedicate a small amount of their time nurturing relationships and connecting people within their sphere of influence.[4]

The top-tier leaders were members of several industry and trade associations, and they often contributed to those groups by writing for the group's magazines or blogs, serving on the board, or by helping to coordinate association events. Many of them were also members of associations outside of their industry. Some of them belong to "unusual" groups (MasterMind and other mindshare groups, creative thinking groups, futurist groups, theater troupes, etc.) that stimulate parts of their minds that their daily work does not.

Daily Behaviors

The best leaders have a set of daily operating habits that distinguish them from the rest. It is not as simple as "listening better," or "setting clearer expectations," though. The very best leaders use all of these habits with all of their people in an everyday context of accountability and high-expectations.

While average leaders are content to hint around at things that are not quite right, the best leaders have found a way to combine absolute candor about performance with clearly-demonstrated respect for them as people in order to broach difficult topics or raise touchy disagreements. VitalSmarts, Inc.'s Crucial Conversations is the best method I know for developing this skill set.

In our research, the top-tier leaders were praised for their focused listening skills. They would insulate themselves from the daily grind long enough to make the person feel absolutely valued and heard. They would also ask many thought-provoking questions that revealed the intensity with which they were listening. The old adage, "I have two ears and only one mouth, so I should do twice as much listening as talking" is a staple for successful leaders.

---

4 More on the importance of "Nurturing Your Network" in Chapter 14.

The best leaders set and communicate crystal clear expectations, with by-name assignments, concrete deliverables, timelines with time-and-date specifics, and they communicate how and with what frequency they will follow up on the team member's progress. It is important to gain agreement on the follow-up expectations so no misunderstandings arise between leader and follower. By agreeing, for example, to expect a progress update and response via email at the end of each day during the last week of the project, both the leader and the follower can manage the others' expectations about goal accomplishment and the need for assistance.

The most effective leaders were quick to say, "I'm sorry" or "I was wrong" when it was true. Beyond the obvious messages about humility, integrity, and respect that an apology sends, it also creates a safe environment for all of the team members to do the same. I am often surprised at the reluctance of some leaders to admit when they are wrong. It's as if they believe they will be surrendering a part of their power or authority by offering an apology. It is my absolutely consistent experience that leaders who will admit their shortcomings and mistakes in front of their team will see their team's respect and level of commitment *increase*. The most effective leaders don't have to say "I was wrong" very often. They know that if they do, it's an early warning sign that maybe their skills or judgment need some improvement.

The best leaders are visible exemplars of the organization's culture. They epitomize the values. They frequently engage people from throughout the company in conversations about what is and what is not culturally acceptable. They use the occasion of values violations from anywhere in the company to spark a team conversation about what happened, and why it is unacceptable. They hold up those who model the values under difficult circumstances as heroes. They demonstrate the culture on a daily basis through their actions and words, and they serve as mentors for people with questions about boundaries.

Leaders who are the "best of the best" push empowerment out to all levels within their team. They talk frequently about empowerment and why it is important. They very visibly grant authority along with the responsibility they give to others. Great leaders will encourage and cajole reluctant teammates to act with empowerment. They create a safety net around the team by encouraging members to ask questions about expectations and where the boundaries are. Perhaps most importantly, the best leaders give public support to team members when others, including superiors, question their level of empowerment or their decision-making ability. Your ability to delegate successfully will be directly proportionate to how much you require others to use the authority they already have.

The leaders at the top of the list did not spoon-feed answers to their members. Instead, they asked higher-level and *guiding* questions that sent the advice-seekers back out to discover the answers for themselves. It seems quicker and easier in the short-term to give our people the answers they seek, but then we create a dependence on us as leaders. Many leaders like that sort of dependence. The best do not. They know that self-sufficient members with a high level of curiosity and critical thinking skills are the ones who will move their team forward and will create the next generation of leaders in that same mold, thus freeing them up to grow those skills in another teammate.

Finally, the leaders who stand out above all the rest are pretty hard on themselves. Self-deprecation seems braided into their DNA strands along with a humility about personal failures that borders on personal shame. They are quick to give credit to others, but hoard blame relentlessly, even when they may not deserve it, to protect the team. Later, behind closed doors, they conduct accountability conversations that get to the root cause(s) of the failure. The best leaders communicate the highest of standards, and hold themselves to those standards even more publically than they do the members of their team.

Congruence

During our research, we knew we were hearing about something else, too. The coaches who had the highest quantitative scores and also seemed to be influential even in situations where they lacked formal power were also mentioned frequently in interviews as being stand-outs by demonstrating a different spirit or attitude about coaching. It was something centered in "authenticity," "sincerity," and "caring." Followers frequently used the word "genuine" to describe them.

As we probed deeper to get to the behaviors, we found that the best leaders—the ones who deliver the best results and are the most highly respected throughout the organization—make an emotional investment in their team that doesn't compromise their professional integrity. They recognize that in order to get the best out of their people, they must recognize them, and connect with them as, what Dr. Stephen Covey calls, "whole people."[5] These leaders recognize that people care about things beyond work and have goals that may have nothing to do with their specific job. They may care about environmentalism. They may be using their current job to fund an education that will help them change careers and even companies. The best leaders engage their teammates in these matters as well, getting to know some details about these topics even if they are not personally interested. By stroking their teammates on the things they care about and hope to achieve, these leaders get teammates who are more fully-engaged, and will unleash more of their discretionary effort on behalf of this team and this leader.

And the final behavior we discovered was what one member called a "liberal sense of interaction." The best leaders make the time to be generous with their time. Just like they had broad internal and external professional networks—and made time to connect with

---

5 Explained in Chapter 6.

them—the best leaders also regularly connected with their teammates on many subjects, both personal and professional.

There is nothing "soft" about this emotional investment. This spirit of caring empowers them to hold members relentlessly accountable. It gives them an ability to engage their people with what is almost a moral authority when teammates are off track or have failed to deliver on expectations. They are empathetic, but not so *sympathetic* that they are unable to remain professionally objective and fair to all.

GREAT LEADERSHIP IS *DOING*

The best leaders in the world are not born that way, and they do not achieve that status because of their personalities. A moment of truth comes in the careers of both the introvert and the extrovert when they realize that their task is to deliver great results through the efforts of others. The best leaders know that interdependency is the highest form of maturity. And they know there are just a few learnable, practicable actions that will deliver the best results, regardless of their personality.

By looking at their own behaviors through The Lens of Leadership, all leaders can improve their reputation and their results.

Summary & Exercise: Chapter 7—Acting Like a Leader: What Great Leaders *Do*

WHAT?—SO WHAT?—NOW WHAT?

What? Leaders are born *and* made. No matter what role you are in, you must learn to balance your personality, functional job skills, and the few behaviors of leadership that will make the biggest difference.

So What? Make sure you know how to apply these tools from your leadership toolbox: Power and Influence, Networking, Daily Behaviors, and Congruence.

Now What?

I will study _____

_____ to learn more about the learnable, repeatable behaviors of the best leaders.

I will reach out to _____

_____ in order to seek more insight, guidance, and advice.

I will ask _____ to hold me accountable for _____

_____.

And I will _____

_____

_____

_____ in order to create an experience with elements/competencies that I have not yet adequately developed by *(date)* _____.

ADDITIONAL RESOURCES FOR YOUR "NOW WHAT?" JOURNEY:

Bennis, Warren. *The Essential Bennis.*

Buckingham, Marcus and Curt Coffman. *First, Break All the Rules: What the World's Greatest Managers Do Differently.*

Cabane, Olivia Fox. *The Charisma Myth: How Anyone Can Master the Art and Science of Personal Magnetism.*

Cain, Susan. *Quiet: The Power of Introverts in a World That Can't Stop Talking.*

Card, Orson Scott. *Ender's Game.*

Deresiewicz, William. "Solitude and Leadership: If you want others to follow, learn to be alone with your thoughts." *The American Scholar.* (Spring 2010)

Gladwell, Malcolm. *Blink: The Power of Thinking Without Thinking.*

Gostick, Adrian and Chester Elton. *The Carrot Principle: How the Best Managers Use Recognition to Engage Their People, Retain Talent, and Accelerate Performance.*

Patterson, Kerry, Joseph Grenny, Ron McMillan, and Al Switzler. *Crucial Conversations, Tools for Talking When Stakes Are High.*

Shaw, Peter J.A. *Making Difficult Decisions: How to be decisive and get the business done.*

Tulgan, Bruce. *It's Okay to Be the Boss: The Step-by-Step Guide to Becoming the Manager Your Employees Need.*

CHAPTER EIGHT

LEADING IS *SERVING*

A leader must remember that he is responsible for his charges. He must tend his flock, not only cracking the whip, but 'washing their feet' when they are in need of help. This approach frees the flock to look out for each other, and for the greater good.
— James Stockdale, The Hoover Institute

Love your soldiers. Love them upon waking up,
and love them as you go to sleep. In the end,
it is the only leadership lesson you need: love your soldiers.
— General Colin Powell

The first paradox of this book is that the best leaders started out as—and continue to be, *simultaneously*—the best followers. The second paradox is that the best leaders are the first to put themselves last.

WHAT IS SERVANT LEADERSHIP?

The notion of servant leadership is highly on-trend in recent leadership literature. Several popular authors have written excellent books about it over the past decade. The term was coined by Robert

Greenleaf, the former head of Management Research, Development, and Education at AT&T from the 1940s through the early 1960s. He also served as a management professor at Harvard and MIT. In his 1970s seminal essay, "The Leader as Servant," Greenleaf wrote:

> The servant-leader is *servant* first. Servant leadership begins with the natural feeling that one wants to serve, to serve *first*. Then conscious choice brings one to aspire to lead. That person is sharply different from one who is *leader* first, perhaps because of the need to assuage an unusual power or drive to acquire material possessions.

> The difference [between leaders and servant leaders] manifests itself in the care taken by the servant-first to make sure that other people's highest-order needs are being served. The best test, and difficult to administer, is: Do those served grow as persons and as professionals? Do they, while being served, become healthier, wiser, freer, more autonomous, and more likely themselves to become servants?

I suggest you re-read those sentences and think about the impact of the paradox on you, your team, and on your leadership style.

I was first introduced to Greenleaf's writings in 1999 when I was teaching leadership at the Naval Academy. I was the course coordinator for the advanced leadership class taught to all one thousand juniors. My department head had received an invitation to the annual international conference of the Greenleaf Center for Servant Leadership. Only half-kidding, he told me to "go to this conference and figure out whether it's a useful principle for military leadership or a Communist plot to undermine good order and discipline." Of course, I discovered that Greenleaf articulated a powerful idea I had already been taught by the Navy with other words. He validated for me that great leaders succeed by putting the development of their teams *first*. We incorporated Greenleaf into the syllabus, and his philosophy is still taught to America's future naval officers.

Military leadership is a 24/7/365 commitment that I found to be wholly encompassing. It was often impossible to discern between "work" and "not work." More than once, I was awakened at three in the morning to bail one of my airmen out of jail because he didn't want to call his spouse. I was also called to rush to the hospital because one of them had been hurt on or off the job and he had no extended family in the area. You might consider those duties as "required" of a military leader because of discipline and readiness, but I also had many opportunities to serve them beyond "discipline and readiness." My airmen—or sometimes their spouses—would reach out to me for advice because they were struggling to pay their bills. Sometimes, it was because their car had died, or because a spouse had been, repeatedly and publically, acting inappropriately back home while we were deployed. They would come to me because they were struggling to understand how to navigate the military healthcare system for a sick child. They would ask for help about deciding between homes to buy, car loans to choose, or whether to marry. These were wonderful, fulfilling opportunities to serve their best interests, but until I had been introduced to Greenleaf, I had no common language to explain why I thought it was important. I was sent to that conference on a mission to gather intelligence on servant leadership. I came back forever-improved as a leader.

I left the Navy after that tour to become a businessman. One of the hardest adjustments to make was the shift away from that total commitment to my teammates' lives. I found civilian leadership to be much less involved, and at first, I played along. Nobody wanted that much involvement in each other's life outside of work. Sure, you might have a social dinner out together, or invite teammates over to your house for a cook-out, but enough energy was expended at work that people seemed to want to get away from their coworkers after hours. Can you imagine one of your junior teammates coming to you for help deciding on a home loan? Would a direct report's spouse call you because their only car was just repossessed?

What about being a listening ear and source of wisdom on what a new-hire might do about an unfaithful spouse? If you are like most people, these would *really* seem to be outside of your normal leadership comfort zone—beyond the "cultural propriety" of the workplace—in businesses and many other organizations. Those events are what Employee Assistance Programs are for, right?

What's the right balance? I communicate the situations from my military past to my current teammates and acknowledge that, although civilian leadership is "different," my commitment to them is still the same. I tell them specifically that "I am always available to you, and am interested in how I can serve you in your professional or personal life." Remember Greenleaf's test: "Do those served grow as persons and as professionals? Do they, while being served, become healthier, wiser, freer, more autonomous, and more likely themselves to become servant-leaders?"

IT SOUNDS KIND OF "SOFT"

Few of today's globally-recognized leaders have a record of being as demanding and also as highly successful as a leader, statesman, and executive of several different types of enormous enterprises as former Secretary of State and U.S. Army General Colin Powell. His record demonstrates that there is nothing "soft" about his quote at the beginning of this chapter, nor about the ideas behind servant leadership.

Servant *institutions*—organizations that exhibit the aggregated characteristics of servant leaders—consider servant leadership and high performance as inseparable. They focus on results *and* relationships; on tasks *and* trust. They recognize that in order to have a strong, sustainable bottom line, they must also have a strong, engaged bench of very agile learners. Such employees are *nurtured* and *shepherded*. They are *served* by their leaders.

I have been impressed over the last decade at how many servant-leader companies consistently earn their way into *Fortune Magazine*'s "100 Best Companies to Work For" ratings. Last year, five of the top ten were companies identified as practicing servant leadership. These companies are also titans in their categories and deliver fantastic business results. The technology company SAS tops the list. Some others in the top 100 include Zappos.com, Recreational Equipment, Inc. (REI), Whole Foods Market, Intel, Aflac, Marriott International, Nordstrom, and Darden Restaurants.

In *Seven Pillars of Servant Leadership: Practicing the Wisdom of Leading by Serving*, James Sipe and Don Frick detail their research on the performance of servant companies with Jeff Pauley of Magellan Executive Resources. They compared the performance of Jim Collins' eleven "good to great" companies with eleven publically-traded companies whose literature and stated intentions demonstrate a servant-leader mindset. Some of these companies included Southwest Airlines, Starbucks, Men's Warehouse, Herman Miller, FedEx, and Medtronic. Their comparison data sets were for the decade ending in 2005. During that time, the S&P 500 averaged a 10.8 percent pre-tax return. Collins' "great" companies delivered an average of 17.5 percent return. The servant-leader companies averaged a 24.2 percent return! In Jerry Glashagel's book, *Servant Institutions in Business*, Sipe says, "The bottom line is that servant-led companies produced far superior financial results, which led us to a startling conclusion: servant-led companies are *even better* than 'great'!"

WHAT DO SERVANT LEADERS *DO*?

Kent Keith, author of *The Case for Servant Leadership* and creator of "Anyway: The Paradoxical Commandments" explains that there are seven behavioral characteristics of the servant leader:

1. Self-Awareness—Everyone benefits from greater self-awareness. It is the *willingness to pursue* self-awareness that can be

the challenge. We may not like what we find, but a person rarely steps into a hole he knows is there.

2. <u>Listening</u>—The best descriptor of great listening I have ever heard is "squinting with your ears." In order to serve, you must understand the served. Ask a lot of thoughtful, probing questions about what your followers think they need.

3. <u>Invert the Pyramid</u>—The typical organizational model gets narrower as you go *up*. Servant leaders avert "loneliness at the top" by creating an environment where opportunities exist for many teammates to act as leaders. Accountability stays with the leader; empowerment lies in those served.

4. <u>Develop Others</u>—Warren Bennis wrote that the best servant-led teams are a "constellation of co-stars." You cannot invert the pyramid unless you are relentlessly using experiences within your organization's business model to build the knowledge and confidence of your teammates.

5. <u>A Coaching Spirit</u>—Coaches lead the fundamentals of a competitive enterprise. They cajole and correct; they motivate and model; they "inspire," or "*breathe life into*" their teams so the team can achieve more than the players think they can.

6. <u>Unleash the Latent Talent in All Members</u>—Servant leaders know their teammates so well that they can get each one to "volunteer" the discretionary talents that are buried in all of us. We all have knowledge, abilities, and passion that our job descriptions do not require we use. Servant leaders get their people to use them voluntarily.

7. <u>Foresight</u>—The ability to "see around corners" takes time, effort, and resiliency to develop. Servant leaders care about the future because they are not just serving today's team—they feel an obligation to prepare the organization or team for a future the leader may not even be part of.

WHO ARE YOU IN IT FOR?

Jim Collins' research has revealed that the leaders of the "good to great" companies demonstrated "a paradoxical blend of personal humility and professional will....'Level 5' leaders channel their ego needs away from themselves and into a larger goal of building a great company. It is not that Level 5 leaders have no ego or self-sense of self-interest. Indeed, they are incredibly ambitious—but their ambition is first and foremost for the institution and not for themselves."[1]

There is a lot of alignment between how various authors have written about examples of servant-leaders and Collins' Level 5 leaders. Words like "humble" and "modest" co-exist with others like "fearless" and "stoic." "But," you are thinking, "I work in *[insert your industry here]*. It's cutthroat, and competitive, and hierarchical, and...did I mention cutthroat? People in my business understand *raw power* and only serve *themselves!*" You may work for a company that wouldn't necessarily reward the behaviors of servant leadership. Maybe you think that because your boss or your boss' boss does not model these behaviors, he might find them evidence of weakness.

All of that may be true. But I know that my career journey and research have taught me two things I believe are universal: 1) Leaders who are leading in a way that is inauthentic to whom they really are will be found out, and then worn out. 2) Bosses may be skeptical of methods that differ from their own—they may even guide you away from those practices—but eventually, they will always recognize and reward *results*, even if those results were not achieved using leadership principles that mirror their own.

It can be hard for people who are still developing their leadership style to lead in a way that is inauthentic to who they really are. If you are working in a culture that rewards behaviors that are inconsistent

---

1 For more detail, read Chapter 2 of Good to Great. It is a short, content-dense description of Level 5 leadership.

with your leadership style, it's time to consider how long you can tolerate it. It's time to find a mirror and ask yourself, "Is it *worth* this?" People will notice that you don't act like the others in the culture, and when they do, they will probably begin to give you advice to conform a little more closely to "the program."

POWER AND SERVICE

Don't be shy about accumulating power. Servant leaders wield power regularly, but they resist its addictive qualities. Servant leaders accumulate and employ power *on behalf of those they serve*, not for themselves. Power, for the servant leader, is a tool for specific instances, and it is always used to achieve noble ends on behalf of many. Those followers will, in turn, grant more power to that type of leader because it is stewarded properly and acted upon as a trust.

SERVING THE WHOLE PERSON

How you communicate with people matters too. In Natal, in northern South Africa, the tribal language conveys a powerful subtlety in its way of communicating between people in the community. The greeting is, "Sawubona," or, "I see you." The response to this greeting is, "Sikhona," which communicates, "I have been seen" or "I am here." Adopting this spirit when communicating with teammates can change each person's perspective in a way that will positively impact a whole team's culture.

In order to say truthfully, "I see you," you must understand the *whole* person, not just the one who shows up for her fifty hours per week. To see somebody as a whole person, you must understand what motivates that person at work, who inspires him to achievement, and what legacy she hopes to leave behind as a human being. If you are listening intently enough to understand people deeply, then you are likely to grant the person some leeway when you suddenly cannot "see" her point of view on a work matter.

In order to reply authentically with "I am here, and I have been seen," you must be similarly committed to a genuine relationship with the other person that is mutually beneficial. You are acknowledging his value to the organization, the community, or the team, and you are communicating that you are willingly engaged with him in improving circumstances for all involved.

Treating people this way—even when it is counter to the prevailing culture—will deliver *better* results because you will be tapping into fundamentally deeper levels of human desire, willpower, and motivation for yourself and for those you serve.

As the former CEO of the Greenleaf Center for Servant Leadership, Dr. Kent Keith sees life not just through The Lens of Leadership, but through The Lens of *Servant* Leadership. He wrote that, "Servant leaders do not work to earn the appreciation of others. Appreciation may come their way, but it is not what motivates them. They derive a sense of meaning and satisfaction from doing a great job. It doesn't matter whether anybody else knows or appreciates what they do—*they* know. And that's enough." Developing the professional skills and personal confidence to lead your way is an important professional milestone. It is hard to describe the liberating feeling that comes from knowing who you are, and being committed to that. You will always serve others, and yet you will never feel like you work for someone else ever again

Summary & Exercise: Chapter 8—Leading is Serving

WHAT?—SO WHAT?—NOW WHAT?

What? The best leaders are the first to put themselves last. A servant leader's impact is measured by whether his or her teammates are "becoming healthier, wiser, freer, more autonomous," and are "more likely to become servant leaders themselves."

So What? You must adapt your leadership mindset to embrace the paradox of the servant leader. It is not soft—quite the contrary. It is because you care so much for those you lead that you can hold them relentlessly accountable to the highest standards. Remember, the servant leader companies in Sipe & Frick's research dramatically outperformed Jim Collins' "good to great" companies during their high-results years.

Now What?

I will study _____

_____ to learn more about servant leadership.

I will reach out to _____

_____ in order to seek more insight, guidance, and advice.

I will ask _____ to hold me accountable for _____

_____.

And I will _____

_____

_____

_____ in order to create an experience with

elements/competencies that I have not yet adequately developed by *(date)* _____.

ADDITIONAL RESOURCES FOR YOUR "NOW WHAT?" JOURNEY:

Autry, James A. *The Servant Leader: How to Build a Creative Team, Develop Great Morale, and Improve Bottom-Line Performance.*

Belasco, James A. and Ralph C. Stayer. *Flight of the Buffalo: Soaring to Excellence, Learning to Let Employees Lead.*

Blanchard, Ken and Phil Hodges. *Servant Leader.*

Collins, Jim. *Good to Great: Why Some Companies Make the Leap... and Others Don't.*

Covey, Stephen R. *The 8th Habit: From Effectiveness to Greatness.*

Glashagel, Jerry. *Servant Institutions in Business.*

Hunter, James C. *The Servant: A Simple Story About the True Essence of Leadership.*

Keith, Kent M. *Anyway: The Paradoxical Commandments.*

Keith, Kent M.. *The Case for Servant Leadership.*

Nelson, Bob and Stephen Lundin. *Ubuntu!: An Inspiring Story About an African Tradition of Teamwork and Collaboration.*

Sipe, James and Don Frick. *Seven Pillars of Servant Leadership: Practicing the Wisdom of Leading by Serving.*

Spears, Larry C. and Robert K. Greenleaf. *Servant Leadership: A Journey into the Nature of Legitimate Power and Greatness.* (25th Anniversary Edition).

CHAPTER NINE

GIVING AWAY YOUR POWER
(TO GET MORE DONE!)

The leaders who work most effectively, it seems to me, never say "I."
And that's not because they have trained themselves not to say "I."
They don't think "I." They think "we;" they think "team."
They understand their job to be to make the team function.
They accept responsibility and don't sidestep it, but "we" gets the credit.
This is what creates trust, what enables you to get the task done.
— Peter Drucker

Give people a chance, and the benefit of the doubt. They will surprise
you with what they accomplish.
— Bill "Freeloader" Freehafer, P-3 Orion pilot & bon vivant

Have you thought very often, or very recently, about how much authority you have? Is it enough? What would the people whom you lead say about the authority they have to get their jobs done? Are you giving away enough of your power?

In the first few weeks of my transition from being a Naval Flight Officer to my first business role as a marketer, I was very concerned about not behaving in a way that would fulfill any stereotypes about military leaders in such a professional, collegial environment as General Mills. I thought through everything I said before I said it. I was cautious not to be too declarative. I didn't want anyone—up, down, or sideways—to think I was overly confident or there to "kick ass and take names."

Lesa was my first manager. She was small in stature, but a firecracker of a marketer and leader. I respected her confidence from the very beginning, and I did not want my outgoing personality to be misperceived as arrogance or even unearned over-confidence, so I erred on the side of being deferential.

After a couple of weeks of working for Lesa, a situation came up that I brought to her attention. I explained what was going on, outlined a couple of options, and asked her what she thought. Her response to me that day still gives me a professional thrill.

She looked up at me from her desk, put down her pen, and after she took a few seconds to form her thought, she asked, "Were you a *good* naval officer, Cory? You had authority over the weapons on your airplane. You flew missions over Bosnia. Were you, you know, a pretty decisive guy?"

I was stunned. Of course I was a good naval officer. Of course I was designated as a Mission Commander because I was decisive. Where was she going with this?

She continued in a determined and confident voice, "I am really good at this marketing stuff, and you're going to have to work really hard to get so far out in front of me that I won't be able to rescue us both. So I want you to start running as fast as you can. *Run* your business. And if I think you are getting too far out in front of me, I'll reel you back in a bit. But for now, just start running. Need anything else from me, Cory?"

That was the most empowering statement a leader has ever said to me. In just a couple of sentences, she expressed a high level of confidence in me, let me know she had my back if I made mistakes, and informed me that she would use those mistakes to *teach* me. And she also let me know that she would prevent me from making mistakes so big that they would hurt either of our careers. Run? Wow! Run I did....

I was surprised to get so much empowerment right away. I expected the business world to be one of tighter controls and little autonomy because so much money is at stake. But Lesa was leading me with some of the same empowerment practices I had experienced in the military. I was right at home with her leadership style. Looking back at it years later, as much as I appreciated and respected what Lesa did, I realized she was benefitting from my very low expectations. She was a very empowering leader, but her trust seemed so great to me because my expectations for empowerment in the business world had been so low.

When I was twenty-eight years old, my Navy squadron peers and I were regularly given assignments I would describe like this: "Fly two airplanes—two crews of twelve airmen each and about ten other maintenance people—to the other side of the world. Live and work for a month there (where none of us spoke the language) without the benefit of being on a military base. Fly training missions against the host nation's ships and submarines. Kick their butts, but be gracious about it. Be a good U.S. ambassador. Work like a team with the local State Department and other embassy people. Live like locals when you're not flying. Keep your planes mechanically healthy. Keep your people fed and out of jail. Call the squadron if you need any help. But don't really call."

I was twenty-eight years old! I didn't fully appreciate the magnitude of my responsibilities as a young officer until it was a distant memory because it was the only professional environment I knew. Didn't every twenty-eight year old have to do things like that to earn a paycheck?

After a decade as a businessman, I started wondering about how the U.S. military is able to give young men and women so much responsibility and authority, yet maintain extremely high levels of professional behavior and results. My first manager Lesa notwithstanding, I have been repeatedly surprised by how "small" certain jobs or roles seem to be, even when held by well-educated and experienced people. I have even found myself from time to time thinking, "I don't have the breadth of responsibilities that I had at twenty-eight." I have even written job descriptions that seemed too "small" for the requirements I was placing on candidates.

I had begun to think that we have become too cautious in the business world, and perhaps a lot more freedom is in order. But then I thought some more. There had to be a process. There had to be a formula. It had to be replicable and repeatable. And there is:

The military invests highly-trained, learning agile members with huge responsibilities, and also the authority to go with them. It forces them to practice, and practice, and practice their operational and decision-making skills until they have demonstrated *mastery* under difficult circumstances. It gives them clear Rules of Engagement that are specific enough to explain what to do in the most expected cases, but that are also flexible enough to enable good judgment for other cases. It imbues them with an ethos that explains that this good behavior and judgment are expectations at all times, not just when it is easy. And it surrounds them with human support.

That support is the component I was forgetting that I had so much of as a young officer. Whether I was flying two hundred feet above the Norwegian Sea hunting a Russian submarine, or twenty-five thousand feet above the troubled villages of Bosnia, I had the benefit of thousands of hours of training and ready access to literally a hundred years of experience. The decision was ultimately mine, and I would stand accountable for that decision. But I had incredible support available. In today's lean business environment, I am not sure companies can spend enough to provide that sort of support for young leaders, and so we make their jobs "smaller."

What can you do to make your peoples' jobs "bigger?"

1. Empower them to be "Strategic Teammates."

2. Give them your "Leader's Intent."

3. Delegate things that you love to do yourself.

4. Give them your authority, too.

5. Remain open to "up coaching."

STRATEGIC TEAMMATES

In January 1999, then-Commandant of the Marine Corps General Charles Krulak published an article in which he pioneered the concept of the "Strategic Corporal." He outlined his intent to train every Marine—even the most junior corporals—to think strategically, independently, and decisively in order that Marine units would be capable of operating independently at a high rate of effectiveness, even when cut off from higher authority.

General Krulak describes the concept like this: "A Strategic Corporal conducts a rapid assessment of the situation, and follows up quickly with *action*. Any Marine, firmly grounded in our ethos, thoroughly schooled and trained, outfitted with the finest equipment obtainable, is infinitely agile, and above all else, a leader in the finest tradition of the Corps, and will make the right decision."

As a leader, you can benefit significantly by committing to build your followers into "Strategic Teammates." For our purposes, let's re-word Krulak's concept to read like this:

A Strategic Teammate conducts a rapid assessment of the situation, and follows up quickly with *action. Any* teammate, firmly grounded in our culture, thoroughly trained and working with the finest equipment and systems available, is learning-agile, and above all else, a *leader* in the finest tradition of [your organization], and will make the right decision.

Why should this paragraph be so powerful and inspiring to you and your team? If all of the elements of that paragraph are in place, then you will have to work hard to live up to its high standards. If any part of it is lacking or rings hollow, then you have work to do. Do you lack a rich, common culture? Are people not very well-trained? Does your team lack fine traditions? Then you have work to do as a leader. Some of it is leadership within your team, but much of it may be leadership "up." You may have to be the catalyst within your organization to develop the culture, ethos, and norms that will allow leaders throughout the organization to create and support "Strategic Teammates."

LEADER'S INTENT

Another tool that is useful to us for creating empowerment also has a military couterpart. "Commander's Intent" is a message or doctrine that each military unit's commander publishes in order to declare his or her desired end state: What is the purpose behind the objective? What must be accomplished for that objective to be considered a "success?" Under what conditions will this intent no longer apply? The Commander's Intent must clearly explain that all efforts are to be focused on achieving this end. Any particular leader's "intent" message will be reflective of the mission of the overall unit to which he or she belongs. Each sub-team will be aligned with the purpose of the larger unit.

For better or worse, any team, military or not, reflects its leader's personality and behaviors. The concept behind Commander's Intent is to describe clearly what work and objectives the team is engaged in achieving so room exists for independent, creative thought in the goal's accomplishment. Commander's Intent is the "Who, What, Where, When, Why?" and leaves the "How?" up to those engaged in the business of "doing."

Developing and declaring your own "Leader's Intent" will help your team achieve clarity around its purpose and mission. Explain to your team members why their daily toils are important to the organization's goals, and why those goals are noble and worthy of their effort. This explanation will give them swim lanes within which they are free to go about doing the work of executing, and doing so creatively. These are the boundaries within which they can be "Strategic Teammates."

If developing your intent message autonomously might seem too autocratic, then I encourage you to develop it collaboratively with your team. Conduct what project management expert Neal Whitten calls "Team Culture Training," a team exercise during which you will develop and declare your operating norms and team culture that all will respect—and hold each other accountable to—as you work toward your common goal. Once a team has a firm grasp of the objective, each member needs to know his or her individual role. In part, delegation is the translation of a team objective into individual roles.

DELEGATE

Pick three tasks right now that you LOVE to do, that you are really great at, and that no longer require you to stretch yourself to accomplish well. Go ahead: pick three tasks that you are a pro at and write them here:

	TASKS	SKILLS	WHO?
1			
2			
3			

Think through these tasks in your head. What are the behaviors, skills, and competencies required to accomplish them with excellence? Write those *skills* above as well.

Now, think of people on your team or an adjacent team that are not great at those skills, but need to be. Write their names next to one or more of the tasks above.

Next, share with that teammate or the person's leader the plan for removing that task from your plate and using it as a developmental experience for the person listed next to it.

You now have more time to do things that are developmental for you, and you have created that additional time by developing others. Don't forget to give them the ongoing support they will need to be successful.

GIVE THEM YOUR AUTHORITY, TOO!

Consider this formula when thinking about delegation:

Responsibility + Authority = OWNERSHIP

Make sure you have truly empowered people by communicating your faith in their judgment and your expectation that they will deliver excellent results. But also give them clear authority to accomplish the task successfully. It may be budgetary authority. It may be clarifying dotted-line and straight-line reporting relationships. It may be declaring in front of others the role that you are asking them to play. If you go out of your way to give them power, they will surprise you with the effort, creativity, and accomplishment that they deliver.

Part of this empowerment is explaining that you want them to be *decisive*. Former Secretary of State Colin Powell has a formula he uses for decision-making. If he has less than 40 percent of the information he thinks he needs to be successful, then he doesn't move forward until he learns more. If he has enough information to give him a 40 to 70 percent probability of being successful, then he goes with his gut. And if he has enough information that he believes he is 70 percent likely to succeed, then he doesn't wait to get closer to 100 percent because that almost always takes too much time.

Powell's "40 to 70" rule may not be the right range for you, but it is a useful model for you to explain to a particular teammate the confidence you have in him or her. Help the teammate to understand how well calibrated you believe her gut is. Maybe for her, you have a "60 to 80" rule. She should work independently until she feels 60 percent sure of success and then come to you for a gut-check. Or maybe once she has enough insight that she is 80 percent confident of success on a particular project, she can give the approval on a particular project herself. Whatever the right numbers are (they will vary by teammate and by project because of timing and risk and budget/profit impact) for a particular situation, be clear and empowering so the teammate can develop good instincts and earn a string of early, small "wins" that will snowball over time into a reputation for great judgment and decision-making.

REMAIN OPEN TO UP-COACHING

A favorite Navy maxim of mine is that "a complaining sailor is a happy sailor." As long as the environment is healthy enough for a little grumbling, then things are still okay. It is when all griping has stopped that the team members have given up and resigned themselves to whatever awful situation they find themselves in.

As leaders go higher in an organization, they become more disconnected and less likely to hear true objectivity from their people. The best leaders create an environment where it is clear they are always open to receiving "leadership up" from their teammates. This openness will create a team spirit of high professionalism and communicate that you are always seeking to improve.

But how can you tell the difference between ordinary, everyday grumbling, and real insight that might keep you from stepping into a hole and ruining a team or your career? I believe the answer lies in how much thought and consideration the people bringing you the insight have put into it before raising the issue.

- Do they raise the issue respectfully?
- Do they explain ways in which they and others might be contributing to the situation, intentionally or unintentionally?
- Do they ask for your insights and contrary facts before explaining their conclusions?
- Do they tell you their conclusions with a tentative tone of voice, as if they are open to learning another perspective?
- Do they explain what specifically they want out of this conversation and what behaviors they hope will be different moving forward?
- Do they explain their motives for raising the issue, and do they connect the issue with a team or organizational goal or purpose?

If they have put enough effort into considering these types of ideas before bringing you the issue, then you should listen to their feedback with great attention and respect in return. If they have given the issue a great deal of consideration, and they still bring the issue to your attention, then they are doing you a great favor, and you should receive the up-coaching with appreciation.

The best leaders grow empowered teammates, who are likely to go on to grow others into empowered teammates. Give away your power (and authority), and you will be able to accomplish ten times as much through others. And always seek out up-coaching. By looking at the results of the next generation of leaders through The Lens of Leadership, you will grow future leaders who will accept responsibility and be more likely themselves to see success and failures through the leadership they provide to others.

Summary & Exercise: Chapter 9—Giving Away Your Power (to Get More Done!)

WHAT?—SO WHAT?—NOW WHAT?

What? The best leaders accomplish more by truly empowering others to get things done. They create "Strategic Teammates." They make their "Leader's Intent" known. They delegate. They give authority along with responsibility. And they are always open to feedback, from anyone.

So What? "Many hands make light work." Great leadership is not necessarily doing more or working harder yourself, but allowing others to come alongside you to get the work done. Not only will your business results improve, but you will grow your reputation as an empowering leader who uses "the work" to develop the next generation of leaders in the organization.

Now What?

I will study _____

_____ to learn more about empowering those I lead.

I will reach out to _____

_____ in order to seek more insight, guidance, and advice.

I will ask _____ to hold me accountable for _____

_____

_____.

And I will _____

_____

_____

_____ in order to create an experience with elements/competencies that I have not yet adequately developed by *(date)* _____.

ADDITIONAL RESOURCES FOR YOUR "NOW WHAT?" JOURNEY:

Blanchard, Ken. *Leadership and the One Minute Manager.*

Blanchard, Ken, John P. Carlos, and Alan Randolph. *Empowerment Takes More Than a Minute.*

Blanchard, Kenneth H., William Oncken, and Hal Burrows. *The One Minute Manager Meets the Monkey.*

Byham, William and Jeff Cox. *Zapp! The Lightning of Empowerment: How to Improve Productivity, Quality, and Employee Satisfaction.*

"Commander's Intent." (Google It)

Goodwin, Doris Kearns. *Team of Rivals: The Political Genius of Abraham Lincoln.*

Hamel, Gary and C.K. Prahalad. "Strategic Intent." *Harvard Business Review.* July 2005.

Heller, Robert. *How to Delegate.*

Kotter, John P. *John P. Kotter on What Leaders Really Do.*

Patterson, Kerry, Joseph Grenny, Ron McMillan, and Al Switzler. *Crucial Conversations: Tools for Talking When Stakes Are High.*

Whitten, Neal. *Neal Whitten's No-Nonsense Advice for Successful Projects.*

CHAPTER TEN

BUILDING YOUR LEADERSHIP BRAND

A good brand is a promise. A great brand is a promise kept.
– Tom Sitati, Brandscape U.K.

I'm not a "businessman." I am a business, man!
– Shawn Corey Carter, aka rapper Jay-Z

Would you invest in "You?"

Think about how others see you. Take a few minutes and search for your name on Google, Facebook, Twitter, and LinkedIn. Read through some of your "press." Revisit some of the posts you have authored. What is "out there" in the public space about "Brand *You?*"

Now, consider what you just found and answer these two questions:

If you had one hundred thousand dollars this year to invest in something in order to earn a reliable and competitive return, would you invest it in "You?"

Circle One: YES NO

Why?/Why Not?

As a leader in what Dan Pink calls this "Conceptual Age," the most precious assets you have are your ideas and your reputation. They are your personal brand, and you ought to build that brand as intentionally and protect it as jealously as Nike has its "swoosh," as Apple has its *pomme*, and as McDonald's has its arches. Your brand is the only thing you can take with you wherever you go, and it usually precedes you on your journey.

Your brand represents the cumulative total history of the *results* that you have delivered for yourself, your teams, and your companies, using all of the tools in your leadership toolbox. Your brand is not just the "What?" It is also the "How?" and the "With whom?" Your brand is what is "there," but it is also what is "not there." And somewhere in your brand also lies the promise of what "will be."

In order to live your brand every day, you need to be authentically "you." In order to be "you," you always need to be in self-discovery mode and be willing to experiment. Once you know who "you" are, you have to steward your brand with the skillfulness of the best brand managers.

SELF-KNOWLEDGE

The most important piece of advice I can give you for getting candid feedback is "be coachable." No matter what your rank or role, always be humble and hungry enough to receive gratefully the constructive feedback of others, no matter their position or role. Candid, accurate self-awareness is your career's *oxygen*. You won't fall into a hole that you know about and can see.

You can't just *act* interested. You have to *be* interested. If your willingness to hear feedback from others is not converted into behaviors that communicate that you were actually *listening*, your brand will be hollow, indeed.

You should seek out several tools for increasing your self-knowledge. Reach out to your organization's Talent Management, Career Counseling, Organizational Development, or Human Resources associate and ask about various assessments that will help you to gain insights and perspective on your leadership traits, potential, strengths, and opportunities. I recommend you seek this feedback from many sources, not just your immediate teammates. Beyond the traditional "360 Degree" methodology (seeking feedback from those over you, your peers, and those who work for you), I suggest you also seek insights from external vendor partners, consumers of your work or services, and teammates with whom you serve on cross-functional projects. Seek feedback from people with whom you have had *close and frequent* contact over at least the past twelve months. If your organization's formal processes don't allow for this kind of feedback, then seek it out on your own. Conduct personal interviews face-to-face or over the phone. Send out a written survey asking for candid feedback.

Be clear in your purpose: Declare up front that you are seeking to improve, and in order to do that, you need many perspectives. This will be very unusual. Most people don't seek out this kind of candor, and so your motives and intentions may be questioned. Some people may never feel "safe" enough to give you the frank feedback you seek. Work hard to demonstrate your desire to be "great," and accept all feedback gratefully and graciously.

This extra effort must be made as a leader—always and forever—especially the higher you go in any organization. The late Dr. Stephen R. Covey wrote, "Leaders, beware! The higher you go, the less likely people are to give you straight feedback. Feedback is your life support system. Without it, you will eventually fail. Do everything you can to create a culture where it is safe to give you feedback." Whether you are in your career's early or ending stages, you should be leading with a spirit that says, "If you see something in my behavior that is inconsistent with my desire to be a strong, successful leader, please tell me about it. I can take it, and I *want* to hear it. How else will I get better?"

That is being coachable.

CREATE "PERSISTENCY": THE "FUSION THAT FITS"

Careers are long things (more about that in Chapter 13), and frequently deviate from "the plan." Most careers will span at least four decades, and each block of eight to ten years will lead to another block of time down a path that might be discovered somewhat serendipitously. In order to find success and fulfillment throughout these years, the one constant, challenging-but-fulfilling companion should be *you*. That is why self-awareness is so important: because you will be spending so much time with yourself.

While you grow, examine the styles of the great leaders you have served or studied. You will naturally adopt the traits and behaviors that get the best results, and you should intentionally discard (without forgetting) the others. You can learn as much about leadership from "bad" leaders as from great ones by committing to yourself what you will *not* become.

Leadership authenticity means finding your own style. To find that style, complete this exercise: Try to remember the last two or three conversations you had with a teammate, a direct report, or a peer where you offered any advice or suggestions.

Now think for a few minutes about each one: Whose style you were using to guide your motivation, words, and tone throughout each conversation? If you are tempted to say, "my own," then think some more about where and when you learned to treat someone that way. Were you acting like your best interpretation of former GE CEO Jack Welch? Like your first manager? Maybe like your championship team athletic coach? Were you doing something you read in another leadership book?

Developing leadership authenticity requires that you observe and adopt the best practices of the leaders and teammates you encounter along your career journey. The best leaders usually adopted a laboratory mindset early in their careers when they experimented with different styles and techniques to create the "fusion that fits" by continually adding on new tools and techniques that match your personal style.

The best senior leaders are deliberate about making sure that their followers know it is okay to experiment, and they should talk openly about what they want to try and why they think it will work. This communication fosters two-way mentoring, and it can drive some of the "20 percent" social learning I write more about in Chapter 13. The best senior leaders make sure that the lab is a safe place to experiment, and they are quick to protect their followers from making "lab" mistakes in "real world" situations. They are close enough with their developing followers to know when (and in front of whom) to let them "practice," and when everyone has to have his or her "game jersey" on. Great leaders don't let their followers get into situations that will hurt careers or jeopardize the business or relationships.

Once you have developed your style, you have to practice what I call "persistency." Persistency is "persistent consistency." Nobody likes a leader who plays, "Guess-Who-I-Am-Today?" Part of building your leadership brand is establishing what that brand will stand for. The best way to do that is to live out "persistency." The experience of buying a sandwich at any of Subway's over 36,000 locations will be absolutely the same. The imagery, the lighting, the major promotions, and the preparation of your meal will be *consistent* across the globe. This kind of consistency is what you are striving for as a leader.

MARKET YOUR BRAND

Once you know who you "are" as a leader, you're practicing persistency at the right things, and you can identify the accomplishments where your approach has made an impact; then you have developed your brand. Now the hard work of "selling" your brand begins.

As a Consumer Packaged Goods (CPG) marketer by education and experience, I have learned that one's personal brand can and should be marketed with many of the same techniques one would manage a beloved brand of cereal, shoes, or computers. You just can't go wrong studying the fundamentals of brand management (see the "Additional Resources" section at the end of this chapter) and applying them to your personal leadership brand. I will use "The Four Ps" as an example, but any marketing model would work.

Product

You are the product. All of your skills, competencies, opportunities, experiences, project results, the way you self-develop and build others, your functional expertise, and your ability to bring to bear a professional network are all parts of your "product."

Price

How much do you cost your organization? You should include your salary, bonus, expense account, and the cost of your benefits package, which often represents an additional 20-35 percent of your pay. A high price can only be merited by creating a lot of value. As you think about *your* value, consider intangibles like your "ease of use." Are you a low-maintenance product, or are your leaders, followers, and teammates spending a lot of their time or emotional energy keeping you operating? What is the opportunity cost of having you onboard as a teammate? Do they wish they had other options with low switching costs? If so, your product may be priced too high.

Place

Are you in what Jim Collins calls the "right seat on the bus?" Are you in the right job for your skills and passion? Are you available to people across your organization who need your product? Do people know where to go to find you? Do you leverage technology to expand your reach? Do you "franchise" yourself by building others with your needed skills and reputation, thereby expanding your reach or "distribution"? Is there some "induced scarcity" built in so you are always just a little unreasonably busy delivering results effectively and efficiently?

Promotion

My favorite part of marketing is developing and executing integrated communications plans: making television ads, developing high-visibility public relations campaigns, and connecting my brand to the right partner brands to increase both of our equities. Getting the word out about the brands I managed was exciting, and finding the right tools with the right reach at the right price was challenging but effective.

How will you communicate your value to your team and organization as both a follower and a leader? The basic blocking and tackling tools are your internal development processes and mentoring programs. But how can you get creative about selling the benefits of your "product" without tarnishing your brand by being too competitive or political?

The best marketing that money cannot buy is authentic word-of-mouth. Let your methods and results speak so loudly for you that others become your brand champions. You will certainly need to think of creative ways to put yourself in position to be chosen by your organization's "consumers." The best place to start is by earning a reputation as a results-oriented, high-value, maintenance-free follower *and* leader who serves his or her customers' needs. A good reputation is a sure way to earn full-price repeat business (the highest-margin kind) and grow your new-business portfolio through inexpensive word-of-mouth advertising.

Manage your career reputation with the care and attention you would manage a global powerhouse brand like Apple, Coca-Cola, or Nike. A brand is always either growing or weakening. You should consider your annual performance reviews as a great time to do a comprehensive business review of your own entrepreneurial business: You!

When people look at their personal brands through The Lens of Leadership, they will be more likely to catch events that might damage a brand earlier, and put more effort into repairing the brand so the blemish fades from consumer memory. They are also more likely to be aware of huge personal brand successes, and leverage those events to take their careers to the next level. We see—and take responsibility for—results much more effectively when we examine our career through The Lens of Leadership.

Summary & Exercise: Chapter 10—Building Your Leadership Brand

WHAT?—SO WHAT?—NOW WHAT?

What? In order to live your brand every day, you need to be authentically you. In order to be "you," you need always to be in self-discovery mode and be willing to experiment. Once you know who "you" are, you have to steward your brand with the techniques and skillfulness of the best brand managers.

So What? You must use every tool at your disposal, from inside and outside your organization, to increase the candid self-awareness of your performance and perceived results in order to manage your personal leadership brand. Once you have that awareness, then shape what your brand becomes in a way that is aligned with your skills and your passions so you can be authentically you—the only "you" that you can be over the long haul of a career. Finding and living in that authentic sweet spot will enable you to over-deliver on expectations consistently across roles and organizations, earning you promotions and influence faster than your peers.

Now What?

I will study _____
_____ to learn more about successfully nurturing and growing my leadership brand.

I will reach out to _____
_____ in order to seek more insight, guidance, and advice.

I will ask _____ to hold me accountable for _____
_____.

And I will _____

_____

_____

_____ in order to create an experience with elements/competencies that I have not yet adequately developed by *(date)* _____.

ADDITIONAL RESOURCES FOR YOUR "NOW WHAT?" JOURNEY:

Aaker, David. *Building Strong Brands.*

Buckingham, Marcus and Curt Coffman. *First, Break All the Rules: What the World's Greatest Managers Do Differently.*

George, Bill, Peter Sims, and David Gergen. *True North: Discover Your Authentic Leadership.*

Goldman, Daniel, Richard E. Boyatzis, and Annie McKee. *Primal Leadership: Learning to Lead with Emotional Intelligence.*

The Marketing Faculty of The Kellogg School of Management. *Kellogg on Branding.*

McNally, David. *Be Your Own Brand.*

Rath, Tom. *StrengthsFinder 2.0.*

Ries, Al and Jack Trout. *Positioning: The Battle for Your Mind.*

CHAPTER ELEVEN

RECRUITING AND HIRING THE BEST LEADERS

Hire people who are better than you are, then leave them to get on with it. Look for people who will aim for the remarkable, who will not settle for the routine.
— David Ogilvy, pioneer of modern advertising

Associate with those of good quality if you esteem your own reputation; for it is better to be alone than in bad company.
— George Washington

One of the most exciting things about being a leader is having the opportunity to recruit and hire high-caliber teammates and other future leaders to your team. But many hiring and promotional processes commit what I call recruiting's "original sin" by assuming that the most highly skilled "doers" are natural choices to be promoted to leaders. Nothing could be further from the truth! The skills required to be an exceptional risk analyst, accountant, machine operator, preacher, pilot, or any of a thousand other "doer" jobs are very different from the skills needed to lead a team of doers or a cross-functional team that has been brought together. But leaders will often be so impressed by someone's year-over-year output results, or his ability to increase quality, or her uncanny ability to find interpretations of regulations that benefit the organization, that they promote the person as a reward for consistently strong individual performance. It is true that sometimes skilled doers will also become accomplished and venerated leaders, but the selection process for leaders should be geared toward measuring them for *that* purpose and not weighing too heavily the impact of just delivering great doer results.

But what if you are hiring a doer? In that case, I suggest you *still* recruit for future leadership potential. I would rather hire a self-motivated, learning-agile candidate who can tell me about her history of taking the initiative to make her previous work areas better—even if she only has 70-80 percent of the job-specific skills I wish she had—than a highly functionally-skilled candidate who lacks demonstrable passion or learning agility. I will use the business to build her job-specific skills and leverage her drive to help me build others. A candidate who is primarily *functionally*-skilled will not progress far as a leader and may struggle as a productive teammate.

GETTING STARTED

If you have a Human Resources partner, then you absolutely should begin by leveraging his or her skills and experience[1]. Human Resources people are *specialists* with deep domain expertise at dancing the recruiting and hiring "tango," that delicate courtship that occurs between hiring teams and candidates. Your HR partner will have an organization-wide perspective on where the deep end of the internal talent pool is and can suggest target-rich environments outside of your organization.

Your HR partner will also have several tools that can help you assess and prioritize your candidates so you can better understand

---

[1] If you are a small organization or a start-up, there are excellent books in the Additional Resources section of this chapter. You should also seek out HR mentorship from within your professional network.

candidates' personalities, work styles, motivators, intellectual capacities, cultural fit, and many other components that are the building blocks of each complicated individual. Your HR partner can help you understand how each candidate's work history translates into the competency models and career paths that exist in your organization.

These tools will also help you understand each candidate's "gaps," and whether those gaps are coachable over time, or whether they will likely keep the candidate from being successful. There are a couple of things to remember, though: 1) Unless the role you are trying to fill is a new role for your team or for the organization, then *you* are the expert in that role. You should, therefore, be leading your HR partner on defining the behaviors and characteristics of the ideal candidate. 2) Recruiting and hiring are more art than science. Your "gut" will play an important factor in determining each candidate's technical and cultural "fit." Experience is, therefore, the best teacher and only time will reveal whether your "call" on the selected candidate was the right one. Hiring and staffing mistakes can be costly. It behooves you to develop a well-calibrated gut.

WHAT TO LOOK FOR: LEADERSHIP FIRST

It is my belief—learned through experience across several different types of organizations and throughout various levels

> You can sharpen your hiring instincts by volunteering to serve on additional interview teams and learn from debriefs with other interviewers. Ask a lot of questions. Find out who is a successful screener in your organization and why.

within those organizations—that you should hire people who act as *leaders first*, and consider their other functional skills second. If they demonstrate the leadership competencies I've written about (including followership), those skills will magnify the effect of their functional competencies. Remember to avoid the "original sin" of searching for a great "doer" when you are really looking for a great (or potentially great) leader-follower. They must certainly meet the minimum functional job skills. I don't mean that their ability to do and understand the functional tasks is irrelevant. But, especially for promotable entry-level roles[2], you should be hiring for leadership qualities and potential, and then use your business model to develop further both their functional and leadership skills.

At General Mills, the recruiting process for Marketing is incredibly rigorous. The first round interview includes scenario-based intelligence testing, creative and personality instruments, and up to six different behavior-based interviews in one day. The company is searching for candidates who can do the job "today," but more importantly, candidates who have the potential to be promoted to *at least two levels* above the role they are interviewing for. When they bring Top-10 MBA candidates in from across the country, they already know they are getting bright and talented people. They narrow the field down to those few candidates whom they believe have the potential to become future marketing directors at their company. They only want to bring onboard those candidates whom they believe possess the ability to deliver results in positions of increasing responsibility and complexity, and who will be able to navigate successfully the internal political and cultural waters. This process is the result of a world-class talent acquisition mindset.

What are some ways to measure a perspective hire's leadership potential? Look at the person's past. In investing, you will often find the disclaimer, "Past performance does not guarantee future results." I would suggest that for recruiting leaders, a better adage is: "Several data points make a trend." Remember, once candidates have exceeded all of the thresholds and you have narrowed the pool down to the few most-qualified, the selection becomes more art than science.

I suggest you look for a track record—going back as far as high school in some cases—of being selected by teachers, coaches, man-

---

2 Even highly-educated, experienced "entry level" roles like associate marketing manager, project engineer, or lab leader.

agers, *and also by peers*, for positions of leadership. Did the person captain several sports teams in high school and in college? Was he or she an Eagle Scout, or Girl Scout "Gold Award" winner? If he did not go to college, what can you learn from his work history or other activities that reveals how he always seems to "bubble up" into formal or informal leadership roles over and over again? In college, did he serve as a Resident Assistant? Did she join a struggling campus extra-curricular activity as an underclassman and eventually lead it to regional or national renown? Can he articulate a long history of roles of increasing responsibility that don't just demonstrate *individual* entrepreneurialism, but that exhibit his leading an enterprise or team to new and highly-accomplished success? This is the track record you want to be asking about. The person should communicate his leadership throughout each of his answers. *How* he talks about his teams and their accomplishments will reveal a lot about his leadership style.

Be sure also to probe into *how they learn*. Are they "earning through learning" new competencies? Have they delivered good results even when in tough environments like down markets or declining companies?

Within the limits of HR legalities, probe into how they learn outside of work. Are they curious, with a broad set of varied interests, or are they focused deeply on one or two hobbies or interests? Neither is wrong—only potentially "wrong" for what you might be seeking for a particular role. The most learning-agile people will astound you with the breadth of their topical knowledge and passions. Learning agility is a better predictor of leadership success than any intelligence instrument.

FOUR "E"S AND A "P"

I am a fan of using Jack Welch's subjective model when I evaluate candidates because they match what I am looking for in candidates. I use a simple scale of 1 to 10 for each attribute.

Does the candidate radiate *Energy*? Based on your total exposure to the candidate—including less-formal situations like a pre-interview dinner or a tour of the plant—does she seem to have an internal generator that keeps her go-go-going? What is your sense of her personal energy, 1 to 10?

Does the person have the ability to *Energize* others? Does he light up the room with his presence and make you glad to be there learning about him? Does his spark get spread to others? Will he enthusiastically accept responsibility? Is he an Eeyore or a Tigger, 1 to 10?

Do her answers convey an *Edge*—a certainty that she arrived at rationally? Does she appear to be healthily competitive internally, and relentless in her pursuit of external competitors? Did she make a tough call even when she only had 70 percent of the information she wished she'd had? Is she decisive, 1 to 10?

Can he *Execute* a plan individually and with a team to realize a vision or accomplish a mission? Is he about "impact" or merely about "activity?" Does he leverage his business acumen and relationships with others to get big things done, 1 to 10?

Finally, the "P": Does the person have the *Passion* to persevere against long odds and rally others to the cause? His passion—for the job, for the team, for the goal, or for the cause—is what keeps him going when it gets tough to deliver on one or all of the "E's." In telling her stories, does she draw you into her cause as well? Does she move to the edge of her chair when she describes a particular challenge? Does she connect it to a motivator that is "bigger" than just herself? Is she mildly fanatical no matter the task, 1 to 10?

Again, these are *subjective* measures and each member of an interview team will arrive at different specific numbers. Using them will give you a common language across a few important measures and a rough scale against which you can compare the candidates.

WHAT ELSE TO LOOK FOR

I look for several, *very* significant accomplishments from each of my candidates, even if they are fairly inexperienced. Their answers are a window into their mental processes and work style. I want their answers framed up this way: First, I want them to tell me exactly what they did—it should be specific and delivered with enthusiasm. Bam! Then I want them to put it in context for me: Why was it significant, and hard to succeed? I want them to explain their thought processes to me: How did they research the problem and come to their conclusions? Were they thinking at a level or two above what the task demanded? Did they take a rational or emotional approach? Was their thinking long-term? Strategic? They will reveal a lot about how they view people, and a lot about their problem-solving process and powers of logic and critical thinking, so listen carefully and "read between the lines" of their answers.

Finally, I want them to explain how they executed the solution. Again, their answers will reveal more than just how they managed the challenge. They will tell you what role they allowed or required others to play. You will hear about how they inspire and encourage others. Are they like Tom Sawyer, influencing others when they lack authority? Are they resourceful and creative? You will learn about whether they have a "can-do" or defeatist attitude as they explain how they overcame hurdles. You will also hear clues to help you decide whether their methodology will be successful within your organization's culture.

Each organization is different. The challenge, as you "pan for gold" through your recruiting process, is to make sure the candidate will be a *cultural* fit as well. Leadership happens *within a culture*. Show the person your organization's mission statement and describe its values. Then ask the person questions about how those ideas and values have been relevant in his or her own life before today. Ask him what his personal mission statement is and see how he responds.

You could hire an exceptionally skilled and accomplished leader whose methods are at odds with the way business really gets done within your organization. You may also have found a new-hire who can bring inspiration and changed behaviors to your team or organization. But you may have, instead, hired someone who will clash with the culture, setting you and him or her up for failure. At this point, it is more art than science, and you are responsible. Develop a well-calibrated gut.

Finally, I like a candidate who "connects" with me frequently throughout the recruiting process and "closes hard." These are more subjective measures, but they are rich with signals and information. Does the person find professional ways to compliment my company and what we do? Or does he flatter in shallow ways that seem manufactured and unauthentic? Does she connect with me as a professional and also as a person? Do his stories help me conclude that I would like to have him as a "neighbor" near my cube and also near my home?

I also want to be wanted. I want candidates to convey subtly to me that their skills are a great match—that they are *exactly* what I am looking for. And I want to believe that their *interests* are aligned with the work, too. Are they trying to build a rapport with me, or am I doing all of the work in this very young relationship? I want to believe they are interested in learning about the next steps in the process. I'm not asking for a commitment—that would be premature. All I want to know is that they are interested enough, and I want to believe they are enough of a match to move to the next step in the relationship.

"A-B-C, A-B-C" is a familiar mantra in professional sales. It means, "Always-Be-Connecting, Always-Be-Closing." I want a candidate to be connecting with me throughout the process. I want him to be "closing the deal" in subtle ways, but also in one final "hard" close at the end, if he is truly interested: "Cory, I have appreciated our conversation, and based on what I have learned from you, from the team, and from the process, I hope I am a very competitive candidate, and I can't wait to learn more about the next steps." That's all. I don't want to hear, "Will you marry me?" but I do want to hear that he is interested in a "next date." The best candidates connect throughout the process, and convey interest with "soft" and "hard" closes.

SOME FOLLOW-UP THOUGHTS...

As you narrow the field of candidates, here are some thinking questions that may help you make your decision:

1. Is the person a cultural fit?

2. If so, is he or she 80 percent of what you were looking for in the "ideal" candidate?

3. If so, does he seem pretty coachable on the other 20 percent?

4. If so, is his other 20 percent *different* from the collective team's "20 percent"? Would you continue to be vulnerable if you hired him, or could he actually reinforce one of the team's deficits and grow into the rest of the role?

If the person meets the functional requirements of the position and you can answer "yes" to those four questions, then maybe he is worth taking a chance on.

...AND A FOLLOW-UP CALL

I also like to make a follow-up phone call a couple of days after the interview to my high-interest candidates. I ask them a handful of questions:

1. How was your interview experience?

2. Do you have questions about any of the assessments?

3. How do you think each of your interviews went?

4. How do you think your presentation went?

5. What did you "nail?"

6. What might you do differently if you could?

7. What did you learn about us?

8. What surprised you?

9. What additional questions do you have?

I may also ask a few questions that subtly address any concerns the interview team might have had.

I have found that this follow-up process gives me insight into the candidate's self-awareness and perception of cultural fit. It also gives the candidate a chance to re-address any of the issues the interview team might be wavering on.

YOU WILL MAKE MISTAKES

No matter how rigorous your process, you will make some bad hiring decisions over the course of your career. Resist the urge to beat yourself up too much. Do *not* resist the urge to beat yourself up at least a little bit. And don't give up on a new-hire too soon. Adjusting to a new organization and a new culture can take time.

My worst estimation of a candidate's potential happened when I was an upperclassman at the Naval Academy. As a junior, I was tasked with evaluating and challenging a young man named Matt, who was a "Plebe," or freshman. I was intensely critical of and unfairly challenging to young Midshipman Matt throughout his Plebe year. My poorly-calibrated and immature "gut" sure was wrong: Matt Blunt became a successful Surface Warfare Officer in the Navy, and then also went on to become the Secretary of State of Missouri, and was then elected the second youngest governor in the history of the "Show Me" state. As I watched Matt's career progress, I was continually humbled at how wrong I had been about him. I always ask myself how I might be wrong about a candidate—even the ones I think will be very successful.

Recruiting mistakes are costly. For some hires, it may cost you 70-80 percent of the position's first year total compensation to fix the problem of a bad hire, and that doesn't include the human costs and emotional stress. As a leader, you have the responsibility to develop the abilities of your followers and teammates, the opportunity to mentor and recruit internal candidates, and the ability to bring in new talent and ideas through external hiring. The best leaders balance all three, constantly on the watch for talent, and always looking for candidates with leadership potential. By looking at recruiting through The Lens of Leadership, you will deliver the best results by hiring and then developing the best leaders.

Summary & Exercise:
Chapter 11—Recruiting and Hiring the Best Leaders

WHAT?—SO WHAT?—NOW WHAT?

What? Recruit and hire people who act as leaders *first*, and who also have the important functional or technical skills you need. Use a rigorous process to find candidates who can describe many, many examples of being learning-agile and delivering superlative results. Introduce them to your organization's culture and develop a well-calibrated gut for estimating "fit." There are no "perfect candidates," just like there are no perfect spouses. There *are* candidates who will grow to become cherished and exemplary colleagues if you choose well.

So What? You must first understand exactly what you are looking for, objectively and subjectively. Next, collaborate with your HR partner and use as many tools as you can to cast a wide net. Then narrow the field down to a great new teammate. Recruiting mistakes are costly, but you can increase your chances of success by focusing on mutual interests as you close the deal.

Now What?

I will study _____

_____ to learn more about re-cruiting and hiring.

I will reach out to _____

_____ in order to seek more insight, guidance, and advice.

I will ask _____ to hold me accountable for _____

_____.

And I will _____

_____ in order to create an experience with elements/competencies that I have not yet adequately developed by *(date)* _____.

ADDITIONAL RESOURCES FOR YOUR "NOW WHAT?" JOURNEY:

Adler, Lou. *Hire With Your Head: Using Performance-Based Hiring to Build Great Teams.*

Charan, Ram. *Know-How: The 8 Skills That Separate People Who Perform from Those Who Don't.*

Colvin, Geoff. *Talent Is Overrated: What Really Separates World-Class Performers from Everybody Else.*

Eichinger, Robert W. *100 Things You Need to Know: Best Practices for Managers and HR.*

Gladwell, Malcolm. "The New-Boy Network." *The New Yorker.* (May 29, 2000)

Gladwell, Malcolm. *Outliers: The Story of Success.*

Gladwell, Malcolm. "The Talent Myth." *The New Yorker.* (July 22, 2002)

Hunt, Steven. *Hiring Success: The Art and Science of Staffing Assessment and Employee Selection.*

Luntz, Frank I. *Win: The Key Principles to Take Your Business from Ordinary to Extraordinary.*

Michaels, Ed, Helen Handfield-Jones, and Beth Axelrod. *The War for Talent.*

Peter, Laurence J. and Raymond Hull. *The Peter Principle.*

Pink, Daniel. *To Sell is Human: The Surprising Truth About Moving Others.*

BUILD

PART THREE

DEVELOPING YOURSELF

Opportunity is missed by most people because it is dressed in overalls and looks like work.
— Thomas Edison

CHAPTER TWELVE

BEING "GREAT" ISN'T GOOD ENOUGH
(SO BE *"SUPERLATIVE!"*)

Everyone thinks of changing the world, but no one thinks
of changing himself.
— Leo Tolstoy

Only as far as we seek
can we go.
Only as much as we dream
can we be.
— Karen Ravn

Every self-development book written will encourage you to be "great." I am not going to do that. I am going to *dare you to become superlative* at what you intend to do and become.

At Johnsonville Sausage, the most enduring and endearing part of its culture is "The Johnsonville Way." The philosophy of "The Johnsonville Way" was developed in the early 1980s. The owner, Ralph Stayer, worked with members (employees) throughout the company to get the words right as a declaration of what they were committing to each other to become, and to give permission to hold one another accountable to those commitments. One of the phrases is, "We will succeed by setting near term objectives and long term goals that will require personal growth and superlative performance by each of us. We will change any objectives or goals that no longer require personal growth and superlative performance to ones that do." When he is asked about that unusual word "superlative," Ralph replies, "I couldn't find a higher adjective than 'superlative' to describe that state of effort and accomplishment. It's the most *superlative* superlative, so I went with it."

In order to achieve "the most" out of your life—whether "the most" means money and career status to you, or becoming a renowned subject matter expert—you must have a *high-achievement mindset*. Perhaps you want to deliver philanthropy beyond measure. Maybe it means having "the most" properly balanced life where you are successful multi-dimensionally at work, at home, and in your community. You cannot achieve a life of "the most" without an ambition to be superlative. Leadership will demand that you inspire others to become their best. The best way for you to be able to inspire others is to have the ambition to become superlative yourself.

You don't have to be born with a Type-A, hyper-competitive spirit in order to become superlative. You can do just a few things that will help you develop your own high-achievement mindset: *Compete With YOU First, Get in "The Arena," Dare Greatly,* and *Cast Out Fear.*

COMPETE WITH YOU FIRST

You should be the most feared competitor that you face in your quest for "the most." And remember, this "competition" is for whatever "the most" means to *you*. Don't dismiss this chapter because you are an altruist who wants to achieve big things for *others*, and you believe I'm writing about aggressive, cutthroat corporate types. I am writing about YOU. You are reading this book because you want to become someone different than who you are today. You will be much more likely to achieve those things if you acknowledge that humans accomplish more when they compete against someone, and that the first competitor who puts a knot in your stomach should be you.

We have all had coaches who pushed us to achieve more than we thought we could by ourselves. As you work on developing yourself as a follower and rising leader, you must *be the coach and the competitor*. The best followers and leaders are hard on *themselves* first. You will recover from, and be forgiven by others for, your inevitable failures and shortcomings if you are able to analyze and critique your performance objectively, admit your opportunities for improvement quickly and in front of others, and articulate a different performance path for "next time." Then you will earn respect from others for your high self-awareness and self-coaching, and you will inspire others with your commitment to continuous self-improvement.

I was raised in a rural Midwestern town by a courageous single mother whom life had robbed of much of her self-esteem. But she knew instinctively how to build self-esteem in me: she taught me to demand excellence of myself, knowing that would result in accomplishment and a high level of confidence and willingness to achieve even more. That such a young boy has become a man with the experiences of my life is a testament to the commitment of a wise woman who does not think herself so. Here is how she did it:

After every single graded, competitive, or merely observed event of my youth that I can remember—academics, athletics, public performances, social interactions—even if I had won, she asked me, "Did you do your *best?*" And she didn't mean had I just given the actual event my best effort. Before answering, she required that I also think about my preparation for the event in the days and weeks prior. Had I given *my preparation* my "best?" Had I primed my heart and spirit in advance for the outcome? Had I given the advice of coaches and teachers my best consideration and application? Had I nourished and rested myself and studied for a "best" performance?

If, after considering all of this, I could still answer, "Yes," then I was worthy of the victory, or I learned to become self-consoling about the defeat, because there was nothing else I could have done. It was a fortunate way to be raised. It was and is a constant reminder to "Compete with *You* first."

GET IN "THE ARENA"

One of my favorite quotes is Theodore Roosevelt's "The Man in the Arena."[1] Read through it slowly and deliberately. *Use a pen to circle or highlight the parts that connect with you:*

> It is not the critic who counts; not the man who points out how the strong man stumbles, or where the doer of deeds could have done them better. The credit belongs to the man who is actually in the arena, whose face is marred by dust and sweat and blood; who strives valiantly; who errs, who comes short again and again, because there is no effort without error and shortcoming; but who does actually strive to do the deeds; who knows great enthusiasms, the great devotions; who spends himself in a worthy cause; who at the best knows in the end the triumph of high achievement, and who at the worst, if he fails, at least fails while daring greatly, so that his place shall never be with those cold and timid souls who neither know victory nor defeat.

A lot of wisdom and inspiration is packed into those words! Depending on how old you are or what stage of development your career is in, different parts of it will resonate more strongly than others. Look back at what you highlighted. Make notes in the margins of this book to complete the sentence, "*This phrase compels me to* ____" for each of your highlighted areas. *Do this now.*

If you are early in your career, or early in a new career transition, maybe you connected with Roosevelt's contempt for "the critic."

1 Excerpted from a longer speech, "Citizenship in a Republic," which Roosevelt delivered at the Sorbonne in Paris in early 1910.

If you have more experience, you probably earned some of your wisdom through "error and shortcoming." Either way, Roosevelt admonishes all of us to avoid underperforming against our potential.

How can you avoid becoming a "cold and timid soul?" Consistently put yourself in a position to be around true greatness. Put yourself in a position to work with people who are better than you are. Hire others who are smarter than you are. Volunteer for roles and opportunities that are a little over your head. Put yourself "out there" relentlessly throughout the several decades that make up a modern career and you will achieve much more than you ever dreamed. You will also develop a network that is stronger than those who live more comfortably and "closer in."

I make no special claim to being highly competitive. As far back as my teenage years, however, I found much satisfaction and joy in the few things I chose to commit more effort to than I would to just a hobby. There have also been things that I had no particular desire to be great at, but that were valued by others as indicators of success, so I took those things seriously too, as a means to achieve my broader goals. You have got to be willing to swim in "the deep end" of life's pool if you want to be superlative. By putting yourself in over your head, you will achieve more out of life, and find life to be more self-satisfying. The deep end of the pool will also introduce you to people who are better than you, have competencies at things for which you will never be truly great, and have experienced life-changing epiphanies that can only be found through the door that is marked, "Push."

DARE GREATLY

I was fortunate to learn as a young man the rewards that come from placing myself in situations where I could be around true greatness. I wish I could claim that I had been intentional about doing so, but I was really more like the blind squirrel that nevertheless finds a nut from time to time. This blind squirrel was also very teachable, however, so I learned to seek out opportunities to get in to places and situations I thought were way out of my league. I learned to "dare greatly."

I knew from a young age that I wanted to attend the Naval Academy, and that goal led me to work harder—at everything—than I probably would have otherwise. Athletics was an early door-opener for me that led to informal leadership opportunities. Those opportunities grew into more formal leadership roles in a part-time job, school clubs, and even a formalized student-to-student mentoring role. All of that led to statewide and national events in swimming, and selection for programs like American Legion Boys' State, where I was suddenly surrounded by high-caliber "#1" students. It was the "deep end of the pool," and I was determined to raise my game to be as good as they were.

I parlayed my high school success into an appointment to the Naval Academy. I was sure I had snuck in, and that they would send me home as soon as they found out how under-qualified I was. I was surrounded by 1,200 of America's morally, mentally, and physically "best and brightest" youth. The deep end had just gotten deeper.

I had not been recruited by the varsity swimming team, but I walked on and made the squad. I only swam in a handful of varsity meets, but I worked harder and learned more about competition and commitment in one year than I had in the previous ten. I was a mediocre Plebe in a sea of people who had been number one in everything they had ever touched. It was a humbling time. But I was being humbled by a national sampling of the very finest young Americans. I went on to volunteer for and succeed in very physically competitive programs like Navy Diver training and Army Parachutist training. I fell in love with the French language and learned it very quickly—quickly enough to live and study in France before my senior year. My overall grade point average was not high enough to be sponsored by the Academy, so generous people from my hometown raised the money so I could go. I was the president of the French Club and hosted the French ambassador to the United States my senior year. I also earned my way into student leadership roles: I failed to become the highest ranking student, but by jumping into that deep pool, I did achieve the top 1 percent of student leadership at what is, arguably, the finest undergraduate leadership institution in the world. I didn't have any other college benchmarks. I thought *all* college kids were surrounded by all-American athletes and Rhodes scholars, and that they all had true American heroes and White House Fellows for professors.

I also *failed* in many ways over those four years: I was underwhelming academically, neither great nor at-risk. I chose to leave a six-week Marine Corps summer training program in the middle of it because I knew I no longer wanted to be a Marine officer. And I failed to earn sponsorship by the Academy to attend summer language training. Each of those failures taught me valuable lessons.

I competed for and earned my way into Naval Aviation as a Naval Flight Officer (NFO). I earned all of the most advanced NFO ratings and served as an instructor in one of the most physically, mentally, and emotionally demanding jobs in the Navy. But I failed to be number one in any of my flight school classes, and I failed one of my most important oral boards the first time, in front of one of the most respected commanding officers in Naval Aviation.

After my flight tour, I went back to teach at the Naval Academy. I was surrounded by top leadership intellectuals and by admirals and generals. I was an aviation professional who had to learn how to drive and captain 100-foot ships and earn the respect of the best small ship handlers in the Navy. I completed my MBA at the University of Maryland, competing academically with people who had been in the business world for a decade. During that time, I almost hit a pier with my vessel while a Navy Captain was on my bridge. I also got three "B"s in my MBA program, each of which I felt was a shameful failure.

To make my transition into Corporate America, I was accepted by Cameron-Brooks, an executive recruiting firm that specializes in transitioning young military officers. It had an 88 to 90 percent candidate rejection rate, but I was accepted into the program. I spent two and a half years preparing for my transition. I converted sixteen interviews into fifteen offers for second interviews. I converted a selection of those into several simultaneous offers of employment, three of which were even from the great business leadership factory of Procter & Gamble. I still think about the one failed interview.

I accepted a marketing offer from General Mills. I was a former Naval Flight Officer with a second-tier MBA who was suddenly competing against really brilliant, experienced business people with MBAs from the Harvard Business School, Northwestern's Kellogg School, UCLA's Anderson School, and the University of Michigan's Ross School. The deep end of the pool gets deeper and deeper.

And that's the point. As you can guess, I went on to various successes, and also failures, in roles at the highly professional General Mills, the strict meritocracy of Newell-Rubbermaid, and the "passionate patriarch" environment at Johnsonville Sausage. With each career move, I entered a world I believed was way over my head and out of my league. But if I were going to fail, I would have failed in the arena, as Roosevelt wrote, "while daring greatly."

CAST OUT FEAR

Once you accept that you are competing against yourself first, that you belong "in the arena," and that you must dare greatly in going after what you want, you must still prepare to face the demons of failure and inadequacy. You will do nothing of any consequence if you fear the deep end of the pool.

I don't know how to make you comfortable with failure. It's a paradox: You cannot grow without failing, yet those who fail—either too often, or perhaps even just once in a very visible way—will not be allowed to continue to grow at an organization. I, and others I know and respect, have found success keeping to this maxim: "Don't be afraid to make mistakes, but never make the same mistake twice." Learn quickly from your mistakes. Demonstrate your adaptive learning by quickly changing behaviors and delivering improved results. Communicate frequently with coaches and mentors about the tolerance at your organization for learning through mistakes. Turn failure into something useful, and move on.

And what about inadequacy? How can you successfully overcome the feeling that you are in over your head based on the people around you?

In his autobiography *Big Russ & Me*, the late, great political journalist and commentator Tim Russert tells the story of getting his job in the U.S. Senate office of the powerful Daniel Patrick Moynihan, a towering intellectual among twentieth century politicians. Russert was feeling out of his league when it came to his own background and education: he was raised in blue-collar South Buffalo, New York, and his degrees were from two small universities in Cleveland, Ohio. Moynihan's intellect was daunting enough, but his office was filled with New York blue bloods who had Ivy League educations. Russert was expressing his concerns to Senator Moynihan, who reassuringly replied, "Tim, what they have, you can learn. What *you* have, they will never understand." And so you, too, must confront your feelings of inadequacy.

You can choose not to go into the deep end of the pool. But if you want to achieve more than you expect, and faster, if you want to lead others better than they expect from you, or if you want to earn the influence to make needed change in the world, you must look at self-development through The Lens of Leadership. The world is in desperate need of leaders. Don't be one of Roosevelt's "timid souls that knows neither victory nor defeat." Be *SUPERLATIVE*!

Summary & Exercise: Chapter 12—Being "Great" Isn't Good Enough (So Be *"Superlative!"*)

WHAT?—SO WHAT?—NOW WHAT?

<u>**What?**</u> You don't have to be born a hyper-competitive, Type-A personality to have the aspiration and discipline to associate and compete with people who are "better" than you are.

<u>**So What?**</u> You must learn to Compete With YOU First, Get "in the Arena," Dare Greatly, and Cast Out Fear. Then you must make consistent career choices to volunteer for and network into positions that are in the "deep end of the pool" if you are to grow your own skills quickly and broadly. Experience is the best teacher of the lessons that are the most useful and indelible.

<u>**Now What?**</u>

I will study _____

_____ to learn more about

setting higher goals and becoming "superlative."

I will reach out to _____

_____ in order to seek more

insight, guidance, and advice.

I will ask _____ to hold me

accountable for _____

_____.

And I will _____

_____

_____

_____ in order to create an experience with

elements/competencies that I have not yet adequately developed by *(date)* _____.

ADDITIONAL RESOURCES FOR YOUR "NOW WHAT?" JOURNEY:

Belasco, James A. and Ralph C. Stayer. *Flight of the Buffalo: Soaring to Excellence, Learning to Let Employees Lead.*

Buckingham, Marcus. *Now, Discover Your Strengths.*

Christian, Ken. *Your Own Worst Enemy: Breaking the Habit of Adult Underachievement.*

Collins, Jim and Jerry I. Porras. *Built to Last: Successful Habits of Visionary Companies.*

Fine, Alan. *You Already Know How to Be Great: A Simple Way to Remove Interference and Unlock Your Greatest Potential.*

Gladwell, Malcolm. *Outliers: The Story of Success.*

Johnsonville Sausage. "The Johnsonville Way." (Google It)

Newberry, Tommy. *Success Is Not an Accident: Change Your Choices; Change Your Life.*

Rath, Tom. *StrengthsFinder 2.0.*

Welch, Jack. *Winning.*

CHAPTER THIRTEEN

BECOMING INTENTIONALLY AGILE: A CAREER IS NOT A STRAIGHT LINE

Luck's a fool. The door to success is always marked, 'Push.'
— Hand-Book of Harvard University, 1908-09

The illiterate of the 21st century won't be those who cannot read or write, but will be those who cannot learn, unlearn, and re-learn.
— Alvin Toffler, futurist

Life is long.[1]

Depending on your current career stage and career fit, that sentence may seem either like a thrill, or a curse.

Think about how much longer you get to work for a living: if you are twenty-five years old, you have got about forty-five years… FORTY-FIVE years…of career still ahead of you. Even if you are fifty years old, you still have fifteen to twenty years left in the journey. That is a LOT of time.

It is really hard to appreciate the number of years ahead of you if you are very early in your career, and maybe it's even a little bit unfair to ask you to try. But no matter how ambitious you are, and regard-

---

1 It can also be short, but that's a different topic for a different book.

less of how "planned out" and deliberate you think you can be in your career management, let me advise you to look at your career this way: a "career" is a string of several periods, each of which is approximately eight to ten years long. The string will not end up where you think it will today.

During each of those eight to ten year periods, you will learn new competencies, deliver various performance results, expand your professional and personal networks, and endure "career crucible" experiences. Most importantly, you will be introduced to new and interesting ideas that will intrigue you so much that you will shift your interests and your focus. Before you know it, you will be beginning a new eight to ten year period—your *next* career stage.

I do not mean that you should just resign yourself to the whims of Fate. You should manage your career strategically, and with intention. New career stages should not be entered into lightly, without methodical contemplation, or without consulting family and mentors. What I want to impress upon you is the importance of living through each career stage *open to signals and relationships that will lead you into your next career stage.*

BE INTENTIONAL

My career stages have been as a Naval Officer, a marketing and brand management professional, and as a leader in corporate Organizational Development and Learning (OD&L). Each of my transitions was made with specific intent, but my journey is what it has become because I was open-minded and deliberate about what I wanted at each of the forks I encountered along my path.

In addition to growing your functional or professional skills, you should also be deliberate about your *leadership* development through each stage. Leadership development has two purposes: 1) To increase your *capacity to lead*—to get scaled results through larger and larger teams, and 2) To prepare you for more significant and sophisticated risks and responsibilities in higher-level roles.

I believe that all results, good and bad, are a result of leadership—good and bad—demonstrated in the course of delivering those results. I look at all results through The Lens of Leadership, which leads me to believe that functional skill development and leadership development are inseparable. *You do not want leadership to be an "accidental career."*

I wrote in Chapter 4 about the significant role that initiative and resourcefulness play in your success as a follower, and that an employee with those traits will always have job security. As you develop your *leadership* skills, you must realize that one of your most important obligations is to ensure, as former General Electric CEO Jack Welch said, that each man and woman in your charge "can see and feel a connection between what he or she does all day, and winning in the marketplace…that's the ultimate job security." As a leader, you will need to make sure that each follower knows how his or her contribution moves the team toward winning. As a follower engaged in self-development, you must constantly add to your *set of competencies* so that you become indispensable.

In order to become indispensable, you must understand your organization's competency system. If there is no formal competency model in place, I recommend the Lominger model, available from Korn-Ferry as Leadership Architect.[2] Regardless of which model you use, make sure you understand which few competencies your leader needs you to be developing in order for you to be highly successful within your organization. Take charge of your own development, and lead "up" if you need to in order to be sure you are developing the right skills for the path you are on in your current stage.

---

2 www.lominger.com. This is based on Michael Lombardo and Robert Eichinger's research at the Center for Creative Leadership.

LEARN FROM EXPERIENCE

I believe in CCL's "70-20-10" model of personal development, which emerged from thirty years of its "Lessons of Experience" research. Think back on how you have increased your professional skills and knowledge since you left formal schooling. How did you learn the lessons that are burned into your mind? How did you learn the fastest? How did you learn when the stakes were highest?

The 70-20-10 model describes that only about 10 percent of what we learn as adults comes through formal programs, books, or seminars. You may have sat through a class facilitated by your training department. Maybe you attended a webinar or completed some e-learning. Perhaps you attended a breakout seminar at a trade conference. All of that is important, but it is only a very small portion of how adults really learn.

About 20 percent of our learning—twice as much as we learn through formal programs—comes from our network of colleagues, mentors, and other developmental relationships. The best analyst may teach you a feature or process within Excel that increases your efficiency or quality of work. Your regional sales manager may give you some negotiation tips and political insights about your toughest client. In today's connected world, there is strong evidence that this "social" learning, enabled by social media, is actually becoming much more than just 20 percent of our learning.

70-20-10's most important lesson is that, by far, the greatest amount of our adult learning comes from *experiences*. The quickest, most indelible, high-stakes learning comes when we are thrown into a situation that is a little over our heads—we are a little under-qualified, perhaps under-resourced, or in a different situation or category—and we have to figure it out, and do so quickly. We make some mistakes, we feel inadequate, and we wonder how our careers will survive. But they do. And *we* do! In fact, you probably surprised yourself with the results you delivered.

Specific types of experiences are necessary for emerging leaders who want to develop into the future's senior leaders. They need roles that grow both the scale and scope of their responsibilities (not necessarily through the same experience). They need to start up something new: create a new division, or lead the company into a new category. They need to take something that is established and mature, and shake it up and accelerate growth. They need to "fix" something that is "broken": turn around a troubled team or product line or customer relationship and deliver a higher level of competitive performance. They need to grow cross-functionally, with accountability for deliverables that are outside their normal function. If their business is global, they will need to grow internationally.

As you develop yourself, and if you are charged with developing others, always construct your development plan using the 70-20-10 model. If you want to get the most out of any formal learning or training event, think about the 20s and 70s you will also need to participate in to convert the new knowledge into improved performance and better results. Write them out before you even take the class and discuss them with your leader. You will notice that at the end of each chapter of this book, the *"Now What?"* section subtly guides you to build a 70-20-10 plan. The most effective learning and development happens through intentional construction of an experience-based learning plan.

SETTING YOUR LEARNING UP FOR SUCCESS

I met Bob Mosher, Microsoft's former Director of Learning Strategy, at an American Society for Training and Development (ASTD) Benchmarking Forum event in 2010. The work he has done (with Con Gottfredson) opened my eyes to another crucial element for the intentional development of myself and others. Once you are on your way to learning something new, five critical "moments of learning need" exist along the path to the mastery of a new skill. Each moment requires different tools and resources to ensure successful completion of the job.

Moment 1 is "When learning something for the first time." It is the obvious moment that most training programs instinctively deliver against quite well. 70s and 20s help reinforce and cement this initial learning.

Moment 2 is "When wanting to learn more." The learner wants to study more deeply or broadly than is covered by Moment 1. Search engines are a frequent source of learning for Moment 2; mentors or experts are another.

The next three moments are the ones that many leaders and training designers forget about and for which they often neglect to design appropriate tools that learners need.

Moment 3 is "When trying to remember and/or apply." This is an on-the-job moment when you need the skill or answer right then in order to be successful. As you develop your own plan, or coach others in their development plan, be sure to create tools like job-aids, checklists, or web-enabled apps for quick reference in Moment 3.

Moment 4 is "When things change." We all run into unexpected hurdles when dealing with systems or processes or structures. Make sure all of your "What-if?" resources (including your human "What-if?" resources) are readily available, *before* you need them. Make sure you have the technical manuals, or the troubleshooting guide, or the 24/7 customer service hotline readily available for Moment 4.

Moment 5 is "When something goes wrong." Moment 5 can use some of the same tools as Moment 4, but you also need to include critical support for crisis situations. You may need to provide emergency checklists and procedures, or develop pre-determined reaction scenarios based on various contingencies.

As a follower and as someone responsible for accomplishing various tasks, you should be aware of these principles in order to develop the tools you need to increase your own and your colleagues' performance. As someone who is personally developing a career by expanding his or her functional and leadership skills, you should consider these principles as you develop your learning plan. This consideration will ensure that *you* have the performance support you need through all five moments of your learning need.

BE AGILE!

As you navigate your career stages, it's essential to understand the concept of "learning agility."[3] People with a high degree of learning agility are *better learners*. That does not mean they are necessarily smarter than others, but they are able to "connect the dots" between apparently unrelated information and synthesize it to create important insights.

People with learning agility generally use more methods for learning, and they are inherently curious and analytical about the new material. That curiosity leads them to explorations that require openness to new situations. They are able to take lessons from previous situations and apply them in a relevant way to the new circumstances. High-agility learners are also more comfortable with ambiguity and use critical thinking skills to adapt on-the-fly. Additionally, they tend to be "people agile," capable of listening, able to "read" people quickly, and adept at navigating conflict in a healthy way that delivers results.

American businesses have found a powerful human resource in hiring former Junior Military Officers (JMOs) as entry-level leaders. The military is exceptional at teaching learning agility. A typical early military career rotation places an officer in a role for which he or she has no educational background or work experience. A time gap often occurs between one person leaving the role and the replacement arriving, so there is little "turnover" information and nobody to show you the ropes. This situation often happens along with a

---

3 The concept of learning agility was developed by Lombardo and Eichinger while they were at CCL.

geographical move, forcing the buying and selling of homes and moving household goods and cars to an unfamiliar city. Through all of this, the officer must learn the job quickly, deliver results at least as good as the previous position holder, and usually within two or three years, leave the role in better condition than he or she found it as the person moves on to yet another, similarly-chaotic transition to another posting. After two or three of these transitions, the military has created a highly agile, flexible person conditioned to respond quickly and effectively. I remember a long-time General Mills employee whom I worked with in marketing making conversation with a newly-hired JMO about the person's onboarding process and learning curve as he adapted to corporate America. The long-time General Mills employee said, "The move, the new job, all the new people, the new expectations—isn't it all so overwhelming?" The JMO replied, "The Bosnian air defense network was overwhelming. This is just getting settled in to a new adventure." That is the spirit of learning agility!

Learning agility is a better predictor of long-term success than intelligence because intelligence is not predictive of being able to acquire *new* behaviors and information. The good news is that learning agility can be learned and improved. As you plan your development, work hard to make yourself a highly-agile learner. One thing you can do is what Korn-Ferry calls "GAG," or "Go Against your Grain." Make conscious choices to do things in different ways, and do things you have never done before at work and in your community. Begin to study different businesses and seek new sources of information. If you read *The Wall Street Journal*, consider switching to *The Economist* or the *Financial Times of London*. Ask to switch to a role that is outside of your direct expertise. Take on a project to solve a long-standing, hard-to-fix problem, and drive it through to completion. Read a book written by a deep thinker with whom you are unfamiliar and connect the book's lessons to your current work. Take a class that is seemingly unrelated to your work. Remember,

Steve Jobs credited a calligraphy class that he took on a whim in college with giving him the insights that led to the creation of various fonts for Mac computers. Learning-agile people seek out different ideas and experiences so they can learn something new and then connect that new learning to problems that exist in their "regular" world. You can train yourself to be more agile by doing different things.

CHEESE MOVES—BE READY!

Spencer Johnson's 1998 best-selling business fable *Who Moved My Cheese?* teaches several lessons about preparing for and adapting to change. The story's metaphor is of mice living in the maze of life, and their "cheese" is how life is experienced. The cheese in the maze moves at unpredictable times and to places that seem without pattern. The book's several lessons reinforce the axiom that "the only thing that is permanent is change." Your career cheese will be moved. How you prepare for and adapt to that change is up to you. When your cheese moves, your attitude about how you will react will make all of the difference in your success finding your way forward through "the maze."

My life has taken several unexpected turns. Fate, or destiny or luck—whatever you believe in—will move your cheese. A mundane twist of fate kept me from attending Naval Aviation's infamous Tailhook conference in 1991. I know several naval careers that were affected regardless of whether the officer had gotten anywhere near the debauchery for which that event is notorious. I was assigned to the Foodservice division at General Mills for my first marketing job instead of one of the highly-preferred (at the time) retail channel brands. And one of my first challenges as the new bratwurst brand manager at Johnsonville Sausage was to convince the sales team—and our customers—to accept not one, but *two* price increases during my first year because of historically-high pork prices.

Every time my cheese got moved, I adapted quickly and my attitude became focused on what I needed to do to be recognized as "the best" in that unexpected situation. I built friendships and a career path through those experiences that I would not trade for the world.

FIND YOUR VOICE

Why do you do what you do today for your job? Why do you work as much or as little as you work? Why are you working toward a particular goal down your specific career path? Are these conscious choices based on preference and aptitude? Are these choices driven by your dreams? Or perhaps by someone else's dreams *for* you? Did you enter your field and find it not to be what you expected?

The late Dr. Stephen Covey describes what he called the concept of "voice" in *The 8th Habit*. Your "voice" is your "unique contribution to the world." There are four elements: What are you truly great at? What do you love to do? Where do you see a need that is going unfilled? And what does your conscience call on you to do to improve the world? Imagine a Venn diagram made of four circles answering the four questions above. *Where those four circles overlap is where you can make your unique contribution to the world.*

Your work should be aligned with your voice. Can you be successful working outside of your voice? Sure. Millions of people do it every single day. But the most successful, satisfied people are engaged in work that fulfills something inside of them that is bigger than that. When we are fulfilled at work, it feels like something we would do even if we were not paid. People who can make a living doing what they love are the luckiest people in the world. And I am one of those people, thanks to Don McAdams.

Don was the Director of Organizational Development and Learning (OD&L) at Johnsonville Sausage when I was the brand manager on Johnsonville Brats. It was a lot of fun: I was making television commercials, hosting corporate clients and partners at NASCAR races, Super Bowl, and Professional Bull Riders events, and working with sports stars and famous chefs as brand advocates. I even got to help host a Hollywood movie premiere party with Jessica Simpson! But Don asked me, "Have you ever thought about helping us build more leaders at Johnsonville? We're just having lunch here—just a conversation—but I want to know if you would ever consider joining our team and helping us build a deeper leadership talent bench? You love leadership. You and I talk about it all the time—more than we do about the sausage business."

What an invitation. It changed my life. It introduced me to the world of corporate training and human performance consulting. Don saw something in me that I was not seeing because I was distracted by the glitzy parts of marketing. I say that I "quit my marketing job at Johnsonville, and started my *career* there" the day I joined the OD&L team. I walked away from a powerful role and began a journey that has given me so much more influence. It afforded me the opportunity to fully develop my God-given talents. It offered me my voice on a silver platter.

It may sound like a cliché, but Robert Frost's poem, "The Road Less Taken" is a powerful admonition to find your voice, and then convert it into a way to make a living.

> *I shall be telling this with a sigh*
> *Somewhere ages and ages hence:*
> *Two roads diverged in a wood, and I—*
> *I took the one less traveled by,*
> *And that has made all the difference.*

In order to achieve personal greatness—in order to bring the skills, the passion, and discretionary effort to bear that is necessary to become truly "great"—you must align your work with your voice.

BE A LIFE-LONG LEARNER

Learning and professional development have incredibly strong support at Johnsonville Sausage for a couple of reasons. The practical one is because investments in the right learning and development programs deliver better business results. The other one is because the owner feels a moral obligation to give Johnsonville members (employees) the opportunity to expand their skill sets in case a day comes when they no longer work at Johnsonville. Ralph Stayer says very publically, "I can't promise you that Johnsonville will be here tomorrow. Who knows what might happen? But I *will* promise you that I will invest in programs that help you increase your skills so that you can provide for your family if you no longer worked for Johnsonville. No one can take those skills away from you, ever. Most companies use people to build their business. We are going to use our business to build people." Ralph has created an environment where the smart, adaptable mice will be preparing for their cheese to move. They will be agile and eager to succeed, despite how the maze may change.

No matter where you are in your career journey, realize that a "career" is a string of eight to ten year periods, during which you will learn and experience things you never expected. Don McAdams helped me see that in every role, inside and outside of the military, I had always risen to a level of mastery that taught others the skills, and that I always seemed to make time to help others. I discovered a new, life-changing eight to ten year block because I was open to signals and relationships that led me to something different.

Seeing your career through The Lens of Leadership means taking responsibility for your career journey. You are the best captain of your own career, and you will be the best, and happiest, when you find ways to align what you love and what you can be truly great at with what you feel called to do in order to fill a need that is going unfilled in this troubled world.

Summary & Exercise: Chapter 13—Becoming Intentionally Agile: A Career is Not a Straight Line

WHAT?—SO WHAT?—NOW WHAT?

What? A career is a long string of eight to ten year periods. Do not let leadership become an "accidental career." Be intentional and strategic about your career moves. Develop the skills of learning agility so you will be prepared for the unexpected career changes outside your control.

So What? You must remain open to signals and relationships that will influence you and lead you into the next stage of your career. Be on the lookout for ways to align your work with your skills, passions, and with what you feel "called" to do. Using the tools available through your company's HR team and in this "Additional Resources" list will help you be more intentional and strategic about your career development, and more happy and successful in the long run.

Now What?

I will study _____

_____ to learn more about managing my career with strategic intent.

I will reach out to _____

_____ in order to seek more insight, guidance, and advice.

I will ask _____ to hold me accountable for _____

_____.

And I will _____

_____

_____

_____ in order to create an experience with elements/competencies that I have not yet adequately developed by *(date)* _____.

ADDITIONAL RESOURCES FOR YOUR "NOW WHAT?" JOURNEY:

Adler, Mortimer J. and Charles Van Doren. *How to Read a Book.*

Bolles, Richard N. *What Color Is Your Parachute?: A Practical Manual for Job-Hunters and Career-Changers.*

Charan, Ram. *The Leadership Pipeline.*

Christensen, Clayton M. *How Will You Measure Your Life?*

Covey, Stephen R. *The 8th Habit: From Effectiveness to Greatness.*

Erickson, Tamara. *Plugged In: The Generation Y Guide to Thriving at Work.*

Godin, Seth. *Linchpin: Are You Indispensable?*

Goldsmith, Marshall. *What Got You Here Won't Get You There: How Successful People Become Even More Successful.*

Gottfredson, Con and Bob Mosher. *Innovative Performance Support: Strategies and Practices for Learning in the Workflow.*

Johnson, Spencer. *Who Moved My Cheese?*

Korn-Ferry International. *FYI for Learning Agility: Korn-Ferry International's practical guide for increasing learning agility.*

Korn-Ferry International. *FYI For Your Improvement: Korn-Ferry International's competency guide for performance improvement.*

McCall, Morgan W., Michael M. Lombardo, and Ann M. Morrison. *Lessons of Experience: How Successful Executives Develop on the Job.*

Porras, Jerry, Stewart Emery, and Mark Thompson. *Success Built to Last: Creating a Life that Matters.*

Rath, Tom and Barry Conchie. *Strengths-Based Leadership.*

CHAPTER FOURTEEN

NURTURING YOUR NETWORK

Learning from others is a gift from them. I honor that gift by building upon it for myself.
— YoYo Ma

Good conversation is as stimulating as black coffee, and just as hard to sleep after.
— Anne Morrow Lindbergh

No matter where you are in your leadership or career journey, you should be putting intentional, discretionary effort into developing your network. I don't mean collecting business cards at professional mixers, or asking people on the periphery of your network a couple of extra, vague questions about their kids. I mean you should make a habit of being gracious and generous with your time in ways that create in others a genuine desire to reciprocate and gift you with some of *their* discretionary time because they find it mutually beneficial.

Exceptional networkers are not just "people" people; they are what researcher Frank Luntz, The Word Doctor, calls "people-centered." In his 2011 book, *Win: The Key Principles to Take Your Business from*

Ordinary to Extraordinary, Luntz explains that being people-centered means you know what makes people tick: "They are constantly looking for personal meaning and benefit from interactions with others. It's not that they are selfish. It does mean that they are always focused on achieving their goals by learning from others."

REMEMBER 70-20-10

As I wrote in Chapter 13, more than twice as much of your learning and growth will come from other people as from traditional learning tools like classes, seminars, and books. In today's always-on, socially-connected world, I would wager that the percentage is much greater than 20 percent. This informal social learning is also *more effective* at improving your performance. The Corporate Executive Board's 2002 "Emerging Mandates for the L&D Function" research concluded that learning from mentors and coworkers delivers three times the performance improvement of traditional programs (9.6% vs. 3.2%).

You cannot develop successfully into the contributor or leader you want to become if you are not genuinely curious and interested in learning about others. Dale Carnegie teaches us to "Be *interested*, not interesting." Countless other authors and programs demonstrate the wisdom of not just "doing" the behaviors, but "becoming" and "being" of this nature: *be* curious about what you can learn from others, *be* inquisitive about how others have overcome their obstacles, *be* a listener and a learner, and *be* open to learning from everyone and in unexpected places and situations. The most agile learners will take apparently disparate pieces of wisdom, reflect upon them, and piece them together in a way that creates something relevant to *their own* needs and challenges.

JOIN A GANG

I am a volunteer pilot and youth mentor in my local Civil Air Patrol (CAP) squadron. CAP is the official auxiliary of the Air Force, and CAP pilots fly about 95 percent of all inland search-and-rescue missions throughout the U.S. CAP also has cadet programs for twelve to twenty year olds. It is a tremendous youth development asset for young people and the communities they live in.

When I am giving a recruiting or informational talk to parents about CAP, I will always say provocatively, "You know, all of your kids are going to join a 'gang.' They will. It's a powerful human drive, especially in the awkward teenage years, to seek out acceptance from people who will give you respect." I let my audience process that for a few seconds, and I follow up with, "CAP is a *good* 'gang' that will help mold your sons and daughters into self-confident future leaders for America. Wouldn't you want them to join *that* kind of gang?" All but the most introverted adults join "gangs" too: The Elks. The Junior League. Rotary International. Which ones are you going to join? I would encourage you to put yourself in the *best* of company.

I stumbled into this philosophy my Plebe (freshman) year at the Naval Academy when I really began to be challenged academically. College chemistry turned out to be way over my head, but James Baca became my lab partner by the luck of classroom geography. James was the opposite of everything I was in chemistry. He was smart, meticulous, and experienced. I, on the other hand, was not very good at chemistry, but I loved to do most of the "grunt work" associated with lab reports and creating presentations, and I didn't mind doing the data crunching. We were a perfect pair with complementary strengths, or at least we were each willing to do what the other didn't like as much. Not only did my lab grades benefit, but James taught me classroom principles I would have otherwise had to spend extra time with the professor to learn. And James had a partner completely willing to do the parts of the lab that took the most time, and time was a valuable commodity to James. Through luck, I discovered a networking philosophy that has been invaluable to me now for twenty-five years: Seek out high-achievers, even those who are a little bit better—and especially a little bit different—than you are. I continued to choose college study and lab partners using this technique. I was successful throughout flight school and during my squadron years because of those I chose to "gang up" with.[1]

I am not encouraging you to be manipulative or insincere. These are authentic, win-win relationships you should be building. Scott Chandler, my constant MBA companion, became and still is my best friend. The fact that we were absolutely complementary in our gifts and preferences was a bonus. And I found Tim Ahrens to be my "other half" when I transitioned from marketing into the world of organizational development and training. Be eager, and be good at the "stuff" your partner is not—or does not want to be—good at. This followership skill is also essential when used to fill in and complement the professional gaps your leader has.

MENTORS: FIND ONE. BE ONE.

Many excellent books about mentoring are available. Find a "superlative" mentor, and approach the relationship in a very respectful way, considering the mutuality of the relationship. What can you offer the mentor? How can you make it worth the time you are asking him or her to invest in you? Be clear in your expectations, mindful of your mentor's schedule, and strategic in the guidance you seek. Get from him or her what you cannot get from peers. One of the most important things to consider as you build your relationship with your mentor is to remain open to the mentor's coaching, even when you are being told something you don't want to hear, or something that conflicts with the way you see the world.

---

1 I also credit it with enabling me to survive the two mandatory semesters of boxing at the Naval Academy.

I was a little too quick to dismiss excellent career management advice a mentor was trying to give me near the end of my flying tour in the Navy. Bing Lengyel saw something in me that I did not see in myself, and he tried to coach me with great advice that I was just not open to hearing. I had already made up my mind to resign my commission and leave the Navy after my next tour when Bing shared with me his insights about why I should consider making the Navy a career. His advice about the value of career trade-offs would have powerfully impacted my life, not just my career, and I very well may have chosen to continue as an officer for another decade if I had listened with more of an open mind. He is still my good friend, and I am quick to use our anecdote to teach mentees about the importance of their mentors' perspective and advice.

Mentors are not always leaders who are higher on the organizational chart or have more authority than you do, however. A mentor is *anyone* who has professional wisdom—be it functional skills, human behavior insights, technical training, or political savvy—to share because it is in your best interest.

One of the strongest mentoring roles in the world is that of senior enlisted military members with their junior officer charges. A young Navy ensign or Army lieutenant technically outranks a senior Non-Commissioned Officer (NCO) like a Chief Petty Officer or a Sergeant First Class, but a young officer would be foolish to do anything but listen intently, accept his NCO's wisdom gratefully, and work diligently to earn his respect. These NCOs are in a powerful role: they serve as mentors up, down, and sideways by virtue of their unique role.

These types of mentor roles are not uniquely military. These chiefs and sergeants exist in every office and factory in the world. They are the influencers—the most respected foremen who happen to have the ears of the "corporate types" and also can still sway the union stewards. They are the experienced territory sales reps who can also drive breakthrough product development. Wherever these potential mentors are in your organization, find them, and build a learning relationship with at least one of them that will benefit both of you.

One of the most valuable pieces of advice I have received lately is to "listen to people who are twenty years older than I am, and twenty years younger, as well." I think this is excellent mentoring guidance.

ASK FOR HELP, AND BE LOYAL TO YOUR NETWORK

In the leadership development program at Johnsonville Sausage, one of the tools we design into case study scenarios and simulation modules is to have unadvertised help available if students or work groups inquire. We do this in hope that students will develop a habit of thinking to ask for help. Human nature being what it is, most groups never drink from the deep well of resources that are available if only they would ask.

If you are early in your career, you may not have had the occasion yet *really* to need to ask for help. I am talking about the, "Man, I *really* screwed up" or "I don't know how my career is going to survive this" kind of insight and support. Being vulnerable is uncomfortable, but there will come a time when you will need to lean on others. Careers are long things. Even if you are a high-flying "Top 10 Percenter" at a Fortune 50 conglomerate, or on the "High-Po" track at an elite Wall Street investment house, you will need help over the course of your career. Cultivate relationships that are authentic enough for you to seek the kind of support that requires personal investment in you by someone else when it is necessary. And when you are sought out and are able to help another, you must do so. People will remember. Your reputation as a follower and as a leader will grow as you earn the roles of confidant, wise counselor, and problem solver.

Loyalty to those in your network is also a "must." Opportunities will arise to demonstrate that loyalty in public and private ways, and they both matter. I recall a social occasion where someone was opining on some public comments made by Clinton-era Secretary of Labor Robert B. Reich. The person was preaching to a sympathetic choir when he made his comment that Reich was "an idiot" for something he had recently written. This conversation happened in front of Ralph Stayer, the owner and CEO of Johnsonville Sausage. Ralph is very politically active and also very conservative. He is a loud, boisterous, brilliant man who likes to be the center of attention. Ralph could have very easily ingratiated himself to the conservative crowd and gotten a laugh out of his audience by agreeing with the comment. But Secretary Reich was well inside Ralph's professional and personal network. Ralph replied with something I'll never forget: "No, that's not right. I know Bob Reich. He's a smart man, and I respect him. He just comes to the wrong conclusions." Ralph was gracious and loyal and did not violate his network relationships—even in private company—to get the easy laugh.

As you navigate the eight to ten year blocks that, collectively, will make up your "career," the most important thing you can collect is relationships. Looking at your development and your leadership potential through The Lens of Leadership, you will see that your "nurtured network" will pay dividends beyond what you can imagine. Your network members will stimulate your own creativity through their intelligence and relative objectivity to your specific challenges. They will serve as a sounding board when you are in need of guidance. They are a source of commiseration and can provide real help if you should need it. And they are a bottomless reserve of praise and pride when you have accomplished something worthy.

Summary & Exercise: Chapter 14—
Nurturing Your Network

WHAT?—SO WHAT?—NOW WHAT?

What? Your personal network will teach you more than twice as much as you will learn from traditional learning.

So What? You must "join a gang" of people who will stretch you beyond what you are today, whose skills and preferences are complementary to your own. Some of these "gangs" should challenge you with divergent thinking as well. You must both find and serve as a mentor. Playing both roles will compound your network's effectiveness. You will be able to seek guidance from colleagues of colleagues. And you must build authentic, long-term relationships (not just collect LinkedIn contacts like points in a video game) that can benefit you through all of the seasons of your career.

Now What?

I will study _____

_____ to learn more about networking and mentoring.

I will reach out to _____

_____ in order to seek more insight, guidance, and advice.

I will ask _____ to hold me accountable for _____

_____.

And I will _____

_____

_____

_____ in order to create an experience with elements/competencies that I have not yet adequately developed by *(date)* _____.

ADDITIONAL RESOURCES FOR YOUR "NOW WHAT?" JOURNEY:

Brafman, Ori and Rod A. Beckstrom. *The Starfish and the Spider: The Unstoppable Power of Leaderless Organizations.*

Carnegie, Dale. *How to Win Friends and Influence People.*

Gladwell, Malcolm. *The Tipping Point: How Little Things Can Make a Big Difference.*

Johnson, W. Brad and Charles Ridley. *The Elements of Mentoring.*

Luntz, Frank I. *Win: The Key Principles to Take Your Business from Ordinary to Extraordinary.*

Mackay, Harvey. *Dig Your Well Before You're Thirsty: The Only Networking Book You'll Ever Need.*

Meier, Dave. *The Accelerated Learning Handbook.*

Sawyer, Keith. *Group Genius: The Creative Power of Collaboration.*

CHAPTER FIFTEEN

NAVIGATING CHANGE LIKE A CHAMPION

Men must be taught
as if you taught them not,
and things unknown
proposed as things forgot.
— Alexander Pope

If you don't like change, you're going to like irrelevance even less.
— General Eric Shinseki, Army Chief of Staff

There is a scene on the "Island of Despair" in Daniel Defoe's *Robinson Crusoe* when Crusoe is at his emotional and physical rock-bottom. He is starving, lonely, and worst of all, despondent. But at the moment when he might just go mad from his hopelessness, he discovers a trove of useful material with which he is certain to improve his circumstances, and likely sustain himself indefinitely. Crusoe should be elated from the very second he makes his discovery, but he is instead quite unsure of what to do, and he is hesitant to gather up what is readily available. Defoe invokes Robert Wild's seventeenth century wisdom to explain: "For sudden joys, like griefs, confound at first."

Even at the moment of delivery from the most awful circumstances, human beings will resist change.

The United States' Declaration of Independence describes it this way: "mankind are more disposed to suffer, while evils are sufferable, than to right themselves by abolishing the forms [of government] to which they are accustomed."

Mark Twain is credited with having written, "The only person who likes change is a wet baby." I believe this is because all change involves grief, and along with the human gift of self-awareness comes the defense mechanism of avoiding unknowns in favor of the known. All change involves unknowns, and so all change will be grieved. Therefore, "Change Management" is a bit of a misnomer: it should be called "*Grief* Management" because the stages mirror a generic grief cycle: a period of denial is followed by anger, then by a period of mental and emotional trade-offs, which is followed by a deeper sadness that, hopefully, is concluded by an acceptance of the loss or change.

The skills associated with managing peoples' *transitions through change* are essential for both followers and leaders to master. The best followers and leaders are capable of managing themselves through change events, of helping small groups of others cope with change and achieve high performance in the new state of things, and they are also capable of *creating* change in order to sustain or improve an enterprise.

A WAY TO UNDERSTAND CHANGE

Several excellent foundational books have been written by big thinkers who deal with managing change events. This chapter's purpose is to give you a few, immediately-applicable ideas and tools that will increase your effectiveness as a follower and a leader through your change events. You should study the resources in the "Now What?" section of this chapter as part of your continuing development. Buy them and put them in your personal library for future reference. You will need them.

I believe an important construct to understand about Change Management comes from William Bridges' work. "Change" is the "stuff" that is different: the new policy that forces you to fly on the company's preferred airline, the time-consuming detour around the construction of a new downtown bridge, or the fact that you now report to Plant Operations for your daily tasking, but Corporate Finance will give you your annual review and decide your pay and bonuses. These things are external, and are usually pretty tangible.

"Transition" is the psychological process of coming to terms with "change." The transition happens internally and is intensely personal. People can experience the same change (like an announcement of

> "Every new beginning comes from some other beginning's end."
>
> — Semisonic, "Closing Time"

the airline policy change), but their transition through that change will likely be very different. For this reason, Bridges inverted his process. Instead of calling the start of the process a new "beginning," the Bridges model starts first with the idea that something is ending. Once people acknowledge that, they can move through their internal acceptance process and "end" their transition by controlling how (and how quickly) they adapt to the new situation.

The important thing to remember is that you can *manage* change, but you must *lead* people through their transitions.

PEOPLE ARE COMPLICATED

What do I mean by "complicated"? I mean that people can be irrational and illogical, even when a change event will be a great benefit to them. Humans tend to overestimate the negative impact of change and underestimate the positive impact. And because we are truly psychologically miraculous and fascinating, we will usually blame external forces for the *bad* things that happen "to" us, and give ourselves most of the credit for the good that results from the change. People are complicated. But if you accept that on its face, and resolve to help people succeed anyway, you will be miles ahead of most transition leaders. One of the most vivid lessons I took away from my two terms as a city alderman in my 50,000-person Midwestern hometown was how irrational people could be about their own self-interests.

Like many municipalities late in the first decade of the new century, Sheboygan, Wisconsin was experiencing financial upheaval: the expense of public employee benefit packages had become unsustainably burdensome, and high private unemployment and national economic trouble prevented us from just raising taxes as a short-term Band-Aid the way previous councils had done. People just could not afford to pay any more in taxes, and I believe we would have been run out on a rail had we asked them to.

I spoke out several times over the course of two years, explaining our financial situation in terms that left no doubt that we needed our employee unions to understand and acknowledge that a different economic era was upon us. I reached out to influential citizens from various groups to support the message: We can't raise taxes in our city because several businesses have already left and unemployment is approaching 14 percent. The unions would not budge. They understood human nature better than I did at the time. They continued repeating their talking points about the hardworking nature of firefighters, police officers, and teachers, while I was talking financial figures and pension liability growth rates. I was working hard to let each local family keep several hundred dollars of their own money each year, and what did I get in return? Nothing but the quiet sound of crickets in the council chamber.

But do you know what created pandemonium in our humble city's government? I mean television coverage from Milwaukee and Green Bay stations, and two hundred sign-carrying protesters with custom-made T-shirts within forty-eight hours? Can you think what might have packed the streets outside with people shouting, and created standing-room-only conditions in our chamber? A proposal to limit leash conditions and walking locations for a

> "Starbucks is not a coffee company that serves people. It is a people company that serves coffee, and human behavior is much more challenging to change than any muffin recipe or marketing strategy." — Howard Schultz, founder of Starbucks

particular breed of dog following an attack on a little boy.

People were willing to ignore foreseeable and avoidable financial conditions that would result in their paying hundreds of dollars more each year in taxes, and we got almost no citizen reaction. But even raise the issue of limiting certain behaviors of a niche breed of dog, and the Bolshevik Revolution comes to town with pitchforks and torches! People are complicated.

HOW YOU COMMUNICATE ABOUT CHANGE

I learned never again to underestimate the power of peoples' passions over their pocketbooks, or how resistant they can be to change. When you talk about change, don't believe that verbal persuasion is your "big gun," no matter what facts you have on your side. The great behavioral scientist Albert Bandura concluded that verbal persuasion is least effective in leading transition conversations about change. Instead, you should find creative ways to get those affected to *experience the change for themselves.* Ideally, you would create circumstances in which they actually experience the negative impact of not changing and the positive benefits of embracing the change. If you cannot put them in that situation, then you should try to create what Bandura called "profound vicarious experiences." Tell deeply poignant stories with direct human impact. Use the power of video and audio to paint a picture of a future that is less desirable without the change. Reveal "hidden victims" who will be affected and illustrate the hard-to-see benefactors of the new situation.

CHOOSE YOUR WORDS CAREFULLY

Joe Galli was brought in as CEO of Newell-Rubbermaid specifically to be a change agent. *Forbes* magazine called him the "Sultan of Sizzle" because of the high hopes surrounding his ability to turn the Newell-Rubbermaid juggernaut into a nimble, effective new-products machine. Rather than say, "We've got to stop doing it the way we do today because 'It's always been done that way,'" he used a very aspirational, *positive* phrase to describe the future: "None of us wants to be trapped by foolish consistency when we could be creating a future together where every American home is filled with several Newell-Rubbermaid products that didn't even exist three years before." "Foolish consistency" is a *fantastic* choice of words!

When NASCAR was at the peak of its meteoric growth rate in the mid-2000s and the founding family was turning over control to Brian France, its third generation, Brian recognized that fans would be skeptical of his youth and wary of change in general. He navigated those waters by saying that he wasn't going to change anything in NASCAR; he was just going to "modernize tradition" a little bit. To a tradition-bound business, that was a wise choice of words, communicating that he intended to make his mark, but that he would be true to the beloved history and culture that others had created. It conveyed respect for people and their past, and it was powerful.

Word choices paint a picture. Peter Tressel was a creative director at one of the advertising agencies from my marketing past. He wanted to push my brand toward a messaging change he felt strongly about. Brand managers are stewards of a business that will long outlast them. We want to make choices that increase brand relevance and brand preference, which will drive higher sales. Brand managers are typically loathe to do anything *too far* "out of the box" for fear of damaging the brand's equity.

Peter had some ideas that he really wanted me to remain open to hearing more about, so he introduced the pitch by saying, "Cory, I think we should give the brand some *stretch marks*." I was so thrown off by that unexpectedly funny, mentally-sticky image that I laughed out loud. That put the room in a more open, receptive mood, and it was well-received. Choose your words carefully to increase your likelihood of winning others over to your new ideas.

THE SECRET TO MOTIVATING OTHERS

Here is the secret: *You cannot motivate others.* I know…what a buzz-kill, right?

What you *can* do is discover the forces that will affect people's motivation and also their ability to adapt to the change, and then build behavioral support around several of those forces in order to do what the authors of *Influencer: The Power to Change Anything* call "over-engineering the inevitability of success."

Influencer is a transition leadership process built around its Six Sources of Influence model. Like any change management model, you start by detailing the specific, measurable result that you want the change to deliver. Then you identify the few "vital behaviors" that are necessary for the change to take hold and succeed. You must also determine any "crucial moments" when people will find themselves at a decision point. A "crucial moment" forces you to choose to do, or choose not to do, the vital behavior that the change requires. By clearly identifying crucial moments and the vital behaviors necessary to succeed in those moments, you give people the power to name the challenges they face, and by naming them, you reduce the power they have to defeat needed change.

The elegance of the "Six Sources" tool is in its simple design: a two-by-three box.

	MOTIVATION	**ABILITY**
PERSONAL	**SOURCE 1** PERSONAL MOTIVATION	**SOURCE 2** PERSONAL ABILITY
SOCIAL	**SOURCE 3** SOCIAL MOTIVATION	**SOURCE 4** SOCIAL ABILITY
STRUCTURAL	**SOURCE 5** STRUCTURAL MOTIVATION	**SOURCE 6** STRUCTURAL ABILITY

© VitalSmarts 2005. Used with permission. No further reproduction or copyright allowed.

In the diagnosis phase, you consider actions and forces from that "box" and their impact on someone's *willingness* ("motivation") *and ability* to perform the vital behaviors, and also the impact of the people and non-human forces acting around them.

Source 1—Personal Motivation

How does the change or the new behavior impact the person? Will it bring more personal pleasure or satisfaction to his or her role? Does it help the person to achieve (or help him to help *others* achieve) something that, itself, is high or noble?

The key to successful transition management is "winning" people's individual motivation to help the cause succeed, or at least adapt their own personal behaviors to those required by the change. By connecting the change to a higher or better view of themselves and the organization, more people will be more likely to "get on board."

When you bring change to a person or to a team, it's easy to blame someone's personal motivation when he fails to live up to expectations. As humans, we are almost pre-wired to do exactly that. But there are five other reasons why people may fail to adapt quickly and easily to change. The power of the Six Source model is that it forces us to explore those other obstacles, and then it helps us to remove them—to "clear the path"—so they can succeed with the new behaviors.

Source 2—Personal Ability

Are people *fully trained and properly equipped* to carry out the new behaviors? Once trained, have they demonstrated mastery of the new behaviors *in the workplace*? Are there any mental tasks or physical barriers, which may prevent them from accomplishing the duties or complying with the new policy, that have not been recently reviewed?

If you are going to bring change to a team, you owe people the training, equipment, and other tools (e.g., checklists, reminders, etc.) they will need to be able to carry out the new tasks.

Source 3—Social Motivation

Source 3 is all about the power of "people pressure." We tend to think of peer pressure as a bad thing because of where it can lead us, our friends, and our kids. During transition leadership, however, you should leverage this pressure for its power to motivate changed behaviors. Are people speaking up and influencing others to do the "right" behaviors, and also speaking up and influencing when they see teammates, and even leaders, doing the "wrong" behaviors?

Source 3 is about the team being accountable to itself. Instead of the leader having to be the "bad cop," Source 3 uses the power of the whole team to encourage people to do the "right things" and not do the "wrong things."

Source 4—Social Ability

Do others *help* when they are supposed to? Do they help even when it is not necessarily their job to help? Do they complete their deliverables on time so the next person in the value chain can start his work on time? As a leader, are you giving people the situational coaching they need to be successful? Are you getting the help you need from above you and also from functional peers?

Sources 3 and 4 leverage the human network to ensure people want to and are able to transition through the change successfully.

Source 5—Structural Motivation

In this model, "structural" refers to non-human influences. Source 5 requires that we examine the incentives in place to drive motivation.

First, have you focused primarily on increasing Sources 1 and 3? Those forces are much stronger than the "reward force" of Source 5. Make sure you have connected people's personal motivation to something of value to them and maybe even to their self-identity. Next, make sure you have the power of the social network supporting the right behaviors and discouraging the wrong behaviors. Then, and only then, apply the rewards of Source 5, which should be modest and be connected to the accomplishment of the vital behaviors or making "right" choices at certain crucial moments.

Source 6—Structural Ability

Are the reporting relationships aligned correctly? Are the new processes and the physical layout of the workspace designed for the accomplishment of the "new way?" Do they have the right equipment, and is it functioning properly? Do the right people have the proper level of authority to navigate the bureaucracy successfully and make timely decisions?

As a leader, it's not really fair to force change without getting the obstacles that are in front of individuals out of their way. Whether you are a follower or a leader, your ability to influence the structural components of change will clearly demonstrate your political and organizational savvy.

TYING IT ALL TOGETHER

Research published in the Massachusetts Institute of Technology's Sloan School Management Review by the authors of *Change Anything: The New Science of Personal Success* found that there is a way to increase your likelihood of successful "change management" by *ten times*.

The Change Anything Labs found that change leaders who were most successful did one important thing that most failed leaders did not. After using the Six Sources model to diagnose all of the potential obstacles to success, the most successful "changers" put in place solutions to problems from *at least four of the six sources* of influence acting against the change. Most change leaders focus on only one or two sources: they spend some money on training, and maybe they pay for an off-site team-building event in hopes of raising personal motivation. Or they re-structure the reporting relationships, and sweeten the pot by increasing potential annual bonuses.

Remember how hard people will "grieve" change, even change that benefits them? And also how they will be more emotional and less rational about accepting change? *Change Anything's* research concludes that you will be ten times as likely to be successful in accomplishing the goals of your change effort if you implement solutions from at least four sources of influence. *That* is a powerful lever to pull.

OVER-COMMUNICATE, AND THEN OVER-COMMUNICATE SOME MORE

Do not underestimate peoples' resistance to change. It is not that they are "bad." It is that they are *human*, and humans dislike change and the grieving process that inevitably accompanies it. You must work hard to develop a multi-media, multi-message communications plan that addresses the many reasons people may resist or dislike the change. Do a lot of internal research. Require that external vendor partners who may be helping you implement the change bring you best practices from previous clients. Enlist the engaged help of senior leaders. And be prepared to be the "cheerleader-in-chief" to promote this change, even if you are not a formal leader, but perhaps only the project leader. If you are the face of the project, then you must also be its voice. Knowledge is the key to driving our fear during transitions: *Fill their void.*

Later in the communications plan—after you have explained the reasons for the change, described the benefits of the change, and acknowledged the impact and personal discomforts brought about by the change—you should ask people three specific questions to get them "on board." Once people have had their chance to be heard, and the time for implementation has come, teach your whole implementation team to look individuals in the eye and sincerely ask these three questions:

1. Are you *willing* to do what is required? *This probes on their motivation.*

2. Will you be *able* to do it? *This probes on their ability.*

3. Is there anything *else* that might get in the way of you being successful at this? *This may surface new obstacles you have not yet discovered, and it gives teammates the opportunity to raise last minute concerns safely.*

Train your team to get two "yes's" out of each member of the organization affected by the change, and to teach others how to overcome legitimate answers to question number three. Be open to what you might learn as people answer these questions—they are a great source of additional data that may affect the success of the transition you are leading.

Whether you are in a followership role, a leadership role, or both simultaneously, you *will* get to lead people through "transitions"— the subtle (and sometimes not-so-subtle) grief that is associated with all change. The better you are at assisting people and teams of people with their individual internal transition experiences, the faster and more effective those people and teams will be at delivering on the external, collective benefits of the change. The best followers and leaders know that by looking at change through The Lens of Leadership they will deliver better results and be seen as more accountable and dependable.

Summary & Exercise: Chapter 15—
Navigating Change Like a Champion

WHAT?—SO WHAT?—NOW WHAT?

What? Human beings will grieve change, even change that benefits them. Knowing this will help you navigate your own personal change transitions, and the transitions you lead. How you communicate about and implement change will make all the difference.

So What? You must lead yourself and others through change gently but firmly. You can communicate in ways that reduce fears by understanding their rational and emotional concerns. By understanding the Six Sources of Influence, you will be ten times more likely to succeed in your change transition.

Now What?

I will study _____

_____ to learn more about

managing "change" and transitions.

I will reach out to _____

_____ in order to seek more

insight, guidance, and advice.

I will ask _____ to hold me

accountable for _____

_____.

And I will _____

_____

_____ in order to create an experience with

elements/competencies that I have not yet adequately developed by

(date) _____.

ADDITIONAL RESOURCES FOR YOUR
"NOW WHAT?" JOURNEY:

Bridges, William. *Managing Transitions: Making the Most of Change.*

Grenny, Joseph, David Maxfield, and Andrew Shimberg. "How to 10X Your Influence." *MIT Sloan Management Review.* (Fall 2008)

Hamel, Gary. *What Matters Now: How to Win in a World of Relentless Change, Ferocious Competition, and Unstoppable Innovation.*

Heath, Chip and Dan Heath. *Switch: How to Change Things When Change Is Hard.*

Herzberg, Frederick. "One More Time: How Do You Motivate Employees?" *Harvard Business Review.* (Jan-Feb 1968).

Johnson, Spencer. *Who Moved My Cheese?*

Kotter, John. *Leading Change.*

Kotter, John. *Our Iceberg is Melting.*

Luntz, Frank I. *Win: The Key Principles to Take Your Business from Ordinary to Extraordinary.*

Patterson, Kerry, Joseph Grenny, David Maxfield, Ron McMillan, and Al Switzler. *Change Anything: The New Science of Personal Success.*

Patterson, Kerry, Joseph Grenny, David Maxfield, Ron McMillan, and Al Switzler. *Influencer: The Power to Change Anything.*

Whitten, Neal. *Neal Whitten's No-Nonsense Advice for Successful Projects.*

Whitten, Neal. *Neal Whitten's Let's Talk! More No-Nonsense Advice for Project Success.*

CHAPTER SIXTEEN

THINKING LIKE YOUR BOSS' BOSS

No problem can stand the assault of sustained thinking.
— Voltaire

Think like a man of action, and act like a man of thought.

— Henri L. Bergson

People are usually promoted to a higher level of leadership because the leaders above or around them have observed that they are ready for it. Being ready will mean different things in different organizations, and in different circumstances. Sometimes you don't feel very ready, but others see something that you don't see, or circumstances may dictate that you are the "least worst" option for the role. Whatever the reason, you and your organization are best served the more ready you *actually are*.

There are four generic levels of leadership:

Lead Self → **Lead Others** → **Lead Leaders** → **Lead an Enterprise**

Being ready for the next promotion means that you can demonstrably think, act, and deliver results commensurate with the next higher level of responsibility. One of the ways to *be* more ready is constantly and consistently to put yourself in situations where you are learning by observing people well above your level.

WHAT TO LOOK FOR

The transitions between leadership levels are the critical times. By observing other senior leaders before you are promoted, you can smooth over your own future transitions. But what are you looking for?

Early-career leaders often struggle with the new skills of delegation, quick decision-making, being responsible for the development of others, conflict resolution, and building self-sufficient, motivated teams. Mid-career leaders have to learn to apply systems thinking to their work, find ways to measure and improve results, navigate the choppy waters of organizational politics, and bring innovation to the current state. Even strong senior leaders climb a learning curve to master dealing with the ambiguity, strategic demands, and the need for "seeing the future."

Leaders at all levels have questions like: "How can I successfully lead change without intimidating others?" "How do I balance the time I spend on strategic thinking with what I spend on execution and follow-through?" and "What can I do today to get my teammates to give more of their attention to the biggest problems we face, instead of fighting the daily fires they're confronted with?"

The best way to find answers to these and other leadership questions is to "get in the room."

GET IN THE ROOM

I am absolutely convinced that the clarity I had about my leadership style and my self-confidence as a junior naval officer was forged in dorm rooms at the Naval Academy. We had very few privileges even during my sophomore and junior years, so I and my closest friends spent much of our non-study time—literally hundreds of hours over several years—confronting and solving the world's problems. I was challenged intellectually and morally by the confounding situations we would place each other in. I had to form my beliefs thoroughly because they were subjected to the utmost scrutiny by my peers, who were establishing their own philosophies. For me, Bancroft Hall (the student dorm) was an unremitting leadership laboratory. My classmates and I created self-managing leadership simulators through these conversations that frequently lasted until two or three o'clock in the morning. We created scenarios that were often more complex than what we faced in our leadership classes. And we were like a pack of dogs, quick to attack intellectual, logical, or moral weak points in anyone's argument.

Being "in the room" means putting yourself in the intellectual arena. Recruit your own mastermind group,[1] a cluster of peers whom you respect for their professional maturity and commitment to professional growth. Create your own challenging leadership scenarios. You won't even have to work very hard at first: all organizations have enough of their own bad situations to provide brain fodder for your talks. Here are a couple of cautions:

Don't allow these conversations to become gossip time. You probably lack a LOT of facts in the case of real-life situations. So instead of judging others and believing your own conclusions, start these kinds of conversations with something like, "Okay, let's assume that these are the facts of the situation" and list out your assumptions.

---

1 Napoleon Hill coined the term "mastermind group" in his book *Think and Grow Rich*.

Then steer clear of using real names or titles to prevent these valuable, challenging conversations from becoming rumor generators.

And don't allow passion for your point of view to overwhelm your ability to learn from others. No matter your experience or education level, you have much to learn from others, and you cannot learn while preaching. Be passionate and challenge others' assumptions. Be just as quick to *listen* as others challenge yours.

GET IN THE *RIGHT* ROOM

While learning from peers is important and safe, you can learn much more by being "in the room" with very senior leaders when they are discussing their biggest challenges.

One excellent benefit that I believe officers from the Naval Academy have because of the Academy's proximity to Washington D.C. is that over their four years as midshipmen they have each had hundreds of opportunities to interact professionally, intellectually, and socially with admirals, generals, senators, congressmen, ambassadors, cabinet secretaries, CEOs, and foreign heads of state. The wisest aspiring leaders take advantage of every opportunity to be in the presence of leaders of this caliber and experience so you can observe and measure them, and potentially adapt what you learn to your own style to increase your decision-making and leadership skills in a way that becomes authentically "you."

Volunteer for high-visibility projects, even if you will be doing grunt work. Put yourself in position to be "in the room" so you can learn through osmosis—not the literal meaning, but rather the subtle but powerful absorption of learning through observation and participation. Earn a reputation for being intellectually agile and professionally mature enough to know when to participate in the discussions, and when to disappear, ready to serve the needs of others when required.

The goal is to become competent and highly-regarded enough for your professionalism that when you raise your hand for extra work involving senior perspectives, you earn a shot at being "in the room." Some risk exists in this learning tactic: You may take on something that is truly over your head or speak up at the wrong time and embarrass yourself (and your leader) very visibly. It has been my experience that it is worth the risk for the professionally mature follower. Here are two examples from my own career:

As a junior grade lieutenant, I offered to use my French language and cultural skills to accompany an American one star admiral to anti-submarine warfare negotiations with the French Navy's leadership in Brest, France. He got my cultural advice and benefitted from my ability to eavesdrop. His reputation was also enhanced among the French because he had an additional escort (naval traditions are sometimes about the entourage, and size matters). I got three days of being "in the room" with admirals from several allied nations as they hashed out future resourcing commitments and rules of engagement on highly classified and strategic matters.

As a new associate brand manager at General Mills, I volunteered to join the team that recruited future hires from the University of Michigan's Ross School of Business. The recruiting team was extra work and extra travel, but I got to network with some of the smartest marketers and business minds in the world. I also got to see the presentation styles and messaging of senior General Mills directors and vice presidents, and adapt their styles to my own. It was also a heck of a lot of fun.

Some sailors say that "NAVY" is an acronym: "Never Again Volunteer Yourself." While it's true that raising your hand can sometimes lead to undesirable work, you will gain an invaluable set of lessons from "smart-volunteering." Some of the benefits are:

- Increased social and professional poise
- Earlier development of strategic thinking and problem-solving skills
- High-stakes negotiation skills
- Development of valuable mentoring relationships
- Collecting a much larger professional and learning network
- More influence

THINK LIKE YOUR BOSS' BOSS

Leaders are desperately in need of followers who are ready and competent enough to be promoted to higher levels of leadership. If you can expose yourself to the higher-level thinking, strategic behaviors, and relationship-management of very senior and successful leaders, and adapt the best and reject the worst of what you see and hear, you will stand out. When your opinion is sought, you will give wiser counsel. When you are confronted, you will react with better instincts. When others are not sure what to do, you will be more confident in determining the right path.

If you can think—and then speak and act—like a leader two levels above you, people will see you through their own Lens of Leadership. They will treat you differently. You will be rotated earlier, promoted faster, and be highly sought out as a teammate and colleague.

Summary & Exercise: Chapter 16—
Thinking Like Your Boss' Boss

WHAT?—SO WHAT?—NOW WHAT?

What? The followers who get promoted quickly are those who can demonstrate how ready they already are for the next role. The way to accelerate your development is to be "in the room" with people who can challenge you and teach you advanced, senior leader competencies through valuable experiences.

So What? You must volunteer for opportunities to take on extra work and extra projects for which you have some aptitude or interest. These projects will often include the opportunity to work with and/or for senior leaders. These experiences will lead you to higher levels of thinking, problem-solving, and judgment. They will also increase your network, which is another way of increasing your effectiveness.

Now What?

I will study _____
_____ to learn more about earning my way into high-level situations.

I will reach out to _____
_____ in order to seek more insight, guidance, and advice.

I will ask _____ to hold me accountable for _____
_____.

And I will _____

_____

_____ in order to create an experience with elements/competencies that I have not yet adequately developed by *(date)* _____.

ADDITIONAL RESOURCES FOR YOUR "NOW WHAT?" JOURNEY:

Brown, Tim. *Change by Design: How Design Thinking Transforms Organizations and Inspires Innovation.*

Charan, Ram. *What the CEO Wants You to Know: How Your Company Really Works.*

Collins, Jim. *Good to Great: Why Some Companies Make the Leap... and Others Don't.*

De Bono, Edward. *Six Thinking Hats.*

Drucker, Peter F. *The Effective Executive: The Definitive Guide to Getting the Right Things Done.*

Gladwell, Malcolm. *Blink: The Power of Thinking Without Thinking.*

Hamel, Gary and C.K. Prahalad. "Strategic Intent." *Harvard Business Review.* (July 2005)

Hammer, Michael and James Champy. *Reengineering the Corporation: A Manifesto for Business Revolution.*

Hill, Napoleon. *Think and Grow Rich.*

Johnson, Steven. *Emergence: The Connected Lives of Ants, Brains, Cities, and Software.*

Kim, W. Chan and Renee Mauborgne. *Blue Ocean Strategy: How to Create Uncontested Market Space and Make Competition Irrelevant.*

Meadows, Donella H. *Thinking in Systems: A Primer.*

Paul, Richard. *Critical Thinking: Tools for Taking Charge of Your Learning and Your Life.*

Peters, Tom and Robert H. Waterman. *In Search of Excellence: Lessons from America's Best-Run Companies.*

Pink, Daniel. *To Sell is Human: The Surprising Truth About Moving Others.*

Surowiecki, James. *The Wisdom of Crowds.*

Thaler, Richard H. and Cass R. Sunstein. *Nudge: Improving Decisions About Health, Wealth, and Happiness.*

Tzu, Sun. *The Art of War.*

PART FOUR

DEVELOPING OTHERS

A man has made at least a start on discovering the meaning of human life when he plants shade trees under which he knows full well he will never sit.
— Dr. Elton Trueblood, Harvard University

CHAPTER SEVENTEEN

LEADING IS TEACHING

Leading and teaching are inextricably intertwined—
where you find one, you find the other.
– Noel Tichy

The best teacher is the one who suggests rather than dogmatizes, and
inspires his listener with the wish to teach himself.
– Edward Bulwer-Lytton

Learning is not something that happens at your corporate university or in the training center of your manufacturing plant. In Chapter 13, I explained the 70-20-10 model of adult learning. Don't fall into the trap of thinking that training is the job of the organizational development team, the training team, or your organization's learning function.

In the history of learning and teaching work skills, the idea that someone besides a direct supervisor would teach a follower new skills and competencies—and do it using something other than the work environment as the classroom—is a fairly new idea. Even workers as recently as the post-World War II business boom in America learned most of their work skills on the job from the people for whom they worked. How has training become so far removed from most current leaders' job expectations? How did leaders come to abdicate their roles as primary sources for the learning their team needs to succeed?

Businesses were growing so quickly—leaping ahead in scale and scope—that the era's thought leaders, who had helped create the victorious U.S. manufacturing war machine, found the business environment ripe to continue spreading their ideas on organizational development (OD) and training. By consolidating the training of new employees, the nascent OD function was able to bring professionalism to the design and development of the content, and consistency to the learning environment and the execution of the training. Scaling up that consistency increased the speed of learning and earned significant cost efficiencies, too. Without the rise of the learning function, the "American Century" would not have been possible, or at least not as likely. But over time, something was lost as well.

Over the past three generations, many followers have gone somewhere outside of their everyday work environment each time they need to advance their skills. The perception among many leaders is that training is something that happens somewhere else, be it a corporate university, a local technical college, or at a conference seminar. Today, many followers can even do some of their training on an iPad at home or in their favorite coffeehouse. The net result is that leaders are in the habit of being somewhat disconnected from their vital role as teachers and trainers.

At least with functional job skills—how to run a piece of manufacturing equipment, use a software tool, or even perform a new medical technique—the new skill can be applied and practiced the very next day or even the same day back on the job. Leadership, teamwork, and communication skills are more abstract and perishable, however. These skills require several applications to "fine tune" because different people will react differently to the same application.

Dr. Robert Brinkerhoff of Western Michigan University found that only 10-15 percent of learners in leadership, communications, and similar soft-skill programs actually converted the learning content into improved business results on the job. That is not only terrible, it is very nearly OD industry malpractice!

Brinkerhoff developed the Impact Map tool at the beginning of this book. It connects the learning content of any program to the expected change in on-the-job behaviors. It also connects those new behaviors to the improved job results that should be achieved, and connects those results to the company-wide metrics that will be positively affected if the learner successfully applies the learning on the job.

The Impact Map, however, is a tool that absolutely requires the involvement of the learner's leader. The leader has an active role to play before and after the training if the learner is to be successful. In fact, in separate research, Mary Broad and John Newstrom concluded that what the *leader* does *before and after the training class* is more important than what either the learner *or the trainer* do during or after the class.

Brinkerhoff found that if leaders will explain why the learner is going to the training, what job skills will be learned, how those new skills will be applied, and how they will improve the business, and then follow up on those expectations back in the workplace, 80-90 percent of those well-prepared learners will convert their new learning into improved business results. That is clear and convincing evidence that should motivate all leaders to reengage in their essential role as teachers.

THE LEADER AS TRANSDUCER

As much as it pains me to do so, I have to give credit to the Behavioral Sciences and Leadership division at my alma mater's arch rival, West Point, for one of my favorite metaphors: the leader as transducer. A transducer is a device that converts one form of energy into another. A microphone converts air pressure from a person's voice into electronic energy that is transmitted to loudspeakers, which convert that electronic signal to amplified air pressure that can be heard by large groups of human ears, which are, themselves, transducers.

One of the most important jobs a leader can do in her role as a teacher is to convert the energy gained in the classroom environment into the appropriate form for use on-the-job. When the learner returns from the class, the leader needs to help him them convert the theory and ideal scenarios from the class into the applications he can expect to confront every day in his workspace. Not only do leaders need to reinforce how the skills should be used on the job, but they also need to coach the learners on any obstacles that may not have been covered in the sterile learning environment of the classroom. What are the "people potholes" to avoid? Are there other teams that might be affected by the learner using the new skills? If they are new to your team, how does your team do it differently than the learner's previous team?

This transducer role is important to the learner's cultural adaptation of the new leadership, teamwork, or communication skills application. But be careful not to over-direct and kill the learner's enthusiasm for bringing new ideas to the team. When that happens, the leader is not being a transducer. She is being a blocker by resisting change and missing an opportunity for herself and the learners to stretch and grow themselves.

WHO MUST BECOME A LEADER/TEACHER?

Timothy Butler and James Waldroop describe "job sculpting" as a process that results in the highest levels of employee satisfaction, engagement, and discretionary effort. In order for a job to be properly sculpted for an individual employee, it must allow the employee to unleash what Butler and Waldroop call a Deeply-Embedded Life Interest (DELI). DELIs are "long-held, emotionally driven passions, intricately entwined with personality and thus born of an indeterminate mix of nature and nurture. Deeply-embedded life interests do not determine what people are good at—they drive what kinds of activities make them happy. At work, that happiness often translates into commitment. It keeps people engaged, and it keeps them from quitting."[1]

I didn't discover Butler and Waldroop's ideas on DELIs until I was already in my current role as a learning professional, but the discovery hit me like a bolt of lightning! I had often struggled to articulate why my journey had brought me to lead a team of training professionals and internal OD consultants. To people who know my background, there is something to them that seems better—I guess maybe more noble, or exciting, certainly more influential—in my history as a Naval Flight Officer and as a marketer. I had struggled to explain why I had left "all that" to be what is basically a corporate teacher. Butler and Waldroop's DELIs are the reason.

Throughout my career, and as far back as high school, I found myself rising to teaching roles in anything in which I was involved. Modeling appropriate behaviors and teaching others the right skills was something I did naturally—I couldn't *not* do it. I was chosen to be a Positive Peer Influence counselor in high school[2]. I earned divemaster certification and taught scuba diving to my fellow

---

1 Butler, Timothy and James Waldroop. "Job Sculpting: The Art of Retaining Your Best People." *Harvard Business Review.* (September-October, 1999).

2 I mention something this far back only to point out that DELIs are so deeply ingrained that the data points develop *early*.

Midshipmen at the Naval Academy, and I led several other teaching and evaluation programs with my peers there. In my role as an aviator in the Fleet, I became a navigator instructor and evaluator. As a Tactical Coordinator, I also became an instructor and evaluator. I was selected to return to the Naval Academy to teach leadership to the next generation of leaders. At General Mills, I became an informal mentor to newly-hired former military officers during their transition as civilians and "showed them the ropes" of our company. I taught what I knew about marketing to several young new hires at Newell-Rubbermaid. At Johnsonville Sausage, I found myself drawn to the Director of Organizational Development—even while I was at the peak of my marketing career—for stimulating conversation about leadership and developing that competency throughout Johnsonville. I ran for election as a city councilman (while I was still a marketer) because I felt passionately obligated to use the role as a teaching platform for educating constituents about the inner-workings of government and financial matters. And I left my marketing job at Johnsonville to finally start the *career* I had been working on…well…my whole career! I became a leader who builds future leaders. That was my Deeply-Embedded Life Interest. I had found my "voice."[3]

I describe my path to realization to explain that the best leaders already recognize their obligations to be teachers and role models to others. Not every leader with a DELI around teaching others will leave his or her function to become an OD or learning professional. And that's the point: all organizations need natural teachers in place as leaders of businesses and other enterprises.

WHAT TO TEACH? MANAGEMENT *AND* LEADERSHIP

Hundreds, if not thousands, of books have been written that split hairs between what is "leadership" and what is "management." This

---

3 Explained in Chapter 13.

is a leadership *handbook*, so I am going to give you what I think is a practical view on both that you can immediately adapt to your toolbox.

I believe that leadership and management are different—one more art, and the other more science. I believe they are *complementary* skills and both are essential to master, model, and to teach.

I believe "management" is the science side of things. Management skills keep the trains running on time. They involve critical thinking, problem-solving, and expectations management. I think helping your followers work within "the system" is also a key management skill. Do you know how to get your followers promoted? Can you teach them your organization's system for getting *their people* promoted? Do you understand the complicated or vague H.R. policies that are keeping them from moving forward? Do you have the right relationships to navigate the human system within your organization?

Leadership, on the other hand, is more art, although I really dislike the term soft skills. When done right, there is nothing "soft" about leadership. Leadership is getting more done through a team of people than they could get done as individuals, and it requires a deft touch because humans are messy, fallible, and sensitive creatures. Whereas "management" is knowledge and application of policies and procedures, "leadership" requires the good judgment to know that life is a case-by-case basis. It also demands the courage to put your reputation on the line when it is time to break a rule or policy and then be held accountable for that decision.

You have to be skilled enough to teach both management and leadership skills. Every interaction with a leader or follower is a chance for you to learn and also to teach. That is a duality my friend Dave Meier of the Center for Accelerated Learning writes about. Dave tells anyone who will listen that future organizational structures will be like the geodesic globe, a structure of strong interconnections. These interconnections drive the new learning paradigm.

Dave says, "Learning is no longer preparation for the job. Learning *is* the job. Therefore, in a networked, geodesic organization everyone is a teacher and a learner simultaneously and continually."

Just as you are simultaneously a leader and a follower, you are also simultaneously a learner and a teacher. As a leader, your impact as a teacher cannot be overstated. In a world where learning *is* the job, the leader must be the primary teacher. As you grow in your own influence, encourage others who are skilled enough to be both leaders and teachers.

HOW CAN YOU BE A TEACHER?

Being a leader/teacher does not have to mean that you stand up in front of a classroom of learners, lead an online webinar, or even be filmed for a teaching video. There are many ways to be a "teacher."

You could collaborate with learning designers to help them identify the learning needs in your organization. As a leader, you are in a prime position to see where people in your organization are struggling with knowledge or experience. Take these ideas to the learning team and make them aware. Offer to explore this need more deeply, and bring what you find back to them.

You can serve as a Subject Matter Expert (SME) on a team that is designing a learning tool on a subject in which you are experienced and/or gifted. Let the instructional designers pick your brain. You can just be "the talent." Another way to contribute as an SME is to blog about the topic on websites to which instructors can refer their students. This process allows you to teach many learners on both the "gory details" of the content, and also the practical applications they should expect to see, along with the business impact.

If you like being in front of a group but don't have the time to lead whole face-to-face learning events, offer to serve as an adjunct and teach a portion of the class. You could also offer to conduct the introduction and the closing of the day, tying the content to real-world application, and communicating your expectations as a leader about how your students should apply the day's learning to improve results.

You can offer to serve as a pre- and post-learning mentor for a student. By connecting with students before and after the class, you can help them understand real life applications of the lessons, and give them a different perspective by explaining to them how it applies outside of their regular work team. Rich mentoring relationships are formed this way and benefit both parties.

You can participate in the beta versions of the content that interests you. You can add a lot of impact by weighing in on the flow and coverage of the topic and by asking difficult questions of the course developers and facilitators.

Finally, you can also offer to coach other emerging leader/teachers. For the leaders-as-teachers philosophy to become really embedded into an organization, a deep bench of talent and passion is required. You can model the behaviors and encourage the spirit of future leader-teachers.

LEAD LIKE SOCRATES

Another technique the best leaders use in their roles as teachers is the artfully-designed question. The best questions are the ones that cannot be answered on the spot. They require some searching, and even perhaps the weighing of alternatives before the person will want to commit to an answer. It is too easy to spoon-feed answers to the people you lead. It is a lot more rewarding to watch them discover the answer when they return to you with knowledge that they did not have the last time.

Vary your open-ended questions by covering micro-topics (like specific techniques or details) and also macro-topics (like the impact of alternative strategic approaches or how another industry might solve the same problem). Engage your teammates in questioning dialogues. Stretch their logic, critical thinking, and problem-solving skills. Teach them to learn from others by asking great questions themselves.

A powerful application of Socratic question-asking is when salespeople ask highly strategic questions of their buyers. What better way to learn of buyers' needs than to ask them? Teach your salespeople to resist the urge to be in "telling and selling" mode, but instead start their initial conversations by focusing on what the buyer or the buyer's organization *needs*. Teach them to go even deeper by asking "Why?" questions around those needs. Teach them to check in with the buyer with questions like:

- "Am I asking the right questions?"
- "What do you need me to *learn* the most out of this conversation?"
- "Are we having the conversation you need us to have to address the things that are keeping you up late at night about your business?"

If they start the sales cycle in the "learning" mode, then when they shift into "selling" mode (probably at the next meeting), they will be talking the buyer's language and addressing his needs instead of (rather selfishly) trying to satisfy mostly their own needs.

BE A LEARNING *AND* A TEACHING ORGANIZATION

Many organizations claim to be learning-friendly environments. In order for that to be true, they must also create explicit expectations around nurturing a *teaching* culture. Teaching is about leaders making *the investment of their time teaching* as much a priority in their lives as they want learners to make a priority of learning and then applying the new skills. A teaching organization lives with a mindset that such an investment is the obligation of those who are in positions of formal or idea leadership.

Leadership development and skill development must happen within the context of the daily work. Great leaders are always looking for "teachable moments" in order to make sure everyone goes home every single day having learned *something* that increases the person's ability to contribute to his or her work team, community, or family. This is the essence of coaching and leading as a teacher. Developing others through The Lens of Leadership acknowledges that the most powerful influence on a follower's learning is his or her leader. If you aren't "using your business to build your people," you are failing as a leader.

Summary & Exercise: Chapter 17—Leading is *Teaching*

WHAT?—SO WHAT?—NOW WHAT?

What? In today's world, the workplace is the most important classroom, and the leader is the most important teacher. The expectations a leader sets before training and the behaviors the leader requires and monitors after the training are much more powerful than anything a trainer can do.

So What? You must take full responsibility for the training and career development of those you lead. Be a transducer who helps them convert classroom learning into on-the-job skills and improved results. Wherever your skills and passions lie, find a way to contribute to the training and learning process.

Now What?

I will study _____

_____ to learn more about my obligation as a leader to also be a teacher.

I will reach out to _____

_____ in order to seek more insight, guidance, and advice.

I will ask _____ to hold me accountable for _____.

And I will _____

_____

_____ in order to create an experience with elements/competencies that I have not yet adequately developed by *(date)* _____.

ADDITIONAL RESOURCES FOR YOUR "NOW WHAT?" JOURNEY:

Betof, Edward. *Leaders as Teachers.*

Brinkerhoff, Robert. *The Success Case Method.*

Broad, Mary and John Newstrom. *Transfer Of Training: Action-Packed Strategies to Ensure High Payoff from Training Investment.*

Butler, Timothy and James Waldroop. "Job Sculpting: The Art of Retaining Your Best People." *Harvard Business Review.* (September-October 1999)

Dyall, Deni. *Rich Questions in Coaching.*

Gray, Dave, Sunni Brown, and James Macanufo. *Gamestorming: A Playbook for Innovators, Rulebreakers, and Changemakers.*

Medina, John. *Brain Rules: 12 Principles for Surviving and Thriving at Work, Home, and School.*

Meier, Dave. *The Accelerated Learning Handbook.*

Pink, Daniel H. *A Whole New Mind: Why Right-Brainers Will Rule the Future.*

Senge, Peter M. *The Fifth Discipline: The Art & Practice of The Learning Organization.*

"Socratic method" and "Socratic question asking" (Google it to better understand the power of asking great questions in order to teach.)

Sugar, Steve. *Games That Teach: Experiential Activities for Reinforcing Training.*

Thiagarajan, Sivasailam. *Design Your Own Games and Activities: Thiagi's Templates for Performance Improvement.*

Tichy, Noel M. *The Cycle of Leadership: How Great Leaders Teach Their Companies to Win.*

Tichy, Noel and Eli Cohen. *The Teaching Organization.*

CHAPTER EIGHTEEN

BUILDING THE FUTURE:
THE ULTIMATE
DEVELOPMENT TOOLBOX

The ability to consistently learn faster than your competition may be the only sustainable competitive advantage.
– Ari De Geus, in Peter Senge's *The Fifth Discipline*

Most companies use people to build their business.
We use the business to build our people.
– Ralph C. Stayer, CEO of Johnsonville Sausage

Beyond the obligation to deliver results, I believe the skill development and career management of others is the second biggest responsibility we have as leaders of teams and organizations. The ability to develop a talent bench is one of the biggest differentiators between *good* leaders and *great* ones. The best leaders see development as their solemn obligation and an opportunity to serve the people they lead. For early leaders, it can seem overwhelming not only to have to develop themselves, but also to be responsible for the career-shaping of the people they lead. It should be a shared responsibility: the best followers are very proactive and want to own their own careers.

In his timeless piece about motivation in the workplace, "One more time: How do you motivate employees?" Frederick Herzberg described that the things that make it *tolerable to stay* in a job are not the same as the things that make us *not want to leave* the job. Let me say that another way: Herzberg teaches us that even if leaders could fix all of the things about our job that may dissatisfy us on a daily basis (like various policies, our supervisor, working conditions, etc.), that would not automatically lead to higher satisfaction and engagement. To achieve real job satisfaction, followers need recognition for achievement, meaningful work, real responsibility, and the opportunity for growth or advancement.

Herzberg's article was published in the *Harvard Business Review* in early 1968. Fast-forward to today, and we have a more succinct model in Daniel Pink's *Drive: the Surprising Truth About What Motivates Us*. Pink describes that employees in today's Conceptual Age need "Autonomy, Mastery, and Purpose" to unleash their full potential. It is incredibly aligned with Herzberg's work.

Pink describes autonomy as "acting with choice" over *what* work will be done, *when* the work will get done, *whom* we do the work with, and *how* we do it. Is this anarchy? No—it is the state to which the modern workplace is evolving for work that is not commoditized and formulaic.

"Mastery" is a mindset that concludes all work is infinitely improvable. The best followers (i.e., the followers who are going to end up leading the future) will want the opportunity to master the competencies required for success. These intrinsically motivated people should be thrown into the deep end of the pool and given several opportunities to fine tune their functional and leadership skills in order to find satisfaction in excellence.

"Purpose" is context that surrounds the other two. It is also the one leaders ought to find a great deal of satisfaction in advertising. Great leaders create a meaningful vision and spend a lot of their time "selling" that vision and connecting it to a noble cause. When followers understand how their work connects to business results that have a purpose worthy of their toil, they will become more likely to give more of their discretionary effort. It is up to leaders to discover that purpose—often collaboratively and iteratively—and then make sure every teammate knows why that purpose is worthy.

THE ULTIMATE DEVELOPMENT TOOLBOX

After years of using different development tools from the military, academia, not-for-profit, government, and business, I finally created what I believe is the best development *process* by stringing together the best individual tools available. They are mutually supportive and were created by the best minds in the field of skill-building to deliver better business results. Used together, they dramatically increase the likelihood of success for those wanting to advance their skills and their careers.

As leaders, we can help even the most committed, skilled, and career-minded teammates by helping them *Find Their "Voice," Get the Skills They Need, Connect Those Skills to Business Results, "Use the Business to Build People,"* and *Surround Them With Six Sources of Support.*

These tools have been described individually in earlier chapters. This chapter's purpose is to explain how they work *together* to help leaders cultivate a deep talent bench, retain the best, most engaged teammates, and earn a reputation as leaders who build future leaders.

FINDING THEIR "VOICE"

In Chapter 13, I explained Dr. Stephen Covey's concept of "voice": your *unique contribution* to the world. You fulfill your voice when you live at the intersection of what you can be truly great at, what you love to do, where you see a need, and what you feel compelled by your conscience to *do* to improve the world.

An experienced leader ought to be able to lead voice conversations with each of his followers. Early leaders or leaders who are still developing their own voices should partner with organizational and personal development professionals to understand what assessments might help. The goal is to help each teammate develop his or her answers to Covey's four questions. The net result is that each of your followers finds his authentic, crystal clear "voice." If that journey leads any of your followers away from your team, you will be forever revered by them for having been an unselfish servant who helped them find their true gifts and place.

GET THE SKILLS THEY NEED

The 2009 Corporate Leadership Council's engagement study found that when high-potential employees understand the link between their work and the organization's strategy, they put in 40 percent more effort. No tool connects skill-learning to daily work, and that daily work to the goals of the organization better than Dr. Rob Brinkerhoff's Impact Map.[1] Once you and your followers understand their voices, you must determine what skills or competencies they need to develop to achieve that goal. They will probably need to develop functional skills (like earning their CPA designations, for example) and also various teamwork, leadership, process-management, and problem-solving skills as well. Identify the top two or three competencies that are essential to develop over the next twelve to eighteen months for them to progress along their path to achieving their voices.

Next, collaborate on what formal learning they will need to complete in order to lay a foundation for application of the learning. What classes do they need to take? Do they need to complete a degree or certification program? Are there industry seminars they should attend? Are there books they could read instead of or in ad-

---

1 Explained in "How to Use This Book to Improve Your Performance and Deliver World Class Results" at the beginning of this book.

dition to classroom work? What webinars could they participate in that might help reduce travel obligations? The purpose of this step is to identify the key learnings that need to take place.

Once you and your followers understand the knowledge they need to gain, then connect that knowledge to the different behaviors they should be able to demonstrate on the job. How will their daily work change? What will they be doing differently or more autonomously? What could be observed by a third party that would indicate increased capacity or performance?

CONNECT THOSE SKILLS TO BUSINESS RESULTS

After identifying those behaviors, connect them to the immediate business results that the team or business unit should realize based on that person's increased performance on the job. Will quality improve? Which safety metrics might be affected? How would a sales or marketing program deliver differently?

Then connect those few improved results to the company's high-level goals. Which organizational metrics will be enhanced directly or indirectly? Even if the company is so large and global that the improved results seem to add only a drop to the bucket, it is vital to create the line-of-sight between what that individual must learn, and connect that to the different behaviors, and those to the affected unit metrics, and those to the organization's benefit. This connection creates alignment between what the individual needs to achieve her voice, and what the organization needs from her in order to survive and thrive. This link, when articulated well and drawn clearly, creates intrinsic motivation, or as Herzberg calls it, the employee's "internal generator" of motivation.

USE THE BUSINESS TO BUILD PEOPLE

Once you have identified the formal learning that needs to take place, you must connect each follower to a network of people who can reinforce the learning and lead him or her to other sources. In Chapter 13, I described CCL's 70-20-10 model of development. In today's networked, socially-connected world, much more than just 20 percent of someone's learning will come from others. It is essential that you help your followers find mentors beyond yourself (and outside of your organization). Renew your commitment to the idea that time spent networking appropriately is not time lost. It is *development* time. It is part of the investment you are making to help your followers achieve their voices and help you develop the bench strength you need.

The next step is to design the *experiences* that will teach them the bulk of the lessons to be learned. Think about the quickest and most indelible lessons from your own developmental journey. Odds are they came from times when you were in a little over your head, out of your depth or field of expertise, and you had to learn while doing. You made some mistakes, and you resolved never to make the same ones again. You were a little scared the whole time. I know a Supply Chain vice-president who says, "If you're not ready to puke in the sink just a little bit every time you think about how you are going to learn how to deliver on the commitments of your developmental plan, then it's not a very worthy plan." That may sound extreme, but as a leader, if you make it safe enough (i.e., earning their trust that you have their backs and will not let them screw up so much that it could hurt their careers), they will learn the fastest and develop the most learning agility through these trials.

SURROUND THEM WITH SIX SOURCES OF SUPPORT

Life gets busy. We get busy, and we forget to follow up despite our best intentions. Our followers get busy and lose sight of the developmental goal because they are mired in the day-to-day. They put off a class because it would take time they "just don't have right now." Their peers fail to give them an important on-the-job demonstration because they are behind in *their* work, too, and the demo would hurt productivity numbers. Mentors get busy and postpone the coaching lunch during which they were going to give your follower some important perspective on the path and the endgame of development. And fourth quarter budgets get tight, so your learner could not fly to the industry seminar with vital learning *and* networking that was important to your follower's development. Life gets busy.

In order to increase dramatically the likelihood that the detailed plan you have put in place (by using this chapter as your guide) will actually be carried out, you need to overcome many forces that will work against you and the teammate you are developing. I described the Six Sources of Influence in Chapter 15. The final step of creating a successful development plan is to apply that learning, too.

	MOTIVATION	ABILITY
PERSONAL	**SOURCE 1** PERSONAL MOTIVATION	**SOURCE 2** PERSONAL ABILITY
SOCIAL	**SOURCE 3** SOCIAL MOTIVATION	**SOURCE 4** SOCIAL ABILITY
STRUCTURAL	**SOURCE 5** STRUCTURAL MOTIVATION	**SOURCE 6** STRUCTURAL ABILITY

© VitalSmarts 2005. Used with permission. No further reproduction or copyright allowed.

First, think about all of the things that could go wrong when it comes to the motivation and ability issues for your follower, his people network, and the non-people forces that will affect the plan. Draw out the two-wide, three-tall matrix with your follower, and write in all of the things that will work against him or create hurdles and obstacles. Work very hard to brainstorm several items for each box.

Then, in a fresh 2 x 3 chart, fill in possible solutions (or at least ideas for solutions) to each of the hurdles you identified above. How will your followers maintain their personal motivation when life gets "busy?" How can you set up peer pressure to work *for* them instead of against them? How can you ensure people who *can* help *will* help? What incentives make sense to put in place without overshadowing the intrinsic motivation they need to muster? How can you clear the path out from in front of them by addressing things like budgets, reporting relationships, seating plans, and other policy issues that might stop them without you having to provide "air cover"? Brainstorm several solutions to each of the problems.

Randy Bernard, the former CEO of the Professional Bull Riders and current CEO of the Indy Racing League, once told me that what makes bull riders so special is that they are full of "try." Saying that a fellow rider is "full o' try" is one of the highest compliments riders can pay each other within that elite fraternity of adrenaline junkies. It means that a rider will not give up, no matter the odds.

Developing skills to achieve your voice is not as physically dangerous as riding a 2,000-pound bull, but the career stakes are just as high professionally for you *and* for your follower. The downside for the follower is obvious. If life gets busy and things get in the way of the plan, he and his career suffer. But his family suffers as well because he becomes less able to contribute to the family's well-being. That family has additional chaos and uncertainty within it. And your reputation as someone who "builds the future" and has a deep talent bench suffers as well, no matter how "full o' try" you and your follower are.

VitalSmarts' research demonstrates that to overcome the potential problems you identified in your 2 x 3 "hurdles and obstacles" matrix, you have to put in place supports from at least *four* of the different boxes from your "possible solutions" matrix. If you plan ahead for what might go wrong by developing a support plan that addresses at least four of the six sources of support, you and your follower are ten times more likely to be successful in completing the plan!

IT IS A MORAL OBLIGATION

Welcome to the club. Being a leader means that you hold others' careers in your hands. They own a lot of it, too, but you have to live with yourself when they fail to promote or do not earn that cross-functional transfer they have been working toward because they did not have the expected skill set. Their families and their community will be affected. And they will remember the support or lack of it they received from their leader.

Are you a "leader who builds future leaders?" Seeing your role through The Lens of Leadership means taking accountability for helping your followers fully develop their voice and achieve their career goals. You can do it. These tools will make it practically inevitable!

Summary & Exercise: Chapter 18—Building the Future: The Ultimate Development Toolbox

WHAT?—SO WHAT?—NOW WHAT?

What? People want a *partnership* with their leader in their career development—a partnership that helps them achieve their goals by delivering what the team and company need from them. As a leader, you have an obligation to serve them by designing a development plan that will help them succeed. Voice + an Impact Map + 70-20-10 + Six Sources of Influence = The Ultimate Development Toolbox.

So What? You must lead brutally candid dialogue about what your teammates need to learn and what skills they need to develop to achieve their deeply-personal goals. Orient your people to their individual voices; get them the skills they need; connect those skills to better results; use the business to build your people.

Now What?

I will study _____
_____ to learn more about developing the people I lead.

I will reach out to _____
_____ in order to seek more insight, guidance, and advice.

I will ask _____ to hold me accountable for _____
_____.

And I will _____

_____

_____

_____ in order to create an experience with elements/competencies that I have not yet adequately developed by *(date)* _____.

ADDITIONAL RESOURCES FOR YOUR "NOW WHAT?" JOURNEY:

Brinkerhoff, Robert. *The Success Case Method.*

Buckingham, Marcus. *Go Put Your Strengths to Work: 6 Powerful Steps to Achieve Outstanding Performance.*

Charan, Ram. *The Leadership Pipeline.*

Eichinger, Robert W. and Michael M. Lombardo. *The Leadership Machine: Architecture to Develop Leaders for Any Future.* 3rd ed.

Gladwell, Malcolm. *Outliers: The Story of Success.*

Gottfredson, Con and Bob Mosher. *Innovative Performance Support: Strategies and Practices for Learning in the Workflow.*

Grenny, Joseph, David Maxfield, and Andrew Shimberg. "How to 10X Your Influence." *MIT Sloan Management Review.* (Fall 2008)

Herzberg, Frederick. "One More Time: How Do You Motivate Employees?" *Harvard Business Review.* (Jan-Feb 1968)

Korn-Ferry International. *FYI For Your Improvement—Korn-Ferry International's competency guide for performance improvement.*

Patterson, Kerry and Joseph Grenny, David Maxfield, Ron McMillan and Al Switzler. *Change Anything: The New Science of Personal Success.*

Pink, Daniel H. *Drive: The Surprising Truth About What Motivates Us.*

Rath, Tom. *StrengthsFinder 2.0.*

"70-20-10 model for learning and development Center for Creative Leadership." (Google it.)

CHAPTER NINETEEN

HAVING PERFORMANCE CONVERSATIONS: EARLY AND OFTEN

No meritorious act of a subordinate should escape [a leader's] attention or be left to pass without its reward, even if the reward is only a word of approval. Conversely, he should not be blind to a single fault in any subordinate, though at the same time, he should be quick and unfailing to distinguish error from malice, thoughtlessness from incompetency, and well-meant shortcomings from heedless or stupid blunder.
– John Paul Jones, on the Qualifications of a Naval Officer

When people know better, they do better.
– Maya Angelou

One of my early inspirations for writing this book was the way I saw certain leaders in business "let their people go"—that is, fire them. I know you have received an email like this one if you've worked in a midsize or large organization: "As of today, so-and-so is no longer part of this organization. Please refer any questions about his workload and deliverables to [a different so-and-so]. Thank you."

I was always shocked by the abruptness of emails like that. I wondered whether the sender realized what a bad light those emails cast on *him*. I finally received an email like that from someone with whom I felt comfortable engaging in a conversation about it. I asked, "What happened with so-and-so?" The answer was, "I had to fire him. He sucked."

So I probed a little deeper: "Did it have to end *that* way—with the 'he no longer works here' email?" He answered, "Well, yeah. I just couldn't let it go on any longer."

I pushed a little harder: "So, you were documenting his performance issues and sat him down and told him about all of that, and he didn't take the hint and *leave*?" He answered, "Well, no, I didn't. But everybody knew he wasn't cutting it. He was terrible. I just couldn't let it go on anymore. I need someone in that seat who can do the job."

I pushed one last time: "What role do you think *you* played in his very public failure?" His shallow answer was telling: "What role did *I* play? I had to fire him. That was hard to do!"

I developed a bit of a habit of engaging people who sent those emails—even people I didn't know very well—in a dialogue about their possible roles in those employees' failures. My experience as a naval officer taught me that a leader bears a great deal of responsibility when someone has to be fired. When a military member is fired from a job (it happens more often than you might think), that person's leader is put under a great deal of scrutiny. Often, the leader bears significant responsibility for the person's failure, and if that is the case, it affects that leader's career. I could not believe how casually people in business would fire a person without it even occurring to them that they may have played a role in the failure.

Often the leaders received my initial questioning with more than just a little indignation. Who was I, after all, to be questioning them? I learned to be clear about my intentions: "Hey, I'm not looking to probe into the H.R. details of why you let so-and-so go. That's between you and H.R. I wonder whether we could just have a quick leadership conversation about how so-and-so left the company?" That has always been received fairly well, and it usually leads to a healthy dialogue, during which I get to ask my progressively "pushy" questions until we get to the part about what role the leader played in what led to "so-and-so no longer works here."

I am sorry to report that in the decade that I have been engaging others in these conversations, only about 10-15 percent of the leaders ever say anything like, "Oh, I know exactly how I failed him. I should have been a lot more candid with him about [*whatever*] six months ago, but I just let it go on. I was too vague right up until the team couldn't function with that deficit anymore. I'll never let that happen again."

That is accountability! That is a leader admitting his role, demonstrating that he has learned something valuable from it, and committing to be better in the future. And that is what should be expected from the other 85-90 percent of leaders. Are there some good reasons to march someone out the door and send the "so-and-so doesn't work here anymore" email? There sure are. But I believe it is used far too often, and I also believe too few H.R. departments engage those leaders in a conversation about *their* roles in that person's failure. Getting, as Jim Collins calls it, "the wrong people off the bus" does not have to be done this way. Great leaders know how.

LEADERSHIP IS NOBLE, BUT IT CAN ALSO BE LONELY

I am sure you have heard the saying, "It's lonely at the top." Well, "the top" means *you* if you are a leader, no matter where you are in the organization. Leaders earn the big bucks because they have the additional responsibility of being accountable for delivering results and for developing the skills and careers of others. Those are two weighty responsibilities. It has been my experience that many leaders focus on delivering results—because they are more easily measured and are often directly tied to incentives—and less time on developing others.

Leading conversations with your followers about skills, standards, and performance expectations can be a difficult part of the job and it takes special skills. Your obligation as a leader to hold these conversations means that you must always maintain an important degree of objectivity. That may require you to maintain a little bit of social distance that didn't exist when you were a follower or a teammate. If you were promoted in-place and now lead people who used to be your peers, you are in the unenviable position of having to create some of that social distance. It is vital to your ability to be absolutely candid.

SPHERICAL COACHING

The verb form of the word "coach" is just as important and powerful as the noun form. In the best coaching environments, coaching happens in multiple directions and even from outside the organization. Unfortunately, this is the typical organization chart:

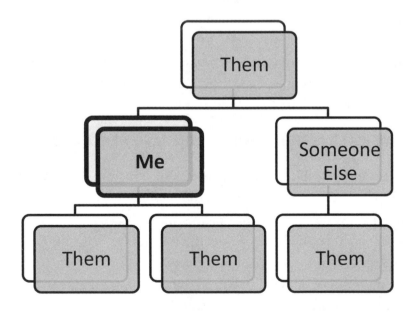

Teams and organizations perform at their best when *everyone* is a coach, and when coaching happens multi-directionally—up, down, and sideways—and multi-dimensionally—from inside and from outside the company.[1] Great coaching looks more like a sphere:

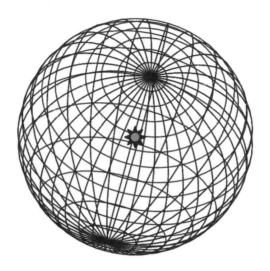

The best leaders are open to "up-coaching" from below, and the best followers are willing to give it, based on a motivation to do what is best for the leader, the followers, and for the organization. On the best teams, up-coaching is an *obligation* that all team members feel compelled to give, because leaders who have teammates looking out for their best interests will lead teams that deliver the best results. For followers, this is another form of demonstrating loyalty (see Chapter 2).

FEEDBACK: HOW, AND HOW OFTEN?

You should never miss an opportunity to give performance feedback. Drive-by coaching should be done "in the moment," based on regular observations. These are "tweaking" comments that con-

---

1 The external view from vendors, agencies, and other suppliers can be invaluable because they see many organizations. Enlist them in giving you feedback.

nect slight modifications to better results. This kind of coaching could be about a hard skill like a manufacturing technique (e.g., hand-positioning during welding), or about a soft skill like political savvy (e.g., up-coaching your leader on how to engage the team on a touchy subject). The key is to use your presence in the work environment as an opportunity to improve teammate behaviors.

Regular one-on-one conversations have significant benefits. They afford you both a little more privacy—a sanctum for candor and raising high-stakes topics in a less-risky way. By keeping the time for these conversations somewhat sacred, it conveys the value you place on both the person and the relationship. It also demonstrates your commitment to his or her development. Depending on the workload and the types of projects the person is working on, you may meet one-on-one daily, weekly, bi-weekly, or maybe only monthly. The most important thing is that the interval be right for *both* of you. And the follower's needs should trump your own. Ask him or her whether the interval is too often or too rare. Adjust it until it is "just right."

Regular team meetings are also important to individual and team performance. Team results and teammate needs should drive how often you meet together. These team conversations should be an open forum for everyone to talk about the things getting in the way of, or contributing to, great performance. Even in a manufacturing environment where these team talks are on the clock and away from the work, these meetings will pay for themselves if carried out with great candor and commitment to better results. I always include what I call "open mic" time for my team members to bring up anything on their minds.

Any time results are published—whether they are annual profit figures, quarterly sales numbers, or daily scrap rates—there should also be team and one-on-one conversations around what led to those results. Great leaders seize every opportunity to connect behaviors to results. The more regularly these happen, the less surprising or even threatening they are. Great teams are comfortable talking about results.

DRIVERS OF PERFORMANCE

During their time at the Center for Creative Leadership, Michael Lombardo and Robert Eichinger created a specific framework for discussing performance. They identified ten performance "dimensions" that may help you better to identify and articulate what you need to say during performance conversations. Before you engage a teammate on his performance, read through these questions and write down fact-based feedback you want to give:

1. Is his quantity of work meeting standards?
2. Is he meeting timelines and deadlines?
3. Is he meeting quality standards?
4. Is he consuming resources (e.g., time, money, materials, people) efficiently?
5. Is his work meeting the expectations of internal and external customers?
6. Is he operating effectively without needing an inordinate amount of direct support?
7. Is he being helpful to and cooperative with teammates?
8. Is he demonstrating productive work habits like prioritization, time management, follow-up, and follow-through?
9. Is he a "learner for life" who is continuously growing his own skill set?
10. Are his on-the-job behaviors aligned with the values, culture, and mission of the organization?

THE VALUE OF MISTAKES

As you develop others, you have to find a way to make it safe for your teammates to make mistakes. The best leader I ever followed said that he had made every single mistake in the book—but only once, and that was how often he preferred we make them too. A manufacturing leader once described mistakes to me as the "tuition we pay for the learning opportunity." That is a powerful perspective for a leader to have and to communicate to her team. I learned another rule of thumb for dealing with mistakes while reading Hammer and Champy's *Reengineering the Corporation*: "Never punish failure. Only punish sloppy execution and a negligent inability to see reality."

The best leaders find a way to carve out some discretionary time (even at "always on" jobs like a manufacturing line) or a certain set of conditions under which they can create a bit of a "laboratory" environment for their people. This is a small slice of time or place when people can experiment a little bit, try a new technique, or fill a position they have never held before. A lab is a little bit safer and the leader is always there to take the reins if necessary. It is essential to create this lab time so people know when they will not be expected to perform at a flawless level of performance. The more they get to do "in the lab," the more skilled and confident they will be when it counts.

STOP-START-CONTINUE

Stop-Start-Continue is a valuable technique for getting and giving performance feedback. You draw up a short list of things you would recommend that the person or team should *stop* doing, *start* doing, and *continue* to do.

Explaining behaviors that you believe should be stopped affords you the opportunity to explain where you perceive inefficiencies and why you believe a particular behavior hurts, or at least does not help, results.

Describing actions that you believe should be started opens the door to creativity and continuous improvement in execution. "We don't, but maybe we should..." is a deep well from which to draw.

Articulating what behaviors and attitudes should continue gives each person the chance to define the parts of the process or system that seem to make the other parts really work well.

You should ask your teammates to do a Start-Stop-Continue on you each time you meet, as well. These coaching conversations should go both ways. You need their coaching as much as they need yours.

HARD SKILLS + SOFT SKILLS = SUCCESS

Leah Glaub, the Vice-President of Human Resources at Johnsonville Sausage, created a comprehensive feedback tool that is smart because of its simplicity.

Across the top of a blank piece of paper, list out the five to eight hard skills that are essential for a teammate to be successful in his or her role. These should be two- or three-word, job-specific, functional skills that might come from a job description or from observing the daily work.

Across the bottom of the page, list out five to eight soft skills that are also necessary for success. These should be specific enough so the desired behaviors are clear. They should describe the few behaviors that will support the hard-skills in delivering excellence. Some examples might be: Drive for Results; Can-Do Spirit; Cheerful and Supportive Attitude, etc.

Near the middle, mark each skill with a checkmark for "on-target," a "+" for above expectations, or a "-" for below expectations. This tool fosters a focused dialogue on the few skills necessary for success. It doesn't overcomplicate an already inherently subjective evaluation. Finally, it recognizes that in order to build professional credibility, trust, and respect, a person must have *both* hard skills *and* soft skills.

CONFRONT MISSED EXPECTATIONS THE FIRST TIME

In *Crucial Confrontations: Tools for Resolving Broken Promises, Violated Expectations, and Bad Behavior,* Kerry Patterson and his fellow authors explain that leaders often hesitate to speak up *the first time* a teammate is late, or *the first time* he breaks safety protocols, or *the first time* he loses his temper. Generally, people hate conflict, and will avoid it when they can. In these first time situations, it can be hard to muster up the courage to hold others accountable. We tell ourselves that maybe it won't happen again. We come up with all sorts of reasons why we shouldn't speak up. It will be hard, and probably not worth it to say anything. But it will never be easier than that first time because of what the authors call the "C-P-R" model: Content, Pattern, and Relationship.

The first time something happens, it is a "Content" issue. The first time someone is late, violates safety protocols, or loses his temper, the conversation is about just that: tardiness, following procedures, or bad behavior. As hard as it can be to bring up those behaviors, it will never get any easier than it is right then.

The second, third, or fourth time the behavior happens, the conversation is no longer about tardiness, or procedures, or bad behavior. Now it is about a *pattern* of offending behavior, and bringing that up is much harder. Why? Now *you* own some of the responsibility for the behavior because you failed to confront it the first time. It is a lot harder to hold someone accountable when we have to admit we also played a role in empowering the bad behavior.

If you fail to confront the pattern, if you confront it poorly, or if the person fails to live up to a promise to change, then you have to have the most difficult type of conversation. The *relationship* is damaged when bad patterns go unaddressed. Once we lose the ability to trust a teammate, begin to doubt his competence, or lose respect for her as a coworker, that relationship may not survive. Those relationship conversations are delicate, but the best leaders engage in them in order to achieve what's best for the team and for all of the teammates.

Crucial Confrontations also explains an airtight way of ensuring accountability for changed behavior. At the end of the conversation, ask the following three questions: "So, are you *willing* to [perform the agreed-to task or changed behavior]?" "Will you *be able* to [perform the agreed-to task or changed behavior]?" and "Is there anything else that would prevent you from keeping this commitment?" These three questions probe on both sources of motivation and ability, and ask an open-ended question that gives the follower another opportunity to voice concern for why he might not be able to live up to his commitment. These questions provide clear accountability for both parties so they are a powerful tool for better performance conversations.

PEOPLE SHOULD NEVER WONDER WHERE THEY STAND

The goal for performance conversations is to provide insights for your teammates about what they are doing well and where they need to improve. These should be both very candid and also very respectful. You should strive to achieve both every time. You have got to let people know where they stand. I believe it is both cruel and immoral not to engage your people in a way that makes them fully aware of their strengths and shortcomings. Hold up your performance "heroes" for all to see. Put your exemplars on a public pedestal that says, "This is what *great* looks like." Tailor your recognition to match the receiver's style, but get the word out about what the best performers are doing, and what results are being driven by those behaviors.

You must also engage the shortcomings, too. Remember to "praise in public and counsel in private" because *everybody* knows who the poor performers are—even the poor performers! When you let inadequate performance go unaddressed, it hurts the team, it hurts your credibility as the leader, and it hurts the poor performer by giving him or her a false sense of security.

People should never wonder where they stand. Give them security or insecurity, whichever their performance merits. I am not advocating being cruel. I am advocating that you engage inadequate performers in well-documented, fact-based performance conversations. If you do that, you will rarely have to fire someone and send the "So-and-so doesn't work here anymore" email. Nobody wants to come to work every day knowing he is a bad fit or underperforming. He will most often self-select to leave your organization. He will go on to find a job that is a better fit, and with the perspective of time, he will be grateful to you for your candor and insights.

I coined the phrase "The Lens of Leadership" during one of my "So-and-so no longer works here" conversations. I encouraged one of my colleagues to look at the firing "through a lens of leadership to see your role." When you look at who is "on the bus" and "who is in which seats on the bus" through The Lens of Leadership, your team's results will be better, your team spirit and motivation will be healthier, and you will build a team of professionals who can hold *each other* accountable whether or not you are around. But it starts with you.

Summary & Exercise: Chapter 19—
Having Performance Conversations Early and Often

WHAT?—SO WHAT?—NOW WHAT?

What? Great leaders have performance and results conversations with individuals and their teams early and often. They engage in spherical coaching, seeking their own feedback from above, below, from peers, and also from vendors and other partners outside of the organization. Feedback should always connect-the-dots between behaviors and results.

So What? You must make a habit of engaging in these conversations so people always know where they stand. Ambushing someone to fire him in a conference room with an H.R. representative is unfair, and it is almost always avoidable. If you have to send a "So-and-so doesn't work here anymore" announcement, take the time to consider what role you may have played in the person's public failure.

Now What?

I will study _____

_____

_____ to learn more about effective performance conversations.

I will reach out to _____

_____

_____ in order to seek more insight, guidance, and advice.

I will ask _____ to hold me accountable for _____.

And I will _____

_____

_____ in order to create an experience with elements/competencies that I have not yet adequately developed by *(date)* _____.

ADDITIONAL RESOURCES FOR YOUR "NOW WHAT?" JOURNEY:

Blanchard, Ken. *Leadership and the One Minute Manager.*

Eikenberry, Kevin and Guy Harris. *From Bud to Boss: Secrets to a Successful Transition to Remarkable Leadership.*

Evans, Henry J. *Winning with Accountability: The Secret Language of High-Performing Organizations.*

Fine, Alan with Rebecca R. Merrill. *You Already Know How to Be Great: A Simple Way to Remove Interference and Unlock Your Greatest Potential.*

Fisher, Roger, William L. Ury, and Bruce Patton. *Getting to Yes: Negotiating Agreement Without Giving In.*

Hickman, Craig, Tom Smith, and Roger Connors. *The Oz Principle: Getting Results through Individual and Organizational Accountability.*

Korn-Ferry International. *FYI For Your Improvement: Korn-Ferry International's competency guide for performance improvement.*

Miller, John G. *QBQ! The Question Behind the Question: Practicing Personal Accountability at Work and in Life.*

Patterson, Kerry, Joseph Grenny, David Maxfield, Ron McMillan, and Al Switzler. *Change Anything: The New Science of Personal Success.*

Patterson, Kerry, Joseph Grenny, David Maxfield, Ron McMillan, and Al Switzler. *Crucial Confrontations: Tools for Resolving Broken Promises, Violated Expectations, and Bad Behavior.*

Tulgan, Bruce. *Not Everyone Gets A Trophy: How to Manage Generation Y.*

INSPIRE

PART FIVE

INSPIRING AND MOTIVATING OTHERS

It is the character of a brave and resolute man not to be rebuffed by adversity and not to desert his post.

— Cicero

CHAPTER TWENTY

LEADING YOUR PEOPLE TO BE LIKE HYBRID CARS

Inspire: *to breathe life into*

All power is a trust, and we are accountable for its exercise.
– Benjamin Disraeli

Here is the ultimate goal of leadership: to consistently exceed your stakeholders' expectations by taking your team to places yet to be discovered by your customers or your competition through the work of bright, ambitious, self-managing teammates who respect and admire you as their leader. Wow! That epic goal, like anything that is worth pursuing, requires you to be on a never ending quest. This chapter is about two important tools that any intrepid leadership Argonaut will need, always and forever, throughout that quest: *power* and *influence*.

This chapter will be your primer on those two fraternal twins. You need to understand their roots and their strengths and limitations. If you can talk in their *language,* and understand when and when not to employ them, you will be a much more effective leader and follower. Being skilled with power and influence will mean the difference between earning a reputation as a people-savvy leader with the deft gift of finesse, and a clumsy bull in a china shop. The benefit of employing power and influence with finesse is that you will be better able to inspire those you lead, and equip them with their own internal motivation "generator." Make them capable of motivating *themselves*, and able to "charge their own batteries." Lead them to be like hybrid cars!

THE FRATERNAL TWINS

Innumerable volumes have been written over centuries about power and influence. This chapter's purpose is to arm you with practical knowledge applicable in the modern workplace. Some people describe power and influence as different sides of the same coin. I see them as fraternal twins: nearly identical and with similar natures, but having a few significant—sometimes subtle—differences that make them distinctly different. The better you understand them, the more likely you will be to get the best out of them *both*, and prevent one from dominating the other—like Cain and Abel—and hurting your team's performance.

"POWER" IS NOT ALWAYS A DIRTY WORD

Power has the bad-boy reputation of the two twins because it is used too often, and it's not very creative. Power is a blunt instrument. Power misused is often a chainsaw when a pocketknife or even a scalpel would have worked. The best leaders understand that there are different types of power, and they use them sparingly-but-intentionally, depending on when each one is the right tool for the job. My favorite model of power is from social psychologists John French and Bertram Raven's 1959 "Bases of Social Power." They divide power up into Positional and Personal Power, with each category having three different types within it.

POSITIONAL POWER: REWARD, LEGITIMATE, AND COERCIVE

Reward power is the ability someone has to grant resources and incentives that are desirable to the potential recipient. Regardless of our title or role, different people have different benefits that they can grant to someone. A divisional finance director may have the discretion to increase a plant's bonus payout by reducing the negative impact of an industry metric that was beyond plant employees' control. A manager on a marketing team may give a team analyst a non-chargeable day off for working a couple of all-nighters while completing an important project. Even a high school student working in an ice cream shop has the ability to scoop extra-large portions for his pals when they come in. How we use our ability to reward others says a lot about our understanding of human material motivation. If you go to the reward well too early or too often, it loses its impact. How and when we use rewards can also reveal a lot about our character.

Legitimate power is the ability to assign work, make final decisions, and conduct other official business by virtue of the authority vested in someone by law, policy, rank, title, or role. Legitimate power can often be a Lose-Lose tool because the authority that comes with it is as powerful as the accompanying responsibility is delicate. If you are regularly resorting to your legitimate authority to get people to do things, you need to reexamine your effectiveness. We have all heard an insecure leader completely misuse his legitimate authority by saying something like, "Do it. I'm the boss and I'm telling you to. Just do it." Before something like that ever comes out of your mouth in front of others, run—don't walk—RUN away from the situation, reread this entire chapter, and apply several other sources of power and influence to the situation when you are thinking more rationally. No matter how good it may feel in the moment to wield this power source, do it only when human safety or other great loss is at risk.

At the other end of the lose-lose continuum, you will also damage your personal leadership brand should you ever fail to own up to the *responsibilities* of your legitimate power. Never fail to own up to failure.

Coercive power is someone's ability to apply punishment or other negative sanctions or withhold desired resources. It is *reward power*'s evil twin, but don't think it is held solely by those with legitimate power of position. Followers can wield this power against leaders through poor quality or the quantity of their work. A union's threat to strike is coercive power, as is a supervisor's threat to fire someone. In either case, this form of power is even more delicate than *legitimate power*. Even just the hinted threat of coercion can blow up in your face if the intended recipient is willing to endure the effects of your power and wield his power against you in return. Use coercion with caution, if ever. There are better, more complete tools.

PERSONAL POWER: REFERENT, INFORMATIONAL, AND EXPERT

Referent power is the power "referred" back to us by the people with whom we have strong relationships. This power could also be called "relationship power," and the stronger the relationship, the stronger the referent power of the leader. It is often rooted in the leader's personal charm or charismatic appeal. Are you a role model whom others try to emulate? Is your personal story inspiring? Is the word on the street that yours is the team to be on? All of these increase your referent power. Be careful, though: this one has the biggest potential to be abused through apathy. This source of power is like a savings account: you need to earn consistent deposits into this account for it to remain powerful. It can stand a big withdrawal from a well-intentioned mistake (especially if the mistake is followed by an apology). But if you make withdrawals that exceed your deposits, this source of power will dry up and leave impacted people going out of their ways to continue to speak ill of your leadership brand.

Informational power comes from someone's ability or perceived ability to be "in the know." This could come from the person's legitimate access to technical or personnel information (releasing that information might, however, be a breach of ethics), or from the person's political or social network. Either way, this power comes from having access to information by virtue of who the person is, what he does, or whom she serves or serves with. This person has power because of information she has, or at least has access to.

Expert power is derived from knowledge and experience. Since generalist leaders are frequently further removed from "the work" than the followers or teammates, it often creates a situation where people in subordinate roles have more of this type of power than the leader does. If you lead in a hierarchical organization, work hard to cultivate strong professional relationships with technical experts so you have close allies on those occasions when you need expert insights. If you treat experts who happen to be subordinate to you like "the help" on a daily basis, they may withhold their power of expertise from you when you need it most. Skilled leaders know who their go-to experts are and go out of their way to cultivate close professional relationships that acknowledge and show appreciation for their domain expertise.

Even in the most progressive and egalitarian organizations, some people have more power than others. It would be shortsighted of you to miss the additional fact that *everyone* in the organization has *some* power. Great leaders know that power used best is used lightest and in conjunction with the levers of influence.

THERE IS NOTHING "SOFT" ABOUT INFLUENCE

Influence may be seen by some as the weaker twin. This just isn't so. Even in hierarchical organizations fueled by legitimate power (like military and police organizations), influence is still the most powerful way to get big things done. Using influence builds allies because it builds better ideas. It has been my experience that in healthy, even moderately-transparent organizations, the best ideas carry the day regardless of the legitimate power brought against them. Remember, like power, any source of influence used in isolation or for the wrong motives can be a huge leadership mistake. *Why* you choose a particular set of influence tactics is as important as which ones you choose. The best leaders work transparently to serve the organization's best interests. I like Temple University researchers David Kipnis and Stuart Schmidt's influence descriptors.

HARD INFLUENCE

Legitimatizing tactics use appeals made under the auspices of your role or position of authority to get things done. These appeals are power as an influence tactic, and that power should only be used lightly and with forethought about all of the effects it will have. When you ask for something from someone and invoke your role or remind him of your authority, it begins to feel like power, not influence.

Pressure tactics are the other "hard" device that feels more like power than influence. Pressure can be as mild as repeated reminders or appeals, but it can be as blatant and negative as direct threats. Stay clear of using pressure tactics yourself. Seek advice or mentoring if someone is using pressure to influence you to do something your judgment tells you is wrong.

RATIONAL INFLUENCE

Ingratiation involves, as Dale Carnegie wrote, "lathering a man before you shave him." Ingratiating yourself to someone only for the purpose of achieving a specific end can earn you false friends and true enemies if you are discovered. Putting yourself in someone's debt, or falsely and shallowly praising him in order to woo him into seeing a particular issue your way, is a risky gambit. In some cultures, you might be required to place yourself in a needy position in order for a solution to be proffered. Seek the counsel of trusted cultural locals when working outside of your own culture. In Western culture, this sort of flattery will probably do more damage than help.

Coalition tactics leverage the power and influence of others to accomplish more than you can alone. For example, if you are the finance member on a cross-functional project team with an idea for a money-saving ingredient change, you might collaborate with Supply Chain to confirm pricing, and with Consumer Research to confirm no critical standard-of-identity will be violated by the change, and win their support before bringing the idea to the brand manager. Used with the best interests of the business or community organization in mind, and used while explaining that you are trying to build consensus around fact-based solutions, will demonstrate that you are not using your coalition as a parliamentary end-run, but rather as a way to get the best ideas out to the most people. Used with the *wrong* motive, this tactic can become a pure power play: "Can I bring more votes or more legitimate power to the decision conversation?"

Exchange involves the swapping of favors or mutually-desired rewards by all parties, creating enough of a "win-win" to earn agreement. Done in a healthy environment, it is the negotiation of outcomes by focusing first on mutual *interests*, and not someone's stated position. Taken to the extreme, this negotiation can be dysfunctional or even unethical. Serving all parties' mutual interests is not easy, and the more parties involved, the more complex the negotiations. Keep it simple, and keep it transparent.

Rational persuasion uses matter-of-fact arguments, factual evidence, and logic to win people over. When the facts are on your side, it is a potent influence tactic. Be careful not to assume that you have all of the facts, though. When making a rational appeal, talk with a tentative nature and ask whether you might be missing anything. This consultative approach will make you less threatening and communicate that you are open to expanding your case by seeking the knowledge of others. Another use of this tactic is to communicate the natural consequences of going against your plan. Talk about what will happen *inevitably*—not because some authority will impose a negative consequence, but because facts are being ignored—the negative consequences are just unavoidable. It is vital to ensure that all of your facts are really facts, and not just *your version* of the facts.

SOFT INFLUENCE

Personal appeals use friendships and other personal relationships to get what you are seeking. "C'mon; we coach our kids' soccer team five nights a week. Can't we make this project at work even more effective by combining these two requirements?" Mixing work and personal lives is often inevitable in today's connected, collaborative world. The strength of friendships is a time-tested way to give and take in healthy situations. All of us will do more for someone with whom we have a "deeper-than-just-work" relationship. But be careful. Personal relationships should not incur debts to benefit your work life. It is hard to get the different currencies to exchange correctly. Drawing from a personal account is an expensive way to bulk up a work or volunteer project. It can cost you a friend or colleague.

Inspirational appeals are designed to seize the moral or enthusiastic high ground and rally groups to your cause. Tie your efforts to a higher purpose or to something that is universally appealing. Seek out and identify by name the role models who are already living out the behaviors you are advocating. Appealing to people's better natures is almost always more effective than burdening them with guilt or regret if they do not come over to your way of thinking. Find a way to frame the conversation so they begin answering "yes" to your rhetorical appeals. Give them something inspirational to agree with and you will be well on your way to influencing for change.

Consultation reaches out to experts and other interested stakeholders in order to expose others to your ideas while receiving their valuable feedback. Consultation may be used as a faster way of getting enough insights on a topic outside of your own area of expertise to make a decision than polling or conducting formal interviews. It should involve a representative sample of stakeholders in order to earn good-faith commitment to the decision.

HOW POWER AND INFLUENCE CONNECT

People will choose their influence tactics based upon the types of power they possess. People with large amounts of referent power will have the widest latitude for influence tactics. People will use the "hard" tactics of pressure and legitimizing when they tend to have an advantage over someone. Otherwise, people will resort to the buffet of other tactics.

My research within Johnsonville Sausage (explained in Chapter 7) is supported by the Center for Creative Leadership's findings as well: the "best" leaders—the ones who consistently deliver the best results and are also held in the highest esteem—are the ones who use the *widest range of power and influencing tactics*. Rather than just use the one or two tactics that seem to "fit" them the best or seem the most natural, they use *all* of the tactics of power and influence at different times as appropriate to the situation. This choosing of the appropriate tactic requires forethought and intentionality, but it delivers the best results.

ANOTHER POWERFUL MODEL OF INFLUENCE

The Kipnis and Schmidt taxonomy is important for describing the forms of influence we use or of which we feel the effects. The simplest, most practical model I know for diagnosing influence failures and influencing the *right* behaviors is VitalSmarts' Six Sources of Influence model (explained in Chapter 15). This 2 x 3 matrix can be drawn on a napkin at a moment's notice. It is elegant in its comprehensive simplicity. What forces are influencing the individual's motivation and ability? What forces are affecting his social network? How is he being affected by non-human factors like incentive programs, technology, and corporate policies? Every leader and follower should understand this powerful device.

LEAD YOUR FOLLOWERS TO BE LIKE HYBRID CARS

I referenced Frederick Herzberg's "One more time: How do you motivate employees?" in Chapter 18 to explain that it is the value a worker gets from the *work itself* that makes him most likely to stay, and stay *engaged*. That sort of engagement requires motivation, but not the kind that a leader can provide. That kind of motivation is a myth, and Herzberg uses his pet schnauzer to bring that myth to life.

He explains that many leaders are tempted to use "Kick-In-The-Pants" leadership (for which he coined the term "KITA") to motivate their employees to get work done. Herzberg writes, "If I kick my schnauzer in the pants physically or psychologically, who is motivated? *I* am motivated. The dog just moves!" Therefore, a negative KITA does not lead to motivation, but to movement.

An incentive, or positive KITA, fails similarly: "Now that my schnauzer has completed obedience training, I hold up a biscuit, and the dog moves. Again, I am the one who is motivated, and the dog is the one who moves. All I did was apply KITA frontally. I exerted a pull instead of a push." And with incentives, the stakes must constantly be raised or their material and psychological value will be diminished.

Herzberg illustrates that a leader cannot place himself in the position of constantly having to recharge his teammates' motivation batteries. Instead, you need to lead your team to be like a hybrid car, which recharges its *own* batteries while it is running on its gasoline engine. But how do you install such a self-sustaining generator in a teammate?

LEAD THE "WHOLE PERSON"

The late Dr. Stephen Covey wrote that we tend to pay a worker for his strong body, or his strong mind, or the combination of the two that he applies to his particular job. But the person also brings a "heart," or things he cares about, to work every day, and he brings his "spirit," his dreams and aspirations, with him too.

Herzberg and Covey agree: The best leaders can accomplish the greatest things only by aligning each of their followers with work they individually believe is noble and worthy of their toil, and by also connecting that work to a future each follower finds value in creating for *himself*, not for the company. This is the essence of installing a "motivation generator" in your teammates. This is why you should lead your team to be like a hybrid car.

TRANSFORMATION TO HIGH PERFORMANCE

Transactional leaders cultivate an exchange-based relationship with their teammates, and they tend to be effective only as long as the transactions are mutually beneficial. Teams can function on a mutually beneficial level for long periods of time, but they will probably not achieve greatness. These leaders tend to be capable of making the trains run on time, but they will probably not adapt well when times change or the "cheese moves."

Great leaders master the forces of power and influence. They also recognize that they play a role in inspiring their teammates, but that each person must find motivation from within, and from the work itself. Leaders who can accomplish that are on their way to becoming transformational leaders instead of remaining merely transactional ones.

Today's "conceptual age"—when change is happening so quickly and competition is so fierce—requires leaders to be capable of building strong bonds with their teammates. They also need to be able to bring forth charisma at important times (even if they are, by nature, introverted) to inspire their teams, grow each teammate as an individual, and communicate a new vision for what is being achieved. Followers will give more of their discretionary effort on teams led by transformational leaders. Transformational leaders are, themselves, more sought after as followers for more senior leaders because their enthusiasm is infectious and people of all levels want to be around them. Transformational leaders are willing to subordinate their own needs to the team's needs, and are willing to be challenged by teammates in order to raise the collective level of skills, ambition, direction, and results. Teams led by transformational leaders are leadership Argonauts, bound tightly together in a quest for greatness.

By looking at power, influence, motivation, and transformation through The Lens of Leadership, you are more likely to inspire your team to achieve better results through more cohesive relationships.

Summary & Exercise: Chapter 20—
Leading Your People to Be Like Hybrid Cars

WHAT?—SO WHAT?—NOW WHAT?

What? You can get your team to deliver better results by understanding the strengths and limitations of the fraternal twins of Power and Influence. The best leaders use all of the tactics at different times as appropriate to the situation. You as a leader cannot motivate anyone else. People must motivate themselves. By using the right tools of power and influence, you can create the conditions under which your followers act like hybrid cars, capable of recharging their own motivation batteries.

So What? In the best organizations, leaders are measured both by the results their followers deliver and by *how* the leaders get those results. If an organization focuses too heavily on just the results, it will be a dreadful, life-draining place to work and will inevitably underperform its potential. If the organization focuses too heavily on just the "how," it will fail to deliver results and will consistently underperform until it ceases to be a going concern. As a leader, you have to find Goldilocks' sweet spot of "just right." Using the right blend of power and influence tools, you will create a team that delivers great results in an environment that is, itself, part of the reward of the work.

Now What?

I will study _____

_____

_____ to learn more about power and influence.

I will reach out to _____

_____

_____ in order to seek more insight, guidance, and advice.

I will ask _____ to hold me accountable for _____.

And I will _____ _____ in order to create an experience with elements/competencies that I have not yet adequately developed by *(date)* _____.

ADDITIONAL RESOURCES FOR YOUR "NOW WHAT?" JOURNEY:

Baldwin, David and Curt Grayson. *Influence: Gaining Commitment, Getting Results.*

Bass, Bernard. *Leadership and Performance.*

Burns, James MacGregor. *Leadership.*

French, John and Bertram Raven. *The Bases of Social Power.*

Gostick, Adrian and Chester Elton. *The Carrot Principle: How the Best Managers Use Recognition to Engage Their People, Retain Talent, and Accelerate Performance.*

Grenny, Joseph, David Maxfield, and Andrew Shimberg. "How to 10X Your Influence." *MIT Sloan Management Review.* (Fall 2008)

Herzberg, Frederick. "One More Time: How Do You Motivate Employees?" *Harvard Business Review.* (Jan-Feb 1968)

Kipnis, David and Stuart Schmidt. *The Language of Persuasion.*

Lundin, Stephen C., Harry Paul, and John Christensen. *Fish! A Proven Way to Boost Morale and Improve Results.*

Machiavelli, Niccolo. *The Prince.*

Pink, Daniel H. *Drive: The Surprising Truth About What Motivates Us.*

CHAPTER TWENTY ONE

PUSHING THEM *BEYOND* WHAT THEY THINK THEY CAN ACHIEVE

If you want to build a ship, don't drum up people together to collect wood and don't assign them tasks and work, but rather teach them to long for the endless immensity of the sea.
— Antoine de Saint-Exupèry

I don't have to like my players and associates, but as their leader, I must love them. And please believe me, gentlemen, my love will be relentless!
— Vince Lombardi, welcoming recruits to training camp

What comes to mind when you think of what it means to be a "team"? That word gets tossed around a lot. It has become, to some degree, like "Mom" and "apple pie"—how could you *not* want more of whatever it is? A few time-tested behaviors and attitudes will create a high-performance team out of a group of individuals. They are known, and they are simple. But "simple" is not "easy." In this case, it is not easy because human beings are messy, fallible creatures with a general tendency to take the easiest path and avoid risk. But becoming a high-performance team requires constant self-discipline and commitment to excellence. Overcoming that "knowing-doing" gap requires an investment of time, energy, and discipline by all of the team members, not just the leader. It also requires constant vigilance to sustain high performance. A team is never in a steady-state. It is always either improving or declining. And whether a team is, as leadership author and speaker Jim Hunter says, "green and growin', or ripe and rottin'," is a reflection of that team's leader.

Many examples of truly high-performance teams can be found in the worlds of business, sports, the military, academia, and medical research. They are the legendary and celebrated: the ones who have the reputation for greatness and the measured performance to back up that reputation. Some examples include the Michael Jordan-era Chicago Bulls, Olympic athletic teams, SEAL Team Six, Cirque du Soleil, and the Blue Angels. They make it look easy, and that is deceptive because they have toiled and sacrificed *unbelievably* to *make it look* that effortless.

THE LEADER AND "MISSIONAL CAMARADERIE"

When you look at teams through The Lens of Leadership, you can clearly see the coach's obligation to equip and push his team members beyond what they think they can achieve. The great NFL football coach Vince Lombardi (whose quote began this chapter) certainly thought so. A leader should be a most difficult taskmaster. But be careful never to be the key stressor at all times, or you risk damaging what I call "missional camaraderie"—the cohesion the team has built by enduring the process of becoming a high-performance team to accomplish its mission. In most civilian high-performance teams, there is a certain point where, if you allow yourself to become the single, consistent source of challenge to the team, you risk being put "outside the team."

In his epic book *Band of Brothers*, Stephen Ambrose recounts the heroic odyssey of an army unit throughout the latter half of World War II. The first commander of "Easy Company" (at its inception during stateside training) was First Lieutenant Herbert Sobel. Sobel was tasked with building a company of inexperienced paratroopers into combat-ready warriors for the European theater. Sobel quickly became despised by his men. It was his job to push them and to prepare them physically, mentally, and emotionally for the rigors of infantry combat. But he pushed them so hard that he turned *himself* into the enemy. He went beyond being a relentless taskmaster with a reputation for honing his men into capable warriors. His men and even his peers believed that he found joy in making them miserable and giving them truly unachievable goals to such a degree that it damaged morale and performance. Sobel had to be removed from command before the company jumped into Normandy on D-Day.

From Sobel, we can learn the importance of separating the roles of leader and stressor. A crucible experience builds confidence and camaraderie through the bonding of shared sacrifices. If a leader fails to highlight some sort of external enemy (even as simple as making the virus that your research team is working against "the enemy") as part of the common goal the team is working toward, the leader risks becoming that enemy. I don't know how to measure where the line is for you and your team, but the best leaders will at least be aware that the line exists and will have tripwires in place (e.g., go-to teammates who can talk with safety and candor, assistant coaches, advisory board members, etc.) that prevent them from going too far and damaging missional camaraderie.

THE BUILDING BLOCKS OF HIGH-PERFORMANCE TEAMS

A team is composed of people who will subordinate their individual interests and opinions to the team's unity and efficacy. Only a handful of attitudes and behaviors are required to forge a high-performance team. Simple? Yes, but not easy.

1) *A Clear, Compelling, Common Goal:* Does everyone on the team know what "success" looks like? Can each team member explain how the team wins? There is the old fable of the stonemasons at a construction site: Some of them will tell you they are bricklayers

day-to-day, but the high-performance members will tell you they are on a team that is building a magnificent cathedral, inside of which people will worship for centuries. Can each of your teammates articulate your team's compelling mission, vision, and strategic goals? I don't mean in a rote way straight out of a Dilbert cartoon, but rather a way that communicates *their individual* passion for "the work?"

Does everyone on your team talk about each member's commitment to team unity? Has your team established its "culture"? That is, have you all had intentional, structured conversations around behavioral and attitudinal expectations? Early enculturation is vital; perhaps second only in importance to effective pre-screening for cultural fit as a condition for long-term success within high-performance cultures.

Do all of you know the boundaries—what is in-scope and out-of-scope—for the team? Do you know the metrics against which victory will be measured? Get this part right, and get it right *first* so the team members can fall back on these items as their guidepost.

2) *A Winning Culture:* The best teams talk about "winning" and "victory" and the yardstick of "the win" frequently and *unashamedly*. Whether you are in business, a not-for-profit that is run like a business[1], a research team, an expeditionary team, or are engaged in creating successful *avant garde* art, the best teams hate to lose. You might be losing market share. You may have failed to earn the endowment of a large donor. A chemical chain may not have sustained its bond in the face of certain conditions in the lab. Maybe a subcontractor let you down and cost you unexpected time or money. A competitor may have crossed the finish line *one one-thousandth* of a second before your team did. However failure is measured by your team, it is an *abomination* to high-performance teams. They aren't afraid to talk about "beating" the competition, "defeating"

---

1 Which is the *only* way you will become a high-performance not-for-profit.

opponents, and sending rival suitors "home"—preferably in tears, bawling for their mommas.

3) *Open, Candid Communication:* Patrick Lencioni writes that high-performance teams have different conversations than other teams.

- They engage in healthy conflict—100 percent candid and 100 percent respectful—to get to the best ideas quickly.
- They are self-policing. It is not up to the "leader" to correct behaviors and hold teammates accountable because each team member is already doing that. This accountability greatly diminishes what sociologists call "social loafing"—the tendency of people to exert less effort when part of a group than they would if they were on their own.
- They do not hold back their thoughts and feelings from one another because they respect each other too much.
- There are no "undiscussables" on high-performance teams. They are unafraid to bring up any topic that is keeping them in any way from reaching their goals, even when the leader may be the problem. They can feel this freedom to discuss items because it is not *personal*: it is about the goal, about the team, and about *winning*.
- These teammates will admit mistakes and confess weaknesses because they like and respect each other. They need each other to fill in their own personal gaps.

4) *High Performance Expectations:* People want to believe they are on a great team chasing a great objective, and that they will all win or lose *together*. They recognize their obligation to hold each other accountable for the necessary, agreed-to behaviors and attitudes required for victory. They recognize the need for unyielding continuous improvement, sometimes at an unreasonable pace.

5) *A "Team" Orientation:* If you had asked Michael Jordan in the mid-1990s what he did professionally, he wouldn't have told you he was an NBA basketball player. He would have told you he was

a Chicago Bull. Like any gang or tribe, high-performance teams create rituals, symbols, and mythologies that perpetuate a focus on *the team*, not the individuals who make up the team. Common expressions of such symbols are team t-shirts, branded water bottles, inside jokes, and maybe even a team quote book for those slips of the tongue that are worth recalling later for a laugh. These form a strong foundation of *esprit de corps*—the team spirit that drives unity and sustains the team members' personal motivation during tough times.

6) *Adequate Resources and Equipment*: It can be an unfair world. Some teams will have better funding. Some will have more team members, and some will have *better* team members. Some may have superior facilities and access to higher quality raw materials. High-performance teams work *together* against whatever disadvantages exist, to achieve their worthy, common goal. One of the most difficult tests for leaders of these teams is how much they can "get" for the team. But the best teams are careful not to use resourcing as a scapegoat. If you lost because the other team's company bought it a new product development lab, you still *lost*. And losing *sucks*. Find a way to win *without* a new lab.

7) *Well-Defined Roles*: Any modern team will have a lot of task interdependence even with differentiated and specialized roles. The best teams know exactly who-does-what, and they have deeply cross-trained team members who know what to do when someone else doesn't. These teams have even prepared for unthinkable scenarios, and have practiced with individual and collective decision-making skills to prepare for the truly unforeseen.

8) *Clear Lines of Leadership*: Great teams have one leader who is ultimately accountable for the outcome—the victory or the loss. That is the entire premise of *The Lens of Leadership*. But high-performance teams are full of situational leaders, who, in the right moments, step up to leading because their skills, their stamina, or their physical position or perspective put them in the best position to lead

at that time. Like a flock of geese, each member leads the formation at the time when he is needed, and the others "honk" in acceptance and appreciation of that leadership.

CREATING *YOUR* HIGH PERFORMANCE TEAM

Okay, you have a pretty good team that understands the fundamentals of high-performance teams. Here are some practical ideas with actions you can lead that will raise your team's game:

A Team is a Reflection of Its Leader

The most important thing you can remember is that any team will reflect the personality and discipline of its leader. I can't emphasize enough the power—for good or for bad—of role modeling. Don't hold your teammates to any standard you are not willing to exceed regularly and visibly yourself. That will breed cynicism and contempt, both of which make it difficult to build a high-performance team.

Your attitude sets the standard as well. When problems come up, do you complain, or do you foster the solutions-based spirit of "Work-the-Problem"? Are you a pessimist in those low moments? I suggest, instead, you live out one of the most powerful examples of "Murphy's Laws of Combat": "Perpetual optimism is a force multiplier."

Protect the Role of the Dissenter

On any high-performance team, you will find that someone— not always the *same* someone—is willing to act as a voice of dissent when something does not seem right. This person doesn't necessarily agree with your latest decision, with the popularly-held organizational opinion, or maybe with current conventional wisdom. People whom history now celebrates as visionaries have often been lifted out of obscurity because they had the courage to be dissenters.

As a leader, you not only have to protect, but to *encourage* teammates to step up to that role, because the dissenter reveals blind spots. My friend and Naval Academy classmate Vic Hyder recently retired from the Navy as a senior SEAL officer. I asked him once to explain how, in a team that is so full of absolute professionals (even in its junior ranks), but that also requires absolute obedience to authority, he managed that dichotomy between dissent and obedience. He looked at me and said, "Cory, sometimes in planning, they would just look at me and say, '*F— you, sir!*' And as long as they said 'sir' at the end, I was pretty inclined to hear them out." The maturity to know when to speak up in planning and when to obey in combat is part of the professionalism bred into Navy SEALs. If those team leaders can nurture the role of the dissenter and still succeed, so can you.

Drill, Baby, Drill!

Not for oil, but for *practice*. When something is high-stakes, deliberate practice and the confidence developed through repetition can be a key success driver. One of the most important lessons of my military years was to "train like you fight." This advice is not just for military teams, though. War gaming is one of the most powerful tools you can use to train and educate your people, but also to develop agile "What if?" contingency plans for you to pull out if your competitor "zags" when you planned for a "zig." How can you use war gaming? Convene "adversary councils" of cross-functional teammates within your organization to study each of your most important competitors. Have them develop a business strategy and tactics from your competitor's perspective and present them to your organization's leaders. Then develop your own counter-attack. You could also reach out to a well-respected business school. The marketing and strategy professors can be hired to conduct more sophisticated, software-based competitive market simulations. Who's afraid of a little friendly internal business strategy competition, right?

Another easy-to-use tool to prepare for high-stakes presentations is a "murder board." During a murder board, your best and sharpest colleagues act like the toughest version of the people to whom you will be presenting. They will ask you the most strategic questions, the most frustratingly detailed questions, the most tangential questions, and the most unanticipated (by you) questions that those in your eventual presentation could *ever* ask you. But they ask you in the safety of a conference room in your own organization (or in the back room of a bar) well before your actual presentation. If you can survive the murder board, then the actual presentation should be a piece of cake. The philosophy is to "train to failure, not to perfection." If you can nail it every time, then you probably have not thought of all that could go wrong. If every time you practice, you "break" something, the final product will benefit from each failure.

To support your efforts to *"Drill, baby, drill!"* and practice relentlessly, you can also use board game and software simulations, create virtual worlds, or study and "solve" any of the hundreds of Harvard Business Cases that apply to your particular situation.

Succession Planning

As the leader of a high performance team, you need to be thinking further down the road than just this season or this fiscal year. You need to be seeking and growing future talent (see Part IV— Developing Others). In *Flight of the Buffalo*, Ralph Stayer writes that the best coaches are "great and efficient sorters of those they can and those they cannot help become world-class." Jim Collins describes it as "getting the right people on the bus, the wrong people off the bus, and getting those on the bus in the right seats." You have to recruit and build for the future today and every day.

Humility

There's nothing "soft" about humility and gratitude. Even in the most cutthroat industries, the best-performing members of the highest-performing teams will, among themselves, have the humility that accompanies high self-awareness. They know that without the complementary power of the team, they will not win consistently over the long run. One of my favorite Michael Jordan quotes is, "Individuals can win games, but *teamwork* wins championships."

Humility is an essential component of teamwork, and it is also required when we are on top to remind us how we got there. Retired Vice Admiral and test pilot Denny McGinn was the head of the Navy's warfare procurement program at the Pentagon when he admonished a team that was pretty pleased with itself: "Don't become a self-licking ice cream cone." High performance teams are rarely satisfied with themselves. They are reluctant to feel like they have ever really "made it."

The Nod of Acknowledgment

The pilots on the Navy's Blue Angels flight demonstration team have a ritual they perform regularly with each other after every flight. Regardless of whether it was the toughest, most physically and mentally demanding airshow performance or a simple relocation flight from one airport to another, they will ask one another, "How'd you fly?" The other pilot will deliver the customary response that shows respect for being part of the team: "I'm just damned glad to be here."

This expected answer demonstrates humility, but more importantly, it acknowledges the superlative level of professionalism of—and mutual respect for—the team's members. No matter the type of flight, they are each always striving for perfection in its execution, and no one is above self-improvement. The highest-performing teams acknowledge and appreciate the company they keep.

Truly high-performance teams are rare because they are superlative. They have very demanding leaders who see their team's performance—and their accountability for that performance—through The Lens of Leadership. Good enough never really is.

Summary & Exercise: Chapter 21—Pushing Them *Beyond* What They Think They Can Achieve

WHAT?—SO WHAT?—NOW WHAT?

What? Truly high-performance teams are rare. What it takes to create one is simple, but "simple" is not "easy." It takes a very demanding leader and self-sustaining teammates who are maniacally committed to victory, and to each other.

So What? In order to build and coach a high-performance team, you must become an "efficient sorter" of those you can help become great and those you cannot. Those who remain must be pushed to their limit—and then beyond—in order for the team to achieve its worthy, noble goal.

Now What?

I will study _____

_____ to learn more about building high performance teams.

I will reach out to _____

_____ in order to seek more insight, guidance, and advice.

I will ask _____ to hold me accountable for _____.

And I will _____

_____

_____ in order to create an experience with elements/competencies that I have not yet adequately developed by *(date)* _____.

ADDITIONAL RESOURCES FOR YOUR "NOW WHAT?" JOURNEY:

Belasco, James A. and Ralph C. Stayer. *Flight of the Buffalo: Soaring to Excellence, Learning to Let Employees Lead.*

Collins, Jim. *How The Mighty Fall: And Why Some Companies Never Give In.*

Gladwell, Malcolm. *Outliers: The Story of Success.*

Gray, Dave, Sunni Brown, and James Macanufo. *Gamestorming: A Playbook for Innovators, Rulebreakers, and Changemakers.*

"Harvard Business Cases." (Google it and search Harvard Business Publishing's site for case topics that will interest you.)

Johnson, Paul. *Churchill.*

Johnson, Steven. *Emergence: The Connected Lives of Ants, Brains, Cities, and Software.*

Krzyzewski, Mike and Donald T. Phillips. *Leading with the Heart: Coach K's Successful Strategies for Basketball, Business, and Life.*

Lencioni, Patrick. *The Five Dysfunctions of a Team.*

Michalko, Michael. *Thinkertoys: A Handbook of Creative-Thinking Techniques.* (2nd ed.)

Pink, Daniel H. *Drive: The Surprising Truth About What Motivates Us.*

Sawyer, Keith. *Group Genius: The Creative Power of Collaboration.*

Welch, Jack. *Winning.*

Wooden, John. *Wooden on Leadership: How to Create a Winning Organization.*

CHAPTER TWENTY TWO

SUCCEEDING IN MOMENTS THAT COUNT

Oh, that a man might know the end of this day's business ere it come.
But it sufficeth that the day shall end, and then the end is known.
– Brutus, in Shakespeare's *Julius Caesar*, Act V, Scene I

On the strength of one link in the cable,
Dependeth the might of the chain.
Who knows when thou may'st be tested?
So live that thou bearest the strain.
– from "The Laws of the Navy" by Rear Admiral R.A. Hopwood,
Royal Navy, 1896

One of my favorite leadership modules to teach at the Naval Academy was Combat Leadership. It was deeply thought-provoking both for me and the Midshipmen because its subject is the essence of why our service academies exist. All midshipmen wonder what challenges combat will bring them. Like hundreds of Henry Flemings, they wonder how they will perform in the heat of battle, and whether they will earn a Red Badge of Courage.

After discussing the readings and class content, I would invite them out into the hallway to conclude the class. High up on the walls on both sides along the length of the corridor were the citations and midshipman photographs of all of the graduates who had been awarded a Congressional Medal of Honor, some dating back one hundred and thirty years. I would have each student line up in front of one alumnus and read his citation to himself. Then I would have him study the hero's black-and-white student photograph above the citation, and I would ask, "What do you see?" Each student would reply with the same kind of answer every time: "He looks like my roommate." "He's got the same smirk as my lab partner." "He looks like he just flunked an exam." "He looks just like us...."

Then I would ask several questions as I walked slowly behind the students, referring to all the men pictured on the wall: "Do you think they *knew* they were going to become war heroes when those student photos were taken?" "What did they *do* while they were here that prepared them for the fateful act that cost many of them their lives and earned them our nation's highest military award?" "Do you think their instructors could have identified who would become the heroes?" "Which one of you will have your student photo up on this wall with a citation for future midshipmen to learn of the heroism you have yet to demonstrate?" "Will you be ready for your moments that count?"

It was always a sobering, incredibly powerful moment in my students' leadership development. Of course, *none* of the heroes expected to become "heroes." None of them wanted to be tested in an *in extremis*[1] moment. In these photos, they were just awkward looking college-age kids, and so, because of the traditions of similar uniforms and short hair, it was easy for my students to identify with them. Each one of those American heroes came to be considered "heroic" for actions that certainly contained courage, but their destinies were driven to their inexorable conclusion by context and circumstance: Nobody wants to fail in his "moments that count."

---

1 One of "extreme circumstances, especially near the point of death."

THE PARADOX OF HUMBLE HEROISM

One of the most heroic people I have known personally was Howard Dignen. Mr. Dignen was my barber at the Naval Academy. I felt very insufficient when I finally learned who Mr. Dignen really was.

As a midshipman, I was full of the arrogance of youth. I couldn't wait to die for my country, and I was sure I would do something great—that Destiny would choose *me*. And I remember Mr. Dignen being a nice, gentle old man who cut my hair. It was only upon my return to the Academy as an instructor that I took the time really to get to know my barber. It took several months of frequent haircuts to coax his story from him, but First Sergeant Howard Dignen had done unimaginably heroic things. He went ashore in the second wave on Omaha Beach. He fought forty-four days of sustained combat before his first shower and change of uniform in France. He turned down two battlefield commissions in order to stay with his men. He led small teams behind enemy lines and was often cut off. He hid in the coal bin of a French bar that German officers were using as a headquarters. He was stunned so deeply by an artillery barrage during the wintertime Battle of the Bulge that he was tagged as "deceased." He was the only one of his twelve closest hometown pals who enlisted together who came home. He returned to become a barber, and a husband, and a father, and a city councilman in his hometown of Annapolis. I realized that Destiny had been right to choose him. And I was humbled by his humility.

My friend and classmate Vic Hyder is the other most heroic person I know. Vic and I spent a summer training block as midshipmen together in the Philippines, Thailand, and Australia. After graduation, Vic went on to become a Navy SEAL. Our paths crossed only once, when I had the great fun of throwing him and his SEAL platoon out of the back of my P-3 Orion for some mid-altitude parachute training jumps. We connected ten or twelve years later via LinkedIn.

He was retiring from the Navy, and I was conducting a business war gaming exercise for the senior leaders of Johnsonville Sausage. I needed someone to connect my company leaders with the concept of business being "combat every day." Vic came and set the tone for the day, and he and I got to catch up on his career, and the impact of 9/11 and the wars in Iraq and Afghanistan on the SEAL community. I was, again, humbled by a friend.

A camaraderie exists between Naval Academy classmates that is hard to describe, but it is an instant thing—years melt away, and we connect as deeply as though no time has passed since we were college-age kids struggling to outlast the Academy's rigorous régime. Vic was measured, but also subtly eager to share with me that he had discussed combat with veterans of World War II's D-Day invasion, the Korean Conflict's battle of the Chosin Reservoir, and from various Vietnam War engagements. He wanted me to know that our classmates and their troops measured admirably against the yardstick of those storied heroes. He was not bragging. He was just letting me know, as a classmate and a friend.

Vic called me "brother" in one of our email exchanges while planning for my company's war gaming event. It was one of the proudest and most inadequate moments of my life: to be considered a brother by a man of such nobility, whose deeds on behalf of our country should be known and revered by our whole society. But Vic and his warriors don't need such reverence. They only need to "measure up" in the eyes of a small circle of their peers: to have demonstrated valor equal to those whose legacy they carry, and to have defeated the enemy. Vic lives the paradox of humble heroism.

For you, measuring up should mean succeeding in the eyes of a small circle of your closest friends, cross-functional teammates, and mentors—not because it will further your career, but because you are humble about moments that count.

HEROISM IN EVERYDAY MOMENTS THAT COUNT

Everyday heroism certainly requires important leadership skills, but mostly it requires *courage*. Courage is central to success during moments that count. C.S. Lewis wrote, "Courage is not simply *one* of the virtues, but the form of *every* virtue at the testing point." In order for an act to be virtuous, it requires courage. It may require the courage to be self-disciplined in a moment of weakness. It may require the courage to temper your personal ambition and instead serve the team's best interests. It may require the courage to say "yes" to something when others are saying "no." Howard Dignen and Vic Hyder were *physically* courageous in the horrible circumstances of ground combat, but there are other important forms of courage that you must demonstrate: *Professional Courage, Managerial Courage, and Moral Courage.*

Professional Courage Puts Others First

The best and most-committed leaders are in it for something they believe in that is bigger than themselves. Because of that, they tend to put the organization—or at least the *mission* of the organization—first. They work for organizations they trust and they believe deeply in their hearts in the good intent and good deeds the organization accomplishes. They believe in and live out the values because they have chosen a team that allows each of them to live out his voice.[2] That belief leads them to put their organization first, their team and teammates next, and themselves last. This notion may seem so idealistic as to be trite, but I have seen it in several business colleagues whom I admire. They are widely revered and are also able to deliver fantastic results because of the commitment they engender in others. They see the typical organizational pyramid as inverted, with the organization on top, the team in the middle, and themselves supporting the whole on the bottom.

---

2 The concept of "voice" is explained in Chapter 13.

Managerial Courage Shows Itself Everyday

My friend Chris Miller, a former Johnsonville colleague who is now a partner at The Praevius Group, writes that the most successful *in extremis* leaders are those who are "the most agile and adaptive. Regardless of the situation, they succeed. They are not committed to a course of action, but to a cause, and intent. They adjust. They accomplish and execute, no matter the level of chaos or order; no matter the audience."

Some important "moments that count" are less dire than *in extremis* moments. For those moments, which are likely to occur in your daily life, here are the important skills needed:

- Conflict management
- Confronting poor results or execution
- Standing alone
- Compassion
- Maintaining integrity and ethics
- Demonstrating loyalty
- Speaking up to arrogance or instances of incompetence

Some of these are big, anticipated moments that you see coming from a mile away, that you can prepare for and practice and even get advice on before they arrive. But many of these will be unexpected and will require you to summon your professional courage, without warning, in a moment that counts.

Moral Courage Does What is Right

Launa Stayer-Maloney, Vice-Chairman of Johnsonville Sausage, taught me that "Business decisions are easy when you know what your values are." She is absolutely right. When you work for an authentic organization, and you know its values and the intent behind them, even the tough decisions become less difficult. You measure the decision against the guidepost of values. Making financial decisions, people decisions, and decisions about whether to step up to career-affecting conversations becomes something you are obligated to do.

YOU HAVE A LOT AT RISK

If you are a police officer, a firefighter, an airline pilot, or a linesman for an electrical company, you are literally putting your life in the hands of others. In some jobs, there is *physical* risk and trust is hard-earned because of that risk. But Roger Cameron, the father of the junior military officer category of professional recruiting, inspired me to pursue a career in business because, he said, "Business is combat every day." Your competitors wake up each day thinking about how they can steal your lunch money and put you out of business.

As you consider what courage means in business, and what moments in your life are moments that count, think about the people of your organization. In most jobs, our *lives* are not at risk, but our livelihoods, our lifestyles, and our self-interests absolutely are. Our ability to provide for our family, and to contribute to our community and to the welfare of others is on the line with every decision we make. Moments that count occur because we put our professional future into each other's hands.

What will make you a hero in the context of your work life? Your teammates need you to be courageous and heroic in both of your roles as a follower and as a leader. There are other ways to be professionally heroic: to inspire others to improve themselves; to speak up when others will not; to defend those who are worthy and in need; to right a wrong you see that others do not. Life is truly like George Bailey's in the film *It's a Wonderful Life*. We can never fully know the impact we have on the lives of others.

TIME: THE LONG LENS OF LEADERSHIP

I was walking through the Père Lachaise cemetery in Paris with my daughter Shelby, who was sixteen years old at the time. We were wandering and visiting some of the famous graves. We stopped at a few from pop-culture, but we mostly searched for the sepulchers of those who had a more enduring impact on Western culture. As we wandered, we suddenly had a heightened awareness of the perspective of time. Many of these eighteenth and nineteenth century politicians, admirals, statesmen, generals, correspondents, scientists, philosophers, and ministers of state had truly been world-famous in their day, having changed the course of human history. They are studied across cultures throughout the world even two hundred years after their deaths. Yet, there on that day, they were only skeletal remains under what were once colossal shrines to their lives, which are now merely moss-covered pieces of granite with decrepit ornamental metalwork and difficult-to-read scripts. My daughter and I recommitted ourselves to the importance of our faith, and to our closest relations. I shared with her Charles De Gaulle's famous quote, "The cemeteries of the world are filled with 'indispensable' men."

What about you? De Gaulle is right: No matter who you are, there is an inevitable future without you in it. Have you prepared your team members for that circumstance in case it comes sooner than you expect? How self-sufficient have you made them? How well cross-trained are they in each other's jobs? Special Forces teams in all services train to be self-sustaining no matter who is lost. Each member is trained in the skills of another—often two other—team members. They are ready for "moments that count." Is your team?

EVERYBODY HAS MOMENTS THAT COUNT

The only remotely heroic thing I have ever done was not "heroic"—it was just my job at the time. I was a poolside safety observer during the evaluation of which midshipmen would earn coveted slots to attend Navy Diver training. I had endured this same program as a freshman and graduated from the Fleet's diver training program. I was now part of the Academy's cadre administering the evaluation program for another group. The candidates were in the pool, each holding his breath while swimming the longest distance he was able to underwater, trying to exceed a certain distance requirement.

Everything was as it was supposed to be: we had healthy, smart, competitive candidates swimming their distances, and our own safety swimmers with mask, fins, and snorkels watching them closely. Everything was going "swimmingly." Until it wasn't....

I was walking the pool deck, watching for surface problems, when up from the pool's depths emerged a safety swimmer and an unconscious candidate who had held his breath to the point of passing out underwater. Everything happened fast, but it happened like it was supposed to. It was all a blur, but my CPR got his systems going again. It turned out he was not just a fellow midshipman, but Greg Collins, a *classmate*. I visited him in the hospital and was happy and grateful to have been successful in my moment that counts. We were not close as friends at the time of the incident—we had different academic and extra-curricular interests and different circles of friends—and we didn't necessarily become friends after the incident. It was an important event in my life, but I didn't focus on it a lot: I was off to the next adventure, and the next, and the next....

Fast-forward twenty years into the future. I was at my twentieth Naval Academy class reunion, renewing all kinds of friendships. All of a sudden, a man appears in front of me at the football game social area and says, "Hi, Cory. Do you remember me?" I knew him instantly. He said, "I want you to meet my family. They know all about you." I was suddenly surrounded by two "tweenagers" shaking both of my hands, and a woman hugging me and thanking me for what I had done for the husband she had not met yet and the children she had not foreseen all those years ago.

Wow. I was stunned. It had been more than just an important moment to Greg. I had minimized in my own mind something that had resulted in an incredible positive effect on people I didn't even know. I will never forget the humbling power of gratitude I felt from that hug. My moment that counted had been important in ways I could not imagine. But you don't have to be involved in saving someone's life to be heroic in a moment that counts.

ANOTHER "MOMENT," ANOTHER OPPORTUNITY

I am equally as proud of the opportunity I had to influence a young man who works in a manufacturing plant at Johnsonville. From time to time, I spend a shift in a plant to keep my head in the game and connect with the members who do the real work of our company, and on this particular day, I was with Brett. Brett was in his early twenties, and he led a team that was different every single day. Each morning, he took a team of seven or eight strangers from our temporary labor provider and molded them into a team doing one specific job. It was a pleasure to watch him lead. He took the Bad News Bears and turned them into the Harlem Globetrotters by the end of the day. And he did it every day.

Later, I was facilitating a class and Brett was one of the students. I had been so impressed by his leadership that I was sure he was on his way to great things. When I asked him what he wanted to do next, he didn't seem to have the fire and ambition I expected. I believed he was capable of great things as a future manufacturing line leader or even a shift leader at one of our plants, and I told him so. But Brett seemed uninterested. My surprise must have shown because he confided that he "would have to go back to school to get a promotion, and high school didn't go that well" for him. "Besides," he said, "two years for an associate's degree? That's a *long* time!"

I asked him whether he had a wife or any children. He told me he was married and would become a father soon. I asked him what he cared about. What did he want to become? He said, "I don't want my wife to want for things, or my kids, either. I grew up poor, and I just want them to be able to have stuff without worrying."

That was my "in." I asked, "Brett, do you know how long you're going to have to work? I mean, at twenty-two, you do realize you're going to be working for another *forty-five* to *fifty* years, right? Twice as long as you've even been alive so far." I let that sink in....

"I never thought about it like that. That's a long time," he replied.

"So, if you're going to work for fifty years," I said, "maybe spending two, or even four of those years in school to get better skills and a couple of promotions might not be a bad investment if you want to provide a better life for your family, right? Working a little extra hard for *less than 10 percent of your work years* may not be too much to ask if it can help you earn more and get better shifts so you can have more time and more money for your family, right?"

Brett left the class that day in a very contemplative mood. I reached out to his coach (supervisor) and told him a little bit about the exchange, and he told me he would continue to push Brett to think about the future and encourage him to consider going to school.

Brett enrolled that fall in an associate's degree program that met regularly in our company's learning center. I saw Brett doing homework and preparing for classes regularly over the next three years. It was hard work for him to deliver a great performance on the job, attend school, get all of his homework and projects done, *and* be a great husband and father to two children. Some days the comments were a good-natured but sarcastic, "What have I done to myself?" And on other days they were about the latest "A" he had received, and how it kept surprising him that he was doing so well.

I was proud to be included in a small group that took Brett out for a beer to celebrate his graduation. He has completed a big accomplishment that will empower him to achieve his goal of economic security for himself and his family. Brett did all of the work. I am pleased I could play a small motivational role that gave Brett some perspective. I am grateful to have passed the test in another moment that counts.

You may not believe you're in a job where you could become someone's "hero." But you don't have to be a Navy SEAL or a fireman or policeman to have an incredibly important impact on the direction and outcome in someone's life, inside or outside of work. And sometimes you don't even have to do very much—you're just one link in a chain of nudges. But you have to be *looking* for the moments. As a leader, some of your precious time has to be spent being on the lookout for moments that count.

Then, you have to be ready with whatever the moment calls for—it might be action, but it also may require *in*action. By having the heart of a servant and the commitment of a warrior, you will surely be ready. By looking at your opportunities through The Lens of Leadership, you will be more likely to find—and succeed in—many moments that count.

Summary & Exercise: Chapter 22—Succeeding in Moments That Count

WHAT?—SO WHAT?—NOW WHAT?

What? Our lives are filled with moments that count. These moments are a test of our skills, our nature, and our commitment to others. In most jobs, our lives are not at stake. But in this interconnected, matrix-structured world, we *do* put our careers, our livelihoods, and our self-interests into the hands of others.

So What? You affect many lives through the behaviors you model, the expectations you set, and the decisions you make. You must be ready for your moments that count by developing professional, managerial, and moral courage.

Now What?

I will study _____

_____ to learn more about

being ready for "moments that count" in business.

I will reach out to _____

_____ in order to seek more

insight, guidance, and advice.

I will ask _____ to hold me

accountable for _____

_____.

And I will _____

_____

_____ in order to create an experience with

elements/competencies that I have not yet adequately developed by

(date) _____.

ADDITIONAL RESOURCES FOR YOUR "NOW WHAT?" JOURNEY:

Adams, Richard. *Watership Down: A Novel.*

Ambrose, Stephen E. *Band of Brothers.*

Dumas, Alexandre. *The Count of Monte Cristo.*

Gerstner, Louis V. *Who Says Elephants Can't Dance?: Leading a Great Enterprise through Dramatic Change.*

Gilbert, Martin. *Churchill: A Life.*

Grove, Andrew S. *Only the Paranoid Survive: How to Exploit the Crisis Points That Challenge Every Company.*

Haynes, Captain Al. "The Crash of United Flight 232." (Google it.)

Kennedy, John F. *Profiles in Courage.*

Kolditz, Thomas. *In Extremis Leadership: Leading As If Your Life Depended On It.*

Lee, Gus and Diane Elliott-Lee. *Courage: The Backbone of Leadership.*

Perkins, Dennis N.T. et al. *Leading at the Edge: Leadership Lessons from the Extraordinary Saga of Shackleton's Antarctic Expedition.*

Stockdale, James B. *Thoughts of a Philosophical Fighter Pilot.*

Treasurer, Bill. *Courage Goes to Work: How to Build Backbones, Boost Performance, and Get Results.*

A FINAL NOTE

*Whether our efforts are, or are not, favored by life, let us be able to say,
when we come near to the great goal, "I have done what I could.
Let he who can, do better".*
— Louis Pasteur

*If you have a goal in life that takes a lot of energy, that requires
a lot of work, that incurs a great deal of interest and that is a
challenge to you, you will always look forward to waking up to
see what the new day brings.*
— Susan Polis Schutz

Followership is *the* prerequisite to leadership. Most great leaders started out as being great followers. This is not a "wait your turn" mindset; it is an "earn your chops" and "learn the skills" mindset. Over the next two decades, America will see tens of millions of experienced leaders from the Baby Boomer generation leave the workforce. There are not enough Generation Xers (born between 1965 and 1980) to fill those empty roles—not enough by about half. Technology and efficiencies will be found to fill some of the work that modern leaders must do, but the fact is that tens of millions of Millennials (or "Generation Y," born between 1981 and 1999) will be sucked up into the leadership vacuum created by the departing Boomers and the limited number of Xers replacements. How these Millennials are different will dramatically change—and improve—the workplace. But Millennials will be promoted into positions of leadership more rapidly than any other generation has without being given time to build leadership skills and confidence. And they will be leading in a world where the rate of change of complexity is increasing faster than the human species' ability to adapt to and master that change.

This need for rapid fundamental leadership development is not unique to America. Emerging markets are growing so rapidly that a whole new balance of global economic power is being created. These economies are in dire need of skilled first- or second-generation business leaders. These leadership principles are *human* principles. They will work in any organization around the world where people interact with other people to get work done.

LEADERSHIP DRIVES ECONOMIC RESULTS

Jim Collins coined the term "Level 5" leadership to describe the humble-but-relentless leaders who drove their companies from "good to great." We know that stronger leadership benches drive better organizational performance. One study measured that improved performance as a 15 percent higher three-year total shareholder return![1] But in the 2009 Corporate Leadership Council's HIPO Survey, only 40 percent of employees identified as having "high potential" say that they "are being asked to contribute to [their] full potential." And only two out of every five leaders are rated as "effective" or "highly effective."[2]

I have spent the last twenty years acting in the paradoxically-simultaneous roles of follower and leader in the military, in academia, in business, as an elected official, and in not-for-profit and community roles. I was fortunate to have been given much more responsi-

---

1 Compared to their competitors with poor leadership development programs, as measured in the 2003 Corporate Leadership Council's "Hallmarks of Leadership Success" report.
2 41 percent in The Corporate Executive Board's 2009 Manager Study.

bility and autonomy than my age and experience warranted at the time. My two earliest leadership influences gave me more than just permission to experiment: they *required* that I vary my followership and leadership techniques in order to find what worked and toss out what did not. They also taught me to see every result—a dirty floor, an undisciplined team, or a wild success—through The Lens of Leadership.

The Lens of Leadership is an accountability mindset. I believe all successes and failures have their roots in leadership, and that people in positions of leadership bear responsibility for those successes and failures. Great leaders are not afraid to have their results examined through The Lens of Leadership.

The best leaders are "students of people" who can help teams overcome human and organizational foibles. They create an environment where teammates believe they are valued, and that they must constantly and forever develop themselves so they can better contribute to their own and to the organization's success. Humans are such complicated, imperfect creatures full of unflattering behaviors and emotions. Some great teammates eventually emerge as great *leaders* and go on to inspire others to achieve their own greatness, despite our human "messiness."

These three time-tested principles will make you a better follower and a better leader. Starting today, they *will* help you become more successful over the course of your career: *Serve*, *Build*, and *Inspire*.

SERVE

As you have read, the first principle of leadership is followership. A "servant follower" serves the best interests of his or her leader by first serving the best interests of the team, not his own personal self-interests. By serving the leader and the team as a follower, you will earn a strong reputation for influence, which will, in turn, get you promoted to the next level of leadership responsibility. After that promotion to leader, you will be both a leader and also *simultaneously* still a follower.

Paradoxically, that spirit of service is also the right mindset for followers to maintain as you grow into leadership. By seeking first to serve the needs of those they lead, servant leaders develop their people to have the skills to achieve the organization's mission and purpose. The best servant leaders "use the business to build their people," not the other way around.

Some of the other essential elements of service are:

- Loyalty—to your leaders and to your team, even when you may personally disagree with certain decisions.
- Integrity, Ethics, and Character—High-trust teams are more efficient, more effective, faster, and cheaper to run than low-trust teams.
- Initiative, Resourcefulness, and Self-Reliance—Lighten your leader's load. Take the initiative to improve things. A "fire-and-forget" missile is a weapon that is advanced enough to adapt to target changes and operate independently all the way to the goal. Be a "fire-and-forget" teammate.
- Professionalism—Setting a sterling example will set you apart. Be Productive, Be Innovative, Be the Expert, and Be Polite.

The most effective leaders give away responsibility *and* authority for mission accomplishment—that is *real* empowerment. This action allows them to compound their own effectiveness through effective delegation. They recognize that their reputation for excellence as a leader is their own personal brand, and they work hard to nurture that brand the way Apple, Nike, and Disney steward theirs.

The best leaders hire the best people. They seek out, network with, and find people who are leaders *first*, who also happen to be exceptional at their functional roles. That requires a very patient, thorough vetting process—one that measures for cultural fit as well as professional competence. By hiring people whom they believe are capable of earning at least two promotions in their organization, they continuously maintain their bench strength and earn a reputation for being a leader to whom others flock.

BUILD

It is a type of service to your leader, your team, and to yourself to pursue your own self-development. The best followers and leaders build their own toolboxes as a method of serving others. You will grow the fastest and achieve the most if you are committed to earning your way into relationships with people who are smarter than you are—people who are *the best* in their category or industry or profession. Work hard to develop your knowledge and judgment so you can consistently maintain professional conversations with people two levels above where you are today.

You should remain curious and inquisitive at all times about professional people and topics that may seem interesting but at first only tangential to your everyday work. A career is a string of eight to ten year adventures, the paths of which are often unanticipated. Don't leave this up to serendipity: seek out mentoring from experts in areas that interest you, and look for opportunities to make a living by moving closer professionally to what you love, what you can be really great at, to fill a need you see, and to do what your conscience compels you to do. Take the time to grow and nurture your professional network. Give away a little bit more than you receive by being a mentor yourself.

As someone's leader, you are the most important influence on his professional development at work. The best leaders are teachers who also recognize that most of the learning occurs on the job, not in a training event. Make sure the people you lead understand your expectations about performance and application following their learning of a new skill. Create experiences that will challenge them beyond what they think they can achieve. They will eventually thank you for that push.

One of the hallmarks of developing yourself and developing others is accountability. The best leaders and teammates do not avoid difficult conversations about performance or expectations. They conduct them in-the-moment, demonstrating 100 percent candor and 100 percent respect.

INSPIRE

The most successful and most respected leaders use *influence*, not rank or power, to lead spherically. They enlist people from all directions on the organizational chart, and also from outside the organization, to accomplish great things. They lead with a servant's heart because they recognize that only by helping others achieve *their* highest goals can they earn their people's highest engagement, and get people to give freely of their discretionary effort.

All leaders should constantly be considering where they and their teammates are on what I call the "Confidence Continuum."

A leader's two biggest worries should be...

Complacency   Hubris

<--->

The "Confidence Continuum"

There is an ideal point where the leader and the team are perfectly balanced on the continuum. They are confident enough to carry out the mission because they have prepared *thoroughly*—they are committed experts. They are also healthfully paranoid enough to be worried about what it is they do not know or haven't considered. This paranoia fuels their insatiable desire to learn more and get better. The best teams recognize that they are always getting better or declining—there is no steady-state. The best leaders don't lie awake nights worrying about complacency and hubris. They lie awake nights worrying about how they can get *their teammates* to lie awake worrying about complacency and hubris. This is the servant-led, self-improving team.

Human beings are capable of unimaginable feats of professional, moral, mental, and physical accomplishment. The more unimaginable the feat, the more inspiration and motivation they require. Many levers exist that leaders can "pull" to motivate and inspire. The best leaders use *several* levers—each at just the right time and in the right circumstance—like tools in a toolbox. In order to be an effective motivator, you must understand your teammates as complete, "whole" people, not just who they are at work for fifty hours a week.

By tapping into these deep reservoirs, leaders unleash extraordinary amounts of commitment and accomplishment. They turn their teams into truly *high-performance* teams. Leaders with the ability to inspire high performance deliver 1.5 times the revenue and 1.8 times the profit of those with poorer skills.[3]

The best leaders and followers are ready for the moments that count. Most jobs don't contain the physical risk or require the physical courage of being a combat soldier or firefighter—we think of *them* as heroes. But no matter what your job is, you place your career and your ability to provide for your family's future in the hands of others every single day. This situation requires that everyone be ready to answer the call when professional, managerial, or moral heroics are required. Courage is an essential ingredient for leadership. That is why *all* leadership—not just service as a police officer or fighter pilot—is a worthy calling. All leadership is *noble*.

WHAT *YOU* MUST DO

You stand on the giant historic shoulders of others, *no matter who you are*. Everything we have is a gift from previous generations. Your

3 Corporate Leadership Council's 2009 "Improving Leader Effectiveness" survey.

obligation is to leave something more behind for future followers, leaders, and their teams.

Your journey now becomes a simple one. But *simple*, is not *easy*.

My friend, bestselling author Patrick Snow, motivates his key-note crowds by having them repeat out loud John Addison's, "I will do today, what others don't, so I will have tomorrow, what others won't." He doesn't necessarily mean material things. There are things you want to "have" that are more important than material posses-sions, and you will only get them by *challenging yourself* to achieve more.

In that spirit,

- I challenge you to review your **Impact Map**. Make sure you know which two or three improved behaviors will increase your effectiveness the most and move you more quickly to-ward achieving your voice. Connect those behaviors to the team and organizational goals you will help achieve by chang-ing your behaviors.

- I challenge you to review the **"What? So What? Now What?"** sections at the end of each chapter that are key developmental areas for you. Create **your customized development plan:** write out the formal learning (books, classes, seminars, etc.) you will need to complete, the social learning (from colleagues and mentors) you will seek out, and *most importantly*, outline the experiences you will need to create with your leader so you can practice these skills on the job. You may have to take on additional work or a modified role. Focus your efforts over the next six to twelve months on specifically improving *these one or two skills.*

- I challenge you to **serve**, beginning with your followership. Also adopt the mindset of service as your reason for being a leader. Are those you lead becoming healthier, wiser, freer, more autonomous, and more likely themselves to become servant leaders?

- I challenge you to **build** by developing the skills and careers of yourself and others.
- I challenge you to **inspire** others to greatness through the example you set, through your skills of power and influence, and through your ability to deliver in the clutch, during moments that count.

Good luck on your journey! Our world is desperately in need of skilled followers, leaders, and teams. Seeing your results through The Lens of Leadership will ensure that you live a life of impact, of worth, and of value to yourself, your family, and our world.

Serve. Build. Inspire.

ABOUT THE AUTHOR

Cory Bouck is the Director of Organizational Development & Learning (OD&L) at Johnsonville Sausage, and is the author of *The Lens of Leadership: Being the Leader Others Want to Follow.*

He is a U.S. Naval Academy graduate, and also served there as a leadership instructor. Cory graduated in the top 1 percent of all student leadership ranks as a Midshipman. As an instructor, he led a team of civilian Ph.D.s and military instructors in managing the content and delivery of the advanced core leadership course.

He is a former Naval Flight Officer. Cory led a globetrotting P-3 Orion combat aircrew, including missions over Bosnia-Herzegovina. His crew was twice named #1 of 48 crews in the Atlantic Fleet.

He led brand and event marketing teams at General Mills, Newell-Rubbermaid, and Johnsonville Sausage. Cory led the team that developed a NASCAR strategy for the Chex cereal portfolio with Richard Petty Enterprises. At Newell-Rubbermaid's Little Tikes toy division, the product development team he led earned a *Parents Magazine* "Best Toys of the Year" award. The Johnsonville brand team he led more than doubled net-margin dollar growth in two years and grew household penetration by 10 percent. That team also earned an "EFFIE" from the North American Marketing Association for effective advertising.

Cory joined Johnsonville's OD&L team to create an internal leader-development system. In three years, the internal promotion rate for leadership positions increased from 40 to 70 percent. He now leads the OD&L function and is responsible for employee development, technical training, and executive coaching.

Cory is active in leadership outside of work. He served two terms as an elected city councilman, chairing several committees while working with state and federal legislators. Cory is a pilot and youth mentor in the Civil Air Patrol.

His personal purpose is to coach the people whose lives he connects with to high achievement in whatever drives *their* purpose.

He tweets as @CoryBouck

BOOK CORY BOUCK TO SPEAK AT YOUR NEXT EVENT

When choosing a professional speaker for your next event, you'll find no one more capable of motivating—or re-igniting—your audience's desire to achieve greatness than Cory Bouck.

Cory has been speaking publically and inspiring others—as a military officer, leadership and ethics instructor, marketing and sales leader, organizational development professional, and politician—for over twenty years.

Whether your audience is 10 or 10,000, in North America or abroad, Cory Bouck will deliver an inspiring message filled with practical, "right now" application for your meeting or conference. Cory will study your organization and conduct personal interviews to understand your business and your people so he can connect quickly and deliver a customized message.

Cory has worked in over a dozen countries in Europe, Asia, and South and Central America, so he is culturally fluent and "global-ready." His **Serve-Build-Inspire** theme touches the universal human desire to live a life of impact and achievement.

Cory's speaking philosophy is not to "teach," but to use his passion for greatness and the power of real-life stories to entertain and inspire your audience to *find it within themselves* to deliver extraordinary results.

To learn more about Cory's speaking topics and to see videos of Cory in action, visit his site below. You can also contact him to schedule an introductory phone conversation.

www.CoryBouck.com

cory@corybouck.com